Praise for the *Roots of Contemporary Issues* series

"Everything around us—policy, population, culture, economy, environment—is a product of the actions and activities of people in the past. How can we hope to address the challenges we face and resolve contentious issues—like inequality, health, immigration, and climate change—without understanding where they come from? The volumes in the Roots of Contemporary Issues series are the tested products of years of classroom teaching and research. They address controversial issues with impartiality but not detachment, combining historical context and human agency to create accounts that are meaningful and usable for any student confronting the complex world in which they will live."

—TREVOR R. GETZ, *San Francisco State University*

"This is a truly innovative series that promises to revolutionize how world history is taught, freeing students and faculty alike from the 'tyranny of coverage' often embedded within civilizational paradigms, and facilitating sustained reflection on the roots of the most pressing issues in our contemporary world. Students' understanding of the importance of history and their interest in our discipline is sure to be heightened by these volumes that deeply contextualize and historicize current global problems."

—NICOLA FOOTE, *Arizona State University*

ROOTS OF CONTEMPORARY ISSUES

CHRONIC DISPARITIES

ROOTS OF CONTEMPORARY ISSUES

Series Editors

Jesse Spohnholz and Clif Stratton

The **Roots of Contemporary Issues** Series is built on the premise that students will be better at facing current and future challenges, no matter their major or career path, if they are capable of addressing controversial issues in mature, reasoned ways using evidence, critical thinking, and clear written and oral communication skills. To help students achieve these goals, each title in the Series argues that we need both an understanding of the ways in which humans have been interconnected with places around the world for decades and even centuries.

Published

Ruptured Lives: Refugee Crises in Historical Perspective
Jesse Spohnholz, Washington State University

Power Politics: Carbon Energy in Historical Perspective
Clif Stratton, Washington State University

Chronic Disparities: Public Health in Historical Perspective
Sean Wempe, California State University, Bakersfield

Forthcoming

High Societies: The Global Drug Trade in Historical Perspective
Ken Faunce, Washington State University

Gender Rules: Gender and Empire in Historical Perspective
Karen Phoenix, Washington State University

Chronic Disparities

Public Health in Historical Perspective

Roots of Contemporary Issues

Sean Andrew Wempe
California State University, Bakersfield

New York   Oxford
OXFORD UNIVERSITY PRESS

Oxford University Press is a department of the University of Oxford.
It furthers the University's objective of excellence in research, scholarship,
and education by publishing worldwide. Oxford is a registered trade mark of
Oxford University Press in the UK and certain other countries.

Published in the United States of America by Oxford University Press
198 Madison Avenue, New York, NY 10016, United States of America.

For titles covered by Section 112 of the US Higher Education
Opportunity Act, please visit www.oup.com/us/he for the latest
information about pricing and alternate formats.

Library of Congress Cataloging-in-Publication Data

Names: Wempe, Sean Andrew, author.
Title: Chronic disparities : public health in historical perspective / Sean
Andrew Wempe.
Description: New York : Oxford University Press, [2021] | Series: The roots
of contemporary issues | Includes bibliographical references and index. |
Summary: "A higher education history textbook that focuses on public
health in world history. This is part of the Roots of Contemporary
Issues series"—Provided by publisher.
Identifiers: LCCN 2020008893 (print) | LCCN 2020008894 (ebook) | ISBN
9780190696252 (paperback) | ISBN 9780197521151 | ISBN 9780197535318
(epub) | ISBN 9780190696306
Subjects: LCSH: Public health—History. | World history. | Equality.
Classification: LCC RA425 .W46 2021 (print) | LCC RA425 (ebook) | DDC
362.1—dc23
LC record available at https://lccn.loc.gov/2020008893
LC ebook record available at https://lccn.loc.gov/2020008894

Printing number: 9 8 7 6 5 4 3 2 1
Printed by LSC Communications, Inc., United States of America

For Ann Marie Kjellerson Wempe
with Love
For my little cousin Riley
and other children taken too soon
by disease.

Public Health policies derived from a particular scientific theory are variable and tend to reflect the political contexts and ideological and other working assumptions of the groups involved. Science does not operate in a value-free or neutral environment, but is given meaning, and creates new meanings, in settings that are specifically social, economic and political as well as intellectual.

—NANCY LEYS STEPAN, *Eradication: Ridding the World of Diseases Forever? (2011)*

CONTENTS

LIST OF MAPS AND FIGURES

Maps

Figures

ABOUT THE AUTHOR

Sean Andrew Wempe is Assistant Professor of History at California State University, Bakersfield. He received his doctorate from Emory University (2015), then taught at Washington State University in the Roots of Contemporary Issues program for three years before moving to Bakersfield. His first book, *Revenants of the German Empire: Colonial Germans, Imperialism, and the League of Nations*, was released with Oxford University Press in 2019. His ongoing research focuses on intersections in the history of empire, the history of internationalism, the history of science, and the history of public health.

ACKNOWLEDGMENTS

A second book, though it may go faster than the first, leaves just as many messages of thanks to be written to the plethora of people who made it possible. Sadly, though, the second book also leaves less word-count for such acknowledgments, so I will strive to thank as many as I can in a short amount of space. For those who I may have had to omit, know that I am deeply grateful for everything you've done for me through the years.

Foremost, thanks go to Jesse Spohnholz and Clif Stratton, not only for giving me my first job at Washington State University, but for envisioning the Roots of Contemporary Issues Program and this book series. Thanks also go to Charles Cavaliere, editor at Oxford University Press, for recognizing the value of this series across many pitches from Clif, Jesse, and even one from myself and Karen Phoenix at the AHA in Atlanta many years ago. Special thanks go to my fellow authors in the first wave of the series: Jesse, Clif, Karen, and Ken. We kept each other going through the process and read so many drafts of each other's work, making it better in the end I think. To my wife, Ann, who has godlike levels of patience, for supporting me as I churned out another book so quickly after my first, both books coming during moves to new homes and new jobs. I promise: more trips to the coast and I'll stick to articles for a little bit. To Matthew Unangst and Jared Secord. Our writing group while we were all working in Pullman, WA helped me frame the writing in its earliest stages. I miss our beers and edits at Café Moro. To Steve Allen and Kate Mulry, two of my new colleagues at California State University–Bakersfield where I did the bulk of the writing on this book— many thanks for your thoughtful perusals of drafts of chapters and your reminders that I should get up from my office desk from time to time to do important things like eat. To Tim Vivian, another great colleague here in Bakersfield, I give thanks for your rapacious appetite for my chapters as I wrote them and your eagle-eye attention to copyediting text. To my CDC friends who I knew during my days at Emory University: our Sunday chats over coffee inspired many of the lesson plans that ultimately led to this book and my courses on the history of public health. My parents, Joseph and Kelly, always pushed us kids to do our best and I still strive to do so. My baby sister, Samantha Robinson, a statistician with a passion for data related to health in society, constantly amazes me with her ability to quantify the most complex of human experiences in a relatable way. My youngest brother, Brian Wempe, with his passion for biology and genetics, makes it clear to the world that though I have two books, he is leaps and bounds smarter than I am.

I am indebted to the many archivists, librarians, collections specialists, permissions experts, and researchers across the globe that granted me access to the sources needed to complete this book. I am grateful to California State University–Bakersfield, the Department of History, and the Dean of Arts and Humanities, Robert Frakes, for their ongoing financial and collegial support in helping me achieve my research and publishing goals. Finally, to all of my students across the years, from my grad school teaching days at Emory, to my RCI students at Washington State University, and those at California State University–Bakersfield, I give thanks to you and wish you well. You all served as "clinical trials" for the lessons in this book and all of you, through the years, taught me how best to reach you. Thank you for making me the teacher I am today.

Connecting Past and Present

Let's begin with events taking place in the last few years. Here's one: in early 2019, Starbucks announced plans to replace plastic straws with recyclable polypropylene lids. "Starbucks is finally drawing a line in the sand and creating a mold for other brands to follow," stated the company's director of packaging. Some supporters see the move as a good example of a market-based solution to environmental damage. Critics warn that it's unlikely that many "green" lids will end up at recycling facilities, since the plan is only slated for stores in two of the seventy-six countries where the company operates, the United States and Canada, which recycle very few polypropylene plastics. Most people agree, though, that plastic pollution has become a problem; worldwide production of plastics in the last few generations has skyrocketed. Many plastics produced today only ever get used for just a few minutes or hours, and then are left for centuries to pollute the earth. Plastics float in enormous masses in our oceans, killing birds, fish, seals, whales, and turtles. They break down into microplastics, making their way into all kinds of organisms. Microplastics found in drinking water are even changing humans' body chemistry. Whose responsibility it is to solve this problem? What solutions are likely to be effective? We will be in a better position to answer those questions if we stop to understand the economic, cultural, political, and social forces that allowed such widespread global plastic pollution to develop in the first place.

Here's another example: On January 28, 2019 the rapper 21 Savage sung a lyric on NBC's *Late Night with Jimmy Fallon* criticizing the US government's policy of separating children from parents who had arrived at the US-Mexico border seeking asylum. A few days later, the US Immigration and Customs Enforcement (ICE) arrested 21 Savage, just a week before the Grammy Awards, for which he had been nominated for his recent collaboration with Post Malone. It turns out the Atlanta-based musician had been brought to the US as a minor by his parents, who failed to renew his visa when it expired. During the Grammys, 21 Savage sat in an ICE detention facility. Supporters of 21 Savage applaud his bringing attention to what they consider an inhumane US immigration policy. Those who disagree with him emphasize the importance of protecting the integrity of national borders and prosecuting violations of American immigration laws. 21 Savage's case became part of a nationwide debate in the US about the arrival of asylum seekers fleeing gang violence in El Salvador, Guatemala, and Honduras, and the US's government's policy of incarcerating children and separating them from their parents. Disagreements on this issue have overlapped with discussions about asylum seekers from the Syrian Civil War as well as about migrants from Latin America who come to the US to work, mostly in the agricultural and service industries, but do not get visas or overstay their visas. But questions about immigration policy and how to response to asylum seekers are by no means limited to the US. In the last couple of years, politicians and ordinary people have been debating similar questions about immigration driven by persecution, poverty, fear of violence, and other hardships in countries such as Lebanon, Turkey, Germany, Britain, India, Bangladesh, Colombia, Brazil, Kenya, and Ethiopia. But too often political dialogue on these issues feels like everyone's goal is to convince others that they are wrong, and treat changing one's mind as a failure rather than as a success. As with the example of plastic, if we work to understand the historical factors that led to these situations, we'll be far better poised to solve problems effectively, instead of contributing to increased polarization.

Here's a third example: a man who murdered over fifty Muslim worshippers in Christchurch, New Zealand in March 2019 was found to have been sharing white nationalist ideas with likeminded people on Facebook and Instagram in the runup to his attack. It turns out that a man who murdered nine African Americans worshipping in a church in Charleston, South Carolina four years earlier had also been using Facebook to exchange hateful and racist ideas with others. Certainly, social media has given people a new platform to spew hate speech, but is there really a relationship between increased racist violence and our new forms of digital communication? After the Christchurch killings, Facebook's executives decided that there was. They announced that the company would remove all white nationalist content from posts on Facebook and its subsidiary, Instagram. Supporters cheered that this massive social media company was taking responsibility to limit hate speech. Critics warned against limiting free speech online. Debate has also centered on whether private companies or governments should be responsible for regulating hate speech and/or protecting free speech. Meanwhile, others worry that extremists are only migrating to new venues, including to the dark web, where they can plot violence free of any oversight. At times one might feel paralyzed by the situation. We want to limit mass violence, but should we accept restrictions on our freedoms to do so? There are other important questions connected to this one. Should anyone be responsible for governing speech on social media? If so, who? And how should do they it? How else could we respond to incidents of mass violence? Often discussions on these topics are guided by people earning ad revenues for every click offering easy-to-understand and/or frantically delivered messages. Fortunately, understanding the longer history of topics like censorship, racism, communication revolutions, and mass violence allows us to take a broader, more mature perspective. Rather than feeling paralyzed, studying the past allows us to make informed decisions about issues and leaves us empowered to help shape the future.

One last example. As the first volumes of this book series entered production in early 2020, a novel coronavirus, which causes the sometimes fatal respiratory illness known as COVID-19, was spreading rapidly throughout the world. First detected in Wuhan, China in late 2019, coronavirus spread to 183 countries and territories in a matter of months. By early April 2020, more than 73,000 people had died, with more than 1.3 million confirmed infections.

In response to this pandemic, national governments have taken uneven measures. South Korea aggressively tested, tracked, and treated in order to slow the spread of the disease. British Prime Minister Boris Johnson faced criticism for his government's more meager response. Johnson delayed the closure of schools, bars, restaurants, museums, and other common gathering spots, even as positive cases in the United Kingdom surpassed 1,300 in mid-March. By early April, Johnson himself landed in intensive care with COVID-19 symptoms.

While we do not yet know the long-term outcomes of the coronavirus pandemic, it has already begun to expose the degree to which the rapid circulation of goods and people throughout the world exposes us all to health threats, even if it does so unevenly. This novel coronavirus has revealed deep global inequities in access to medical care, adequate nutrition, and stable employment that make one more or less likely to contract and survive disease. It has left many societies caught up in a web of just-in-time supply chains woefully underprepared to combat the health threat. The pandemic has exposed the dangers of rapid global travel in spreading disease and highlighted humans' reliance on that same global transportation to share medical supplies and health care personnel. Many advocates of open borders around the world, for example, are supporting border closures to slow the spread of the disease. At least in April 2020, many politicians in the United States seem to be rapidly shifting their positions on policies related to incarceration, debt collection, health care, and guaranteed basic income. The pandemic has also raised important questions about the threats to public health from the intentional and unintentional spread of disinformation. In short order, coronavirus has made us all comprehend just how dependent we are on our fellow humans, for better and for worse. Coronavirus did not create the problems that it has exposed. A purely medical response to the disease will not solve those problems either. But understanding the historical origins of intertwined economic, political, and social developments that shape its spread will put all of us in a better position to address current and future problems rendered acute by disease.

It is the premise of this book series that addressing the aforementioned issues and others facing us today requires understanding their deep and global historical roots. Today's problems are not simply the outcomes of decisions yesterday—they are shaped by years, decades, and centuries of historical developments. A deep historical understanding helps us understand the present-day world in more sophisticated, mature, and reasoned ways. Humans have been interconnected with faraway places for centuries; solving the central problems facing our world means understanding those connections over time.

Too often our popular political dialogue—increasingly driven by social media, partisan politics, and short-term economic interests—ignores or discounts the complex historical dimensions of current issues and thus fails to provide useful contexts for those issues that could help citizens and leaders resolve them. Historians can help their fellow citizens make decisions by explaining the historical developments that created the world we inherited.

Rather than survey all of world history, each book in this series begins in the present with a pressing or seemingly intractable problem facing humanity (i.e., climate change, terrorism, racism, poverty). It then helps us better understand that not only is that problem not intractable but it has historical origins. That is, it has not been a problem since time immemorial, nor is it unique to the present. Rather, problems have historical lives, have undergone changes both subtle and dramatic, and are the outcomes of human decisions and actions. The book in front of you and others in this series will help you: (1) understand the deep historical roots of a pressing and controversial issue facing the world today; (2) understand its global context; (3) interpret evidence to make reasoned, mature conclusions; (4) evaluate the arguments of others surrounding those issues; and (5) identify and utilize research skills to make independent conclusions about contemporary issues of interest to you.

The Case for the Roots of Contemporary Issues

Five central arguments shape this series' scope. First, every book explains why history matters now. Widespread consensus abounds that history helps individuals make reasonable decisions about the present and future. This is why so many governments require that their citizens study history. And yet, in the United States at least, history is pretty consistently among the least popular subjects for high school and college students. Why is this? The answer is probably in part because it is required and because we give so much attention in our society to prioritizing personal and short-term interests, such that studying history seems impractical. Books in this series are explicit about how essential, practical, and empowering studying history is.

Second, all books in the series offer world history, rather than histories of "civilizations" or continents. None of these books, for instance, stops at the history of the "West." There is a good reason for this: the very idea of the "West" only emerged as an effort to imagine a fundamental civilizational distinctiveness that has never existed. The "West" developed in response to interactions between people in Europe and North America with peoples around the world. The "West" offered a politically motivated myth of a linear inheritance from Greece and Rome to modern Europe, and from modern Europe to the United States. But many facts had to be omitted (intentionally or unintentionally) to sustain that argument.

The idea of the "West" had its core in some kind of definition of Europe, and tacked on the majority-white populations in settler colonies in North America, Australia, and elsewhere. That is, the definition of the "West" is rooted in ideas about race and in global racism, which were not just products of internal developments (i.e., developments taking place exclusively within Europe and the United States), but also of the centuries-long interactions of people around the globe, including systems of colonialism and slavery. In short, these volumes recognize that humans have interacted across large spaces for centuries, and that many of the geographical terms that we use to understand the world—the West, Middle East, the Far East, Europe, America, Africa—only came to exist as products of those interactions.

Third, while all volumes in the series offer world histories, they are also different from most world histories in that they focus on the history of a specific issue. In our view, a central challenge facing a lot of world history is the magnitude of coverage required by adopting a global scope. Some solve this problem by dividing up the world into continents. That approach can be effective, but suffers from the same challenge as books that adopt civilizational paradigms like "the West." Others attempt to solve the problem by adopting global narratives that replace older civilizational ones. Global approaches can help us see patterns previously overlooked, but risk erasing the complexity of human experiences and decisions in order to tell universalizing stories that can make the outcomes look inevitable. They often do not capture the extent to which even major outcomes—political revolutions, technological changes, economic transformations—are the products of decisions made by ordinary people. Neither can they capture the logical counterpoint: that those people could have made other decisions, and that ordinary people actually do transform the world every day.

The fourth argument that shapes the scope of this series relates to the interconnection between premodern and modern history. What does "modern" signify in the first place? Most understandings of the past rely on this concept, but its meaning is notoriously hard to pin down. One easy way to think about the options is to look at how historians have divided up history into premodern and modern eras in textbooks and classes.

One common dividing point is 1500. The argument here is that a set of shifts between roughly 1450 and 1550 fundamentally transformed the world so that the periods before and after this period can be understood as distinct from one another. These include global explorations, the information revolution associated with the invention of the printing press, a set of military campaigns that established the boundaries of lands ruled by Muslim and Christian princes, and the spread of Renaissance capitalism.

Another common dividing point between the modern and premodern is 1800. Critical here are the development of industrial production and transportation, democratic forms of governance, waves of anticolonial revolutions in the Americas, novel forms of Western imperialism that came to dominate much of Africa and Asia, the intensification of scientific understandings of the world, and the spread of new secular ideologies, like nationalism. There are other dividing points that historians have used to separate history, but these two are the most common.

Regardless of which breaking point you find most convincing, there are at least two problems with this way of dividing histories along "modern" and "premodern" lines. First, these divisions are usually Eurocentric in orientation. They presuppose that "modernity" was invented in Europe, and then exported elsewhere. As a result, peoples whose histories are divided up differently or that are less marked by European norms wrongly appear "backward." The second problem with these divisions is that they are less capable of identifying continuities across these divides.

We are not arguing that distinguishing between "modern" and "premodern" is always problematic. Rather, we see advantages to framing histories *across* these divides. Histories that only cover the modern period sometimes simplify the premodern world or treat people who lived long ago as irrelevant, often missing important early legacies. Meanwhile, histories that only cover premodern periods often suffer because their relevance for understanding the present is hard to see. They sometimes ask questions of interest to only professional historians with specialized knowledge. This series seeks to correct for each of these problems by looking for premodern inheritances in the modern world.

The final argument that shapes the series is that we have a stronger understanding of developments when we study the interrelationships among large structures of power, processes of change, and individual responses to both. The books work to help you understand how history has unfolded by examining the past from these three interactive perspectives. The first is structural: how political, economic, social, and cultural power functioned at specific times and places. The second explains what forces have led to transformations from one condition to another. The third looks at how individuals have responded to both structures and changes, including how they resisted structures of power in ways that promoted change.

Historians distinguish between structure, change, and agency. Leaving out agency can make structures and changes look inevitable. Leaving out change flattens out the world, as if it were always the same (hint: always be skeptical of a sentence that begins with: "Throughout history"!). Leaving out structures celebrates human choices and autonomy, but naively ignores how broader contexts limit or shape our options. Understanding how structure, change, and agency interact allows us to create a more realistic picture of how the world works.

Doing History

When we talk to authors about writing these books, we urge that they do not need to provide all the answers to the issues about which they write, but should instead provide readers with the skills to find answers for themselves. That is, using the goals just described, this series is meant to help you think more critically about the relationship between the past and the present by developing discrete but mutually reinforcing research and analytical skills.

First, the volumes in this series will help you learn how to ask critical historical questions about contemporary issues—questions that do not beg simplistic answers but instead probe more deeply into the past, bridge seemingly disconnected geographies, and recognize the variety of human experiences. Second, you will learn how to assess, integrate, and weigh against each other the arguments of scholars who study both historical and contemporary issues. Historians do not always agree about cause and effect, the relative importance of certain contributing factors over others, or even how best to interpret a single document. This series will help you understand the importance of these debates and to find your own voice within them.

Third, you will learn how to identify, evaluate, interpret, and organize varieties of primary sources—evidence that comes from the periods you are studying—related to specific historical processes. Primary sources are the raw evidence contained in the historical record, produced at the time of an event or process either by a person or group of people directly involved or by a first-hand observer. Primary sources nearly always require historians to analyze and present their larger significance. As such, you will learn how to develop appropriate historical contexts within which to situate primary sources.

While we listed these three sets of skills in order, in fact you might begin with any one of them. For example, you may already have a historical question in mind after reading several recent news articles about a contemporary problem. That question would allow you to begin searching for appropriate debates about the historical origins of that problem or to seek out primary sources for analysis. Conversely, you might begin searching for primary sources on a topic of interest to you and then use those primary sources to frame your question. Likewise, you may start with an understanding of two opposing viewpoints about the historical origins of the problem and then conduct your own investigation into the evidence to determine which viewpoint ultimately holds up.

But only after you have developed each of these skills will you be in a position to practice a fourth critical skill: producing analytical arguments backed by historical evidence and situated within appropriate scholarly debates and historical contexts. Posing such arguments will allow you to make reasoned, mature conclusions about how history helps us all address societal problems with that same reason and maturity. We have asked authors to model and at times talk through these skills as they pertain to the issue they have contributed to the series.

Series Organization

Each volume in this series falls under one of five primary themes in history. None attempt to offer a comprehensive treatment of all facets of a theme but instead will expose you to more specific and focused histories and questions clearly relevant to understanding the past's impact on the present.

The first theme—Humans and the Environment—investigates how we have interacted with the natural world over time. It considers how the environment shapes human life, but also how humans have impacted the environment by examining economic, social, cultural, and political developments. The second theme, Globalization, allows us to put our relationship to the natural world into a greater sense of motion. It explores the transformations that have occurred as human relationships have developed across vast distances over centuries. The third theme, the Roots of Inequality, explores the great disparities (the "haves" and "have-nots") of the world around us, along lines of race, gender, class, or other differences. This approach allows us to ask questions about the origins of inequality, and how the inequalities in the world today relate to earlier eras, including the past five hundred years of globalization.

Diverse Ways of Thinking, the fourth theme, helps us understand the past's diverse peoples on their own terms and to get a sense of how they understood one another and the world around them. It addresses the historical nature of ideologies and worldviews that people have developed to conceptualize the differences and inequalities addressed in the inequality theme. The fifth theme, the Roots of Contemporary Conflicts, explores the historical roots of conflicts rooted in diverse worldviews, environmental change, inequalities, and global interactions over time. Its goal is to illuminate the global and local factors that help explain specific conflicts. It often integrates elements of the previous four themes within a set of case studies rooted in the past but also helps explain the dramatic changes we experience and/or witness in the present.

Our thematic organization is meant to provide coherence and structure to a series intended to keep up with global developments in the present as historians work to provide essential contexts for making sense of those developments. Every subject facing the world today—from responding to COVID-19 to debates about the death penalty, from transgender rights to coal production, and from the Boko Haram rebellion in Nigeria to micro-aggressions in Massachusetts—can be better understood by considering the topic in the context of world history.

History is not a path toward easy solutions: we cannot simply copy the recommendations of Mohandas Gandhi, Sojourner Truth, Karl Marx, Ibn Rushd, or anyone else for that matter, to solve problems today. To do so would be foolhardy. But we can better understand the complex nature of the problems we face so that the solutions we develop are mature, responsible, thoughtful, and informed. In the following book, we have asked one historian with specialized knowledge and training in this approach to guide you through this process for one specific urgent issue facing the world.

—Jesse Spohnholz and Clif Stratton

ROOTS OF CONTEMPORARY ISSUES

CHRONIC DISPARITIES

INTRODUCTION

Purpose

August 1, 2014, 8:22 a.m.: "Stop the EBOLA patients from entering the U.S. Treat them, at the highest level, over there. THE UNITED STATES HAS ENOUGH PROBLEMS!" Donald Trump—at the time a reality television star—tweeted. As the President Barack Obama's administration rushed to bring home American citizens and aid workers who had been infected overseas, protests erupted at Emory University hospital in Atlanta, Georgia, which received and treated these individuals. "It was that tweet that created a level of anxiety in the country," said Amy Pope, a senior Obama administration counterterrorism official who worked on the outbreak. "That was a crystallizing moment."[1]

Two months later on the *Today Show*, celebrity doctor Mehmed Oz trafficked in erroneous hysterics over Ebola during an interview with Matt Lauer while discussing the case of Thomas Duncan, a Liberian citizen with Ebola who had travelled to Dallas, Texas. Duncan was visiting family when he felt ill and tried to tell doctors at a hospital he had recently come from Liberia, a site of an Ebola outbreak. Doctors ignored this statement and sent him home with antibiotics. Seemingly inspired more by the 1995 science fiction film *Outbreak* than actual medical knowledge, Oz even went so far as to claim what he was "hearing behind closed doors" was that Ebola was mutating and could become airborne "like the flu."[2] The Centers for Disease Control (CDC) had to refute Oz's absurd claim for months afterward in an educational campaign.[3] On October 8, 2014, Duncan

---

1. Reid Wilson, "How Ebola Entered the American Consciousness: A Trump Tweet," *The Hill*, May 8, 2018.

2. Matt Lauer, Interview of Dr. Mehmed Oz, *The Today Show*, NBC, October 2, 2014.

3. "Why Ebola Is NOT Likely to Become Airborne," US Department of Health and Human Services and the Centers for Disease Control and Prevention, April 30, 2015, http://www.cdc.gov/vhf/ebola/pdf/mutations.pdf.

died from the disease. About a week later, American congressional lawmakers, both Democrat and Republican, called for travel bans against African countries, even as Thomas Frieden, Director of the CDC, counseled such a ban would be ineffective in curbing the spread of the disease and detrimental to African communities in need of the aid workers seeking to travel there. Frieden further stated there was no cause for panic, as there were a handful of well-contained cases in the United States.[4]

But panic and misinformation proliferated nonetheless. Parents in Dallas pulled their children out of school, fearful the disease was spreading rapidly. By October 24, in New York City, eleven-year-old Amadou Drame and his thirteen-year-old brother Pape, Senegalese migrants, were beaten by classmates. Their tormentors called them "Ebola."[5] Politicians positioned themselves to cast blame on both sides of the aisle in the lead-up to the 2014 midterm election year. Discrimination reared its ugly head and all Africans in the United States were labeled with the stigma of Ebola. All of this was the response to fewer than a dozen US cases of Ebola—a disease endemic to central Africa. In the United States, all but Duncan survived. Meanwhile, over the next two years the death toll in Liberia, Guinea, and Sierra Leone—the hardest hit countries—ballooned to a combined 28,610 cases resulting in 11,308 deaths.[6] What historical and social contexts explain the disparity? What factors led to the stigmatization of Africans in the United States during this disease outbreak? One of the many places you might start your investigation of those questions is in the social and cultural history of public health.

This book has two primary purposes. The first is to argue inequalities in public health access and outcomes, like those described here, are the results of broader social, economic, and political inequalities emerged and changed over centuries. In other words, there are historical reasons for the negative reactions of some Americans to migrants from Africa as media coverage of Ebola outbreaks increased in late 2014. And there are also historical reasons for the high death toll in Africa compared to other places where Ebola cases emerged. Those historical reasons often have little or nothing to do with medical science on its own. Further, public health initiatives, however well-meaning, have at times deepened inequalities ranging from race to class to gender. In other words, I argue that in order for public health initiatives to achieve the desired positive outcomes for

---

4. Will Dunham, "U.S. Lawmakers Blast Government's Ebola Response, Urge Travel Ban," *Reuters*, October 16, 2014.

5. Josh Sanburn, "Ebola Brings Another Fear: Xenophobia," *Time*, October 29, 2014.

6. "Years of Ebola Virus Outbreaks," Centers for Disease Control and Prevention, last reviewed April 3, 2019, https://www.cdc.gov/vhf/ebola/history/chronology.html.

humans, it is imperative we understand them within its particular social and historical contexts. A failure to do so will exacerbate—not close—the equity gaps public health is meant to address.

What we call "public health" as a field of study and profession did not emerge until the nineteenth century. Many of the strategies, agencies, institutions, and cultural attitudes toward managing the collective health of a population, however, were present centuries earlier. To increase the depth of historical coverage, I define public health more broadly here. Rather than focusing solely on the professional field itself, my definition of public health for this book will include any organized efforts and policy directives of governments as well as public and private organizations to promote human health in a society.

The second purpose of this book is to provide a model for how to conduct further historical research into this and other contemporary issues. Each chapter follows the format of structured research essay—and the case studies contained within include models for how to analyze evidence and discussions of scholarly debates. The intent is to equip you with analytical tools and opportunities to practice using them so you can go on to conduct your own research into the historical—rather than immediate—cultural and social roots of contemporary issues like the one presented here.

This book is a work of history, not a medical textbook. It explores the historical, social, and cultural contexts that shape medical crises and policies in specific regions and time periods. Additionally, even though my analysis will at times critique certain public health projects, the goal of this volume is not to discredit medical science. Public health and medicine have done a great deal of good for many people. Let's take smallpox, for example.

Between 1966 and 1980, the World Health Organization (WHO) organized programs and distribution networks to provide affordable or free smallpox vaccinations. While earlier efforts led to the disease's eradication from Europe, Australia, and the Western Hemisphere, Africa and Asia still experienced outbreaks. By combining resources from a host of countries to educate communities about the vaccine and deliver doses, the WHO managed to successfully eradicate smallpox everywhere. It is hard to put a value or a number on how many lives this program saved in the intervening decades. One of the deadliest diseases humanity has ever faced is now restricted to laboratory samples. Unless someone makes the horrible decision to weaponize those samples, no one, regardless of the happenstances of socioeconomic status or where they are born, will have to face smallpox again.

The book you are about to read, however, does encourage you to think about disease, treatment, and public health in their social and historical contexts. Scientific thought is not crafted in a vacuum. Even though we often consider—or desire—science to be objective, and even though scientists strive for objectivity, science is a product of human action. The humans that produce it are, like all of us, influenced by their unique historical and social contexts.

Those contextual influences can create undue or unintentional harm. This was true in the case of smallpox a century before the WHO began its eradication program. In the nineteenth century, mandatory vaccination programs in Great Britain met resistance from poorer segments of the community who were wary of government intrusion. The historian Nadja Durbach outlines in her work how this first "antivaxer" movement evolved. She points out how nineteenth-century British doctors and elected officials were predisposed to view the poor as recalcitrant and illogical. Rather than meeting individuals to address their concerns and educate them on the benefits of the vaccine, they crafted punitive systems that were ineffective, received backlash, and ultimately hindered efforts to vaccinate the community for decades.[7] Humanities, like history, can help public health officials and doctors make better decisions to hopefully avoid some of those unintended consequences.

Structure

The book is organized into five chapters following a rough chronology from the fourteenth century to the present. Each chapter offers a case study that illustrates the development of public health protocols for issues as policymakers, physicians, medical officers, and government officials addressed what they deemed to be threats to the health of their communities. Across the book as a whole, we can see how decision-makers modified their approaches as the considered local, national, regional, and global contexts of each issue while managing matters affecting the health of populations.

Through a set of examples in each chapter, you will see how local efforts to manage health increasingly centralized into national and later international organizations, movements, and agencies. The chapters also demonstrate how the systems of public health formed in Western and Central Europe spread across the globe by means of imperialism and other forms of domination and influence. This process of replication has at times benefited populations in Africa, Asia, and the Pacific—the best example being the global eradication of smallpox mentioned earlier. In many instances from the nineteenth century to the present, however, you will also see that "Western" health interventions reinforced disparities in the standard of care and living for disenfranchised groups in several

---

7. Nadja Durbach, *Bodily Matters: The Anti-Vaccination Movement in England, 1853–1907* (Durham, NC: Duke University Press, 2005). This book has a rich, complex argument and I highly encourage you to read it!

societies as these interventions displaced older and more localized systems of health management.

Chapter 1 explores the social and religious contexts of different communities responding to disease before the discipline of public health emerged. This chapter looks at how local governments in Christian-dominated Europe and Muslim-dominated Southwest Asia and North Africa understood and attempted to control *Yersina pestis*—popularly known as Plague—during the Second Pandemic in the fourteenth century and several recurrent outbreaks well into the late seventeenth century. People living in these regions in the premodern era did not use the same terminologies we do to describe "modern" biology, medicine, and healthcare. Yet their premodern conceptions of disease and views of health as a "public utility" did have an impact on how our modern views and approaches to disease control developed. The inequalities addressed and created by the policies and beliefs of these earlier societies—which at times targeted social outsiders and the poor as the source of contagion—represent an impactful pattern of social and government interactions with the health of communities.

Chapter 2 looks at how prejudiced views of the poor merged with racism in the responses of national and imperial governments to cholera outbreaks in India, Great Britain, Germany, and the United States during the nineteenth century. The expansion of European empires across the globe in the eighteenth and nineteenth centuries increased the frequency of outbreaks and epidemics of disease on a global scale. Initial public health responses to cholera reinforced false ideas certain groups were the cause of the disease through their behaviors, leading to policies that made these targeted groups more vulnerable to cholera. The chapter will also explore key transformations that later improved conditions for the poor, including the centralization of sewer and drinking water infrastructure, legislation empowering the national government over the local during public health crises, and the chlorination of water. Although these policies were increasingly used in the Europe and the United States, British colonial governments in India refused to adopt the costlier approaches, insisting such measures would be ineffective among "unhygienic natives." The end result was a growing global health disparity as cholera outbreaks decreased in Europe while becoming deadlier and more frequent in India.

Chapter 3 covers the history of global colonial empires and medical and policy efforts to control and limit the spread of sexually transmitted diseases (STDs). Imperial notions of race explored in chapter 2 emerge again in chapter 3 alongside nineteenth- and twentieth-century European and American perceptions of gender. These worldviews impacted how policymakers viewed the role of the imperial state in regulating and controlling sexuality and reproduction. Any history of STD controls is closely linked to the history of reproduction and gender roles, as well as the history of eugenics: a racialized pseudo-science calling for extreme government control over reproduction and sex. This chapter outlines the history of how doctors and colonial officials regarded women as the "vectors" of STDs, the Euro-American belief in a "tropical origin" for diseases like syphilis, and how "prostitution controls" morphed into attempts by Euro-American empires to prevent racial mixing. Finally, this chapter will show you how all of these threads come together alongside the eugenics movement in the Tuskegee syphilis experiment (1932–1972).

Chapter 4 looks at how national and imperial governments forged internationalist institutions in the early twentieth century in response to a different public health threat: opium addiction. This chapter examines drug controls in the Kingdom of Burma, the Chinese Empire, the British Empire, and international organizations like the League of Nations after World War I. Opium controls are an excellent example of how "Western" approaches to public health disrupted local, non-European systems of public health through imperialism. Older substance abuse controls in Burma and China were destroyed by the arrival of Britain's global trade in narcotics. As Great Britain experienced an "epidemic" of opium addiction in the nineteenth century, British officials adopted drug control policies with different standards of care and prevention for the rich versus poor and different regulations for British citizens versus colonized subjects. When international organizations such as the League of Nations and later the United Nations and World Health Organization attempted to regulate narcotics globally, their efforts rested upon imperial foundations.

The last case study, chapter 5, looks at disparities created and exacerbated by worldwide connections and national responses to a truly global crisis: the HIV/AIDS pandemic. The first part of the chapter explores the history of the pandemic itself, the identification of "risk groups," and how some government officials, such as those in the United States, initially responded to the HIV outbreak. The chapter pays special attention to the initial demonization of homosexuals and Haitians as sources of the disease and the impact this had on those communities and on global perceptions of HIV/AIDS. The second half of the chapter examines programs intended to care for AIDS on a global scale. The intention and stated goal of these ongoing programs is to help bridge global financial disparities and inequalities in access to care. However, the system of dependency created by global HIV aid programs, run largely by European countries and the United States, has also created ideological flaws in care protocols and left Africans, like denizens of the sub-Saharan state of Uganda, vulnerable to forms of exploitation by Europeans and Americans.

Finally, in the conclusion, I come back to the Ebola crisis. Here, the Ebola crisis is not presented as another fully developed case study, but rather as a model of how to begin researching such a paper on the topic on your own.

Selecting a Topic

In writing an abbreviated history of something as socially complex and geographically far-reaching as a global history of public health, I had to make choices regarding content. I attempted to balance in-depth case studies with breadth of geographic and temporal coverage. The choices made to keep this book relatively brief have meant less attention to other regions of the world and other diseases and health concerns that are no less important. For example, a chapter on the important developments in public health in Enlightenment Europe was set aside in favor of covering developments for a similar period in Chinese and Burmese history in chapter 4 to provide geographical balance. The 2014 Ebola outbreak in Guinea, Sierra Leone, and Liberia that inspired me to write this volume ultimately did not become a chapter in this volume either. I hope some of you go on to explore the deeper historical reasons behind why the 2014 outbreak was so devastating, particularly in the West African countries.

In choosing your own research projects, start by looking carefully at the world around you. What events or ideas or regions of the world appear more frequently in the news or arise in your everyday life? Do any of those stories or moments prompt you to ask questions about how things got the way they are? Perhaps the impact of the COVID-19 pandemic that began in late 2019 could prompt a project looking at public health and racism, comparing microaggressions and violence towards Asians in different parts of the world; or possibly investigating the historical roots behind vast inequalities in access to COVID-19 testing, personal protective equipment, and ventilators in countries such as China, Iran, South Korea, Italy and the United States. Personally, my interest in the history of public health began during my final graduate school years at Emory University, which coincided with the 2014 Ebola outbreak in West Africa. Emory, located next door to the CDC in Atlanta, Georgia, provided care and treatment for a few of the American Ebola victims in specially designed wards at the university hospital which was less than 500 yards away from the history department. I saw first-hand the protocols and drills put in place for disease containment, alongside a media frenzy and the at times hateful public backlash against bringing these individuals to the United States for treatment. It sparked my interest and made me want to know more about the history of public health and societal perceptions of disease.

Or consider selecting a topic another way: is there a time period or society from the past in which you are particularly interested? What public health issues did that society face? Instead of analyzing the historical connections between public health and inequality, you might take a completely different approach. For example, you could explore the environmental impact of certain public health programs. How were natural landscapes transformed by historical efforts to control disease-carrying tzetse flies in Tanzania or mosquitoes in Florida or to combat rabies in the United Kingdom? The possibilities for scholarly exploration are endless.

Finding Sources

When it comes to locating sources as you pursue your own projects, the best place to start is—as I did—at the library, either the physical building or its online catalogue. Begin your search by looking for books and articles written by scholars and experts. In writing this book, I relied heavily on such secondary sources as I explored the topics in this text in their local, national, regional, global, and cultural contexts. Do not be discouraged if results do not materialize in the first search. Try different key words. Look carefully at each entry the search catalogue provides in response to your query. Even if the title does not exactly match your topic, it may still be useful. Also consider searching for aspects of your topic. If you are interested in the history of Ebola, for example, try looking for books on the history of the Congo, Guinea, Sierra Leone, or Liberia in addition to searching for the disease itself. Cast a wide net.

In the case of articles, JSTOR and other online databases to which your university or school library subscribes will yield several pieces related to your topic. If you can do so through your library's subscription, download and save those pieces to read and refer to later. The same will be true of books in the library catalogue when you search online. eBooks will likely appear in your search and are convenient and easily accessible online. Even though eBooks are easier to bookmark in your search engine from the comfort of your home, I would still encourage you to investigate the hardcopies suggested to you by your library catalogue search. There is an added benefit to going to the physical stacks and grabbing those books yourself. When you go to the shelves to grab a title from your search, you will often find other, related books sitting right next to it. Collect some of those as well.

My research also included primary sources: documents and other evidence produced during the historical period being analyzed. To locate primary sources, I relied on a range of options. In some instances, I relied on documents and images I had discovered in my archival research abroad for other projects. I requested older published documents through interlibrary loan systems. I looked through subscription-based databases like JSTOR or online newspaper archives available through my university library. I also took advantage of open-source collections available online like the Wellcome Library, the British Library, Google Books, Harvard's Open Collection on Contagion, and the WHO's IRIS database, which are incredibly helpful if you already know exactly what you are looking for.

In a few instances, documents or images were particularly difficult to locate and I contacted other scholars who I knew to be specialists in the subfield for copies they had or advice on how to acquire a copy.

Another strategy for locating more sources is to look at the footnotes, endnotes, and bibliographies of the books and articles you collect. Good scholars cite their sources so that future students and researchers can see what works and archival documents they used. In citing material, they are encouraging you to seek out those sources and use them yourselves. In this book, I cite my sources in the footnotes and I provide others in Further Reading sections at the end of each chapter. There are so many options for you to pursue sources for your research. Follow where they lead.

FURTHER READING

Packard, Randall M. *A History of Global Health: Interventions into the Lives of Other Peoples*. Baltimore: John Hopkins University Press, 2016.

Porter, Dorothy. *Health, Civilization and the State: A History of Public Health from Ancient to Modern Times*. London: Routledge, 1999.

Scally, Gabriel, and Justine Womack. "The Importance of the Past in Public Health." *Journal of Epidemiology & Community Health* 58, no. 9 (2004): 751–55.

Spray, E. C. "Health and Medicine in the Enlightenment." In *The Oxford Handbook of the History of Medicine*, edited by Mark Jackson, 82–99. New York: Oxford University Press, 2011.

Stepan, Nancy Leys. *Eradication: Ridding the World of Diseases Forever?* Ithaca, NY: Cornell University Press, 2011.

HEALTH AS A PUBLIC UTILITY

LOCAL PLAGUE RESPONSES IN THE CHRISTIAN AND ISLAMIC WORLDS

The existence of contagion has been proved by experience, deduction, the senses, observation, and by unanimous reports . . . It is not a secret to whoever has looked into this matter or has come aware of it that those who come in contact with [Plague] patients mostly die, while those who [have no contact] survive . . . to ignore the proofs of plague contagion is an indecency and an affront to God and holds cheap the lives of Muslims.

—LISĀN AL-DĪN IBN AL-KHATĪB, *a fourteenth-century Muslim physician living in Moorish Spain*[1]

In 1347, a boat filled with dead sailors docked in Italy, ushering in a wave of fleas and rats infected with *Yersina pestis* and spreading illness across Europe, Southwest Asia, and North Africa. At least, this is the standard narrative we normally receive about one of the earliest pandemics in recorded history. This story of a boat full of the dead became a common literary trope. We see it repeated, from Cairo to London, from Istanbul to Marseilles, as the Plague spread in the mid-fourteenth century to the sixteenth century.[2] This was not the first time Plague had arrived in the Mediterranean, though. The disease broke out in Europe, Africa, and Asia repeatedly from antiquity forward. Genetic research in 2014 confirmed the "plague of Justinian," which swept much of the Mediterranean world, central Asia, and eastern Africa from 541 to 542, was caused by different strains of the same bacterium as the outbreak over seven centuries later: *Yersina pestis*.[3]

1. Lisān Al-Dīn Ibn Al-Khatīb, *A Very Useful Inquiry in the Horrible Sickness, 1349–1352*, as quoted and translated in John Aberth, *The Black Death: The Great Mortality, 1348–1350: A Brief History with Documents*, 2nd ed. (Boston: Bedford/St. Martin's, 2017), 90–93.

2. Stuart J. Borsch, *Black Death in Egypt and England: A Comparative Study* (Austin: University of Texas Press, 2005), 1–3.

3. David M. Wagner, Jennifer Klunk, Michaela Harbeck, Alison Devault, Nicholas Waglecner, Jason W. Sahl, Jacob Enk, et al., "*Yersina pestis* and the Plague of Justinian 541–543 AD: a Genomic Analysis," *Lancet Infectious Diseases*, 14, no. 4 (April 1, 2014): 319–26.

Still, the pandemic of 1347 to 1350, known as "the Black Death," represents an important place in the history of public health. Over the next three centuries, Plague swept through Europe, North Africa, and Southwest Asia repeatedly, leaving a massive death toll in its wake (see Map 1.1).[4]

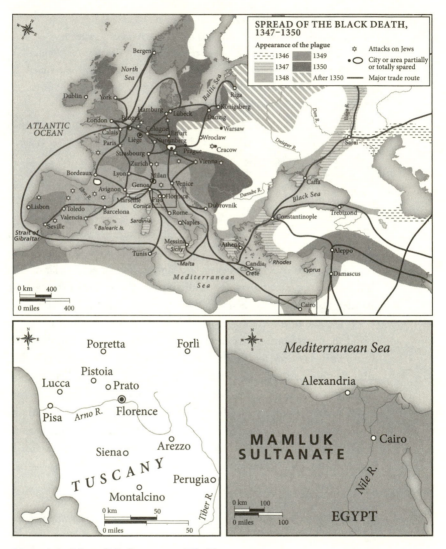

MAP 1.1 Map of Mediterranean World

---

4. You might have noticed that I capitalize "Plague." This is to distinguish the actual disease Plague, caused by *Y. pestis,* from the general, common meaning of the word "plague" as any disease sweeping through a community.

Scholars have debated whether the fourteenth-century pandemic started in India, China, or Central Asia before spreading to the Mediterranean. The preponderance of evidence from contemporaries and later historians favors the Central Asian origin. Regardless of where the outbreak originated, we do know how it spread. Overland trade networks across the Silk Road—heavily protected by offshoots of the Mongol Khanate—and sea routes in the Indian Ocean, the Red Sea, and the Mediterranean provided easy transmission as people, livestock, goods, and rodents and fleas connected societies. Conflict in these centuries also provided a means for transmission, in the form of numerous wars between European principalities and kingdoms before and during the Protestant Reformation, the expansion of the Ottoman Empire, and the decline and ultimate collapse of the Byzantine Empire with the Ottoman capture of Constantinople in 1453. The destruction of infrastructure and movements of soldiers helped spread Plague. Although other illnesses followed pathways of commerce and war, Plague was by far the most effective in its death toll, wiping out between 10 percent and 33 percent of afflicted populations with each outbreak from 1348 to the 1700s.[5]

You may recall in the introduction I stated "modern" public health and epidemiology did not emerge until the nineteenth century. You may wonder why the first chapter of the book covers a period centuries earlier in societies that did not view disease or disease control in explicitly epidemiological terms. The reasons I chose to cover the responses to Plague in chapter 1 are threefold. First, the Black Death is one of the premodern diseases heavily researched by historians and epidemiologists alike. Second, most people have some general knowledge of Plague in the history of epidemic disease. For this reason, it is an excellent starting point—a common foundation upon which to build—in our textbook. Third, and more importantly, how Renaissance Europeans and Southwest Asians and Africans living in the final centuries of the Islamic Golden Age responded to this health crisis set important precedents for understandings and policies related to communal health. Other societies, such as the Chinese Empire and the Mughal Empire in India, also interacted with Plague, but research confirming the presence of Plague and outlining the societal impacts of the responses is more complete in the cases of Europe and Southwest Asia.[6]

People living in these societies did not operate with the same terminologies or practices we associate with "modern" biology, medicine, or healthcare. Yet their

5. Michael Dols, *The Black Death in the Middle East* (Princeton, NJ: Princeton University Press, 1977), 13–67.

6. For more on whether or not Plague was in China and India in this era, see George Sussmann, "Was the Black Death in India and China"?" *Bulletin of the History of Medicine* 85 (2011): 319–55.

conceptions of disease, health, and community and the inequalities addressed and created by the way these earlier societies responded represent a pattern of social and government interactions with the health of communities that persists to this day. We will see this pattern in later chapters, related to other health concerns, in, for example, pre-nineteenth-century Burma and China. The global pattern in the history of response to real and perceived health crises, not a specific era of public health, is what we are exploring in this text.

In the times and places we explore in this book, some far removed from our own, we should remember context. It is easy for us to mock those in the past as irrational or illogical, particularly for the "medieval" world. In doing so, however, we ignore how scientific and religious thought about disease is a product of its own social, economic, geographic, and ideological circumstances at the time of its creation. This is true even today. As we examine how social inequalities were amplified in public health responses in any era, we must not excuse hatred and persecution, but we cannot write these decisions off as "illogical." To do so would damage our ability to assess where our own biases and prejudices we believe to be logical or rational, objective science in our own time themselves create and perpetuate inequalities even when trying to address them.

In the first two sections of this chapter I will cover what Plague is and earlier fourteenth-century religion-based reactions to the disease. Fourteenth-century responses sought to aid the poor, primarily in their spiritual well-being, but some severely persecuted religious minorities. Here, we will analyze how and why religious responses to Plague, though benefitting the economically bereft, led to the murder and torment of Jewish populations across Europe, but not in Southwest Asia or North Africa. The second half of the chapter will discuss responses to Plague in the fifteenth and sixteenth centuries. By the fifteenth and sixteenth centuries, new ideas challenging the religious responses emerged in the Italian principalities, Egypt, Muslim-dominated Kingdoms in Southern Spain, and the Ottoman Empire. Advocates of new ideas on health and city management contributed to a growing view of health as a *publica utilitas,* a public good or utility, coinciding with an understanding of disease as "contagion": something spread from one person to another regardless of morality. Muslim physicians, like Lisān Al-Dīn Ibn Al-Khatīb, were the first to hit upon and advocate contagion theory. Italian physicians and officials adopted the theory, with developments of their own, later.

Rather than viewing disease as a divine punishment, new ideas on contagion encouraged governments both local and kingdom-wide to institute "controls" to prevent the spread of illness. Some segments of the population, however, experienced stigma and persecution as a result. The shift in thought to contagion as the cause and labeling poverty as a sign of sin transformed perceptions of the poor as disadvantaged to views of the poor as an amoral threat to public health in some parts of the Mediterranean world, but not in all. Community leaders introduced controls such as quarantine and compulsory burial of Plague dead in special pits on the outskirts of communities. City officials placed restrictions on travel and commerce regionally to block the spread of the illness. Local governments levied taxes and provided compensation for loss of livelihood sustained by various industries impacted by these controls.[7]

What we might term the earliest public health responses were profoundly local. In Europe, Southwest Asia, and North Africa, chief decisions on how best to manage Plague outbreaks were made by city and regional officials. For this reason, this chapter uses fourteenth- to seventeenth- century responses to Plague in the Italian city-state of Florence and the city of Cairo, a sprawling metropolis on the Nile River in then Mamluk- and later Ottoman-controlled Egypt, as its core case studies. Florence is regarded by many historians as having laid the groundwork for several key aspects of sanitary policy in the Western world and Cairo represents one of the best-researched case studies of response to Plague in the Islamic world.

Throughout this chapter, we will explore the impact emerging *publica utilitas* and changes in views on disease transmission had on charitable groups and states in their policy decisions. From supernatural, to environmental, to contagion factors as the vector for disease, the association of "wrong-living"—either morally or in terms of hygiene—was a causal factor in disease encouraged policymakers to link poverty with disease. Accusatory public health perceptions had far-reaching historical implications. Sanitary and disease control policies built on prejudices and perceptions of certain groups as a "threat" to the health of the community evolved into national and international public health paradigms, accentuating inequality of health along class, race, and gender lines.

The "Horrible Sickness"

What was Plague? You may have a general knowledge of the Black Death and how it was and is spread, but you might not be familiar with the origins of this bacterial illness, its symptoms, and its forms. Plague bacteria of the various species in the *Yersina* genus most likely evolved in rodents first, with the most probable point of origin being the steppes of Central Asia. To this day, rodents are the primary animals impacted by Plague. These diseases are often spread among

---

7. Sheldon Watts, *Epidemics and History: Disease, Power and Imperialism* (New Haven, CT: Yale University Press, 1997), 1–39.

populations of rodents and can jump over to other animals, such as horses, dogs, and cats, via fleas that bite infected creatures (see Figure 1.1). A build-up of the bacteria in the flea's proboscis makes it unable to ingest blood during its attacks, prompting it to try to suck blood from multiple hosts as it slowly dies of starvation, spreading the disease in the process. Only one species of this bacteria, however, infects humans: *Y. pestis*. Infection occurs one to six days after exposure and death can come in ten days or less without antibiotics, which were not available until the twentieth century. *Y. pestis* comes in three disease forms: Bubonic, Pneumonic, and Septicemic Plagues. Bubonic Plague is usually spread by an infected flea bite. Pneumonic Plague occurs when the bacteria infect the victim's lungs and is the only form spread directly between humans by coughing up infected droplets and sputum. Septicemic Plague occurs when the bacteria directly

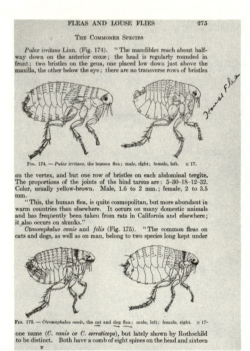

FIGURE 1.1 An image of a "human flea" (*P. irritans*) from a 1915 entomology textbook, after the connection between fleas, the microbe, and Plague had been established. *P. irritans* may be responsible for transmission of Plague to and among humans, but other species of flea more frequently transmit it between rodents and other animals. The Oriental rat flea (*Xenopsylla cheopis*) is the primary vector for Plague.

Source: Herms, William Brodbeck. *Medical and Veterinary Entomology*. New York: Macmillan, 1915, 274. Courtesy of Metcalfe Collection at North Carolina State University, digitized and placed on The Internet Archive. Public Domain. https://archive.org/details/medicalveterinar00herm/page/274

infects the blood stream, can cause sudden death, and is transmitted by contact with bodily fluids, handling an infected animal, and flea bites.[8]

All three are caused by the same bacteria and all three were most likely present during the outbreaks of Plague from the fourteenth to seventeenth centuries. This issue of historical distance and ever-changing technologies and ideas are some of the reasons trying to match modern diagnoses to older accounts of disease is tricky for historians researching epidemics in earlier times. From the 1970s to the 2000s, however, a small community of bacteriologists and historians questioned the larger body of historical scholarship that identified bubonic and pneumonic plague as the cause of the Black Death. These "plague deniers" speculated the "Great Mortality" may not have been caused by a single disease, let alone infections of *Y. pestis*. Their main arguments were a) Black Death spread too quickly among humans and animals to have been caused by a bacterial agent; b) descriptions of symptoms by chroniclers living in the fourteenth century could map on to an array of diseases and did not match neatly with "modern" diagnoses of Plague; and c) because these earlier societies had no understanding of microbiology to definitively distinguish between diseases, individuals might generally have referred to outbreaks of any illness as "plague."[9]

"Plague deniers" were proved wrong in the 1990s and 2010s. The debate ended with the genetic testing of remains of fourteenth- to seventeenth-century victims of Plague buried in mass graves across Europe, Southwest Asia, and North Africa. Anthropologists, historians, and bacterial geneticists worked together to locate and survey the historical geography of Plague, using historical records to locate remains to excavate and test for the bacteria. In blood, teeth, bones, and hair, traces of *Y. pestis* DNA were found in every victim (human and animal), at every site, across this vast geographic area. Further testing of other sites around the world revealed outbreaks of *Y. pestis* far earlier, such as Justinian's Plague (541–542 CE), and far later, like the "Third Pandemic"—a global plague outbreak in India, China, Europe, and the United States at the turn of twentieth century.[10]

"Plague deniers" questioned the validity of symptom descriptions by contemporaries. Plague in humans, however, can present different symptoms and

---

8. Borsch, *Black Death*, 1–9; "Plague," Centers for Disease Control and Prevention, https://www.cdc.gov/plague/index.html, last updated November 27, 2018.

9. Examples of "plague denial" include J. F. D. Shrewsbury, *A History of Bubonic Plague in the British Isles* (Cambridge: Cambridge University Press, 1970); Graham Twigg, *The Black Death: A Biological Reappraisal* (New York: Schocken, 1984); Samuel K. Cohn Jr., *The Black Death Transformed: Disease and Culture in Early Renaissance Europe* (London: Arnold, 2003).

10. Aberth, *The Black Death*, 5–10.

is not entirely uniform. Sometimes, Pneumonic and Septicemic cases may not present any signs of illness before death. Let us consider the medical descriptions of Plague. As this text is designed to give you content, but also teach by example the basics of conducting historical research, I hope you have been looking at my citations of sources. Please go to the Centers for Disease Control (CDC) website, found in footnote 8 of this chapter. Select the tab marked "Symptoms" and read. Now, compare to Plague descriptions from Louis Sanctus of Avignon, France in 1348:

> The plague is of three types of infection. First . . . men feel pain in their lungs, from which there comes a shortness of breath. He who has this malady . . . will not live more than two days . . . Many dead bodies were cut up and opened and it was found that all who die so suddenly have an infection of the lungs and spit up blood . . . There is another kind of plague . . . namely that certain *apostemes* [essentially: boils] suddenly appear on both armpits, from which men die without delay. There is even a third plague . . . it runs its own course: namely that people of both sexes are stricken in the groin, from which they die suddenly.[11]

These symptoms seem similar to the description you saw on the CDC website. We see *apostemes*—which are the *buboes* mentioned by the CDC—infected lungs and blood, lumps under the arms and in the groin, and death. All of this could negate claims contemporary accounts do not match modern diagnosis.

Still, we need to remember our source. Sanctus was a musician, not a physician, so we might suspect his account. Yet Sanctus was in Avignon, France, where the Pope of the Catholic Church resided for much of the fourteenth century.[12] Since the Catholic Church was a powerful economic and cultural force during the Renaissance, some medical experts of the time would have been present in Avignon, plying their trade. As a musician entertaining wealthy individuals and high-ranking clergy, Sanctus likely interacted with "learned men" who knew more than he about the illness. What about errors in his account, such as the rapidity of death? Sanctus's own fear may have played a role in these supposed exaggerations. We need to remember that Sanctus was a fourteenth-century European, which means he had no knowledge of bacteria nor of incubation periods, which might also explain why, to him, death seemed so sudden. Associations

---

11. Louis Sanctus, *Letter*, April 27, 1348, as quoted in Aberth, *The Black Death*, 30.

12. Wondering why the Pope was based in France instead of Rome in this century? Read Joëlle Rollo-Koster, *Avignon and Its Papacy, 1309–1417: Popes, Institutions, and Society* (London: Rowman & Littlefield, 2015).

of bacteria, viruses, and other microbes as causes of illness did not emerge until the nineteenth century, as we will see in chapter 2. *Y. pestis* itself was not identified until 1894, when Swiss bacteriologist Alexandre Yersin (1863–1943) found it under his microscope.

To confirm the connection between Plague and the disease we know to be caused by *Y. pestis*, good researchers collaborated with geneticists and microbiologists once new technology was available. One of the most important steps in the research process is to corroborate your findings, sometimes working with scholars and experts in other fields. Genetic testing of mass graves enabled historians, archaeologists, and anthropologists to confirm it was indeed Plague, and confirmed Sanctus's account is the same disease. You should always analyze your sources and corroborate your findings when you conduct your own research.

You now know what Plague is and have seen contemporary accounts. You have a greater understanding of how and why this disease was so terrifying to populations in the premodern era before antibiotics. Keep that context in mind as we analyze the responses societies had to Plague and how societal inequalities were impacted by these policies and reactions. In the next section, we will examine initial religious responses in Christian Europe and Muslim Southwest Asia and North Africa to what contemporaries perceived as a plague of Biblical proportions.

Charity and Conspiracies: Religion, the Poor, and Persecution of Jews

Most communities in the Mediterranean world were, as they are today, incredibly diverse, containing populations of diverse ethnic, linguistic, and religious backgrounds. We tend to think of Europe as "Christian" and Southwest Asia and North Africa as "Muslim," particularly in the medieval era. That is not an accurate description of those societies, which contained members of both faiths and countless religious and ethnic minorities. For our purposes, it is more appropriate to refer to these parts of the globe as "majority-Christian/Christian-dominated" or "majority-Muslim/Muslim-dominated."

Initial fourteenth-century responses to Plague based on Christian and Islamic beliefs tried to reconcile horrible outbreaks with religious thought. Christians often viewed the disease as a punishment for individual sin while Muslims interpreted it as the will of Allah and a form of martyrdom. Although members of both religious identities saw it as their responsibility to administer aid to the poor, Christian societies did not distribute assistance evenly among members of these communities. Due to differences in popular religious interpretations of Plague in Christianity and Islam, disparities were more pronounced in majority-Christian than in majority-Muslim communities. The most frequent targets of this inequality were practitioners of the first of the three Abrahamic Faiths: Jews. We do not have sufficient scholarship on Jewish religious interpretations of Plague, with more research having been done on Christian and Muslim responses, but we do see frequent mention of Jews during outbreaks of Plague. Unlike in majority-Muslim regions, some leaders, clerics, and movements in majority-Christian areas often falsely blamed Jews for the disease. Jews were frequently cast out of their communities or killed as a result.

Before we launch into the religious reactions to Plague by Muslims and Christians in the fourteenth century, you may need a short history on the shared heritage of Judaism, Christianity, and Islam. These three monotheistic religions originated in Southwest Asia. The first, Judaism, according to tradition was founded by a man named Abraham (hence "Abrahamic Faiths") in Canaan circa 1850 BCE. His god, Yahweh, became the focal point for worship by a group of people in Southwest Asia who came to refer to themselves as the Israelites or Jews.

Over a millennium later, circa 30 CE (AD or "Year of Our Lord" in some older texts), tradition holds that a practitioner of Abraham's Faith—Jesus of Nazareth, often called Christ—started preaching a message of reform for Judaism. According to Christian tradition, Jesus was descended from the line of King David, a great King who according to Jewish lore was anointed by God (Yahweh) in antiquity. Originally viewing themselves as Jews reforming the faith, centuries after his crucifixion, Jesus's followers later branched from Judaism and founded a new religion, Christianity. Early Christians worshipped the same God, but most versions of this faith regard Christ as God's son—the key difference with Judaism.

In 313 CE, Christianity was legalized in the Roman Empire, which dominated the Mediterranean world from 27 BCE to 480 CE in the West and 1453 in the East, enabling the faith to spread more easily through the Roman Empire and later the Byzantine (Eastern Roman) Empire. As the Christian faith grew over the centuries, its leaders took the religious texts of Judaism—the Torah, the Pentateuch, and the Talmud—in an expanded version known as the Septuagint, relabeled it the "Old Testament," and added new scriptures on the life and teaching of Christ called the "New Testament" to form the "Bible" after centuries of debate about what should and should not be included in this religious volume. Debates over biblical content continue to this day between the denominations of Christianity.

Islam emerged in 622 CE over a half a millennium after the death of Jesus in part of the Mediterranean world partially controlled by the Christian-dominated Byzantine Empire. Muhammed, the founder of this Abrahamic Faith, was born to a polytheistic group in Southwest Asia. According to religious texts, Muhammed was approached by the angel Gabriel (the same angel who in Christian tradition heralds the birth of Jesus in the New Testament Gospels) and introduced to the faith of Abraham and chosen to be the "final Prophet" to introduce Allah's (God's) new additions. In the Qur'an, the holy text of Islam which incorporates pieces from Jewish and Christian texts as well as new material, Muhammed preached the "People of the Book"—Jews, Christians, and Muslims—are of one God.

All three faiths have global distributions, a process started long before the Black Death in the mid-fourteenth century. All three religious traditions outline a code of rules by which individuals should live with some variations. There are many branches of each of these faiths, each with its own unique subset of interpretations of religious texts, traditions, and beliefs. Despite their differences, Islam, Christianity, and Judaism and all their denominations share a belief in a single god and advocate a responsibility to care for the sick and poor along with compassion for one's neighbors and family, sometimes even one's enemies.[13]

We can readily observe this commonality of care for the sick and poor in the teachings of these faiths in medieval societies dominated by the Christians, Muslims, and/or Jewish enclaves within them. Despite drastic economic inequalities between the ruling elite and the everyday person, in many European, Southwest Asian, and North African societies prior to the outbreak of Plague, providing charity and a degree of medical care for the poor was expected and commonplace. Governments and religious institutions took this responsibility seriously in major European cities dominated by Christian rulers, including but not limited to Paris, London, Rome, Florence, Madrid, and Salzburg. Monarchs, princes, and high-ranking clergy like Catholic and Orthodox cardinals and bishops funded public hospitals to shelter the poor and provide a modicum of palliative care.

In some instances, rulers paid physicians to make home visits to impoverished members of the community to provide limited medical services. Priests, monks, and nuns often took care of nutritional needs and tended to the dying. In Mamluk-controlled Cairo and Damascus, Muslim emirs and sultans had done the same for centuries, paying for physicians for the poor, providing funeral expenses for the destitute, and even going so far as to invite the poor into their own homes to reside for a time. Jewish rabbis, craftsmen, and economic leaders of Jewish communities often played a key role in contributing to the construction and maintenance of charitable hospitals in the communities they resided in, regardless of whether the rulers were Muslim or Christian. There were also many Jewish physicians in the era across the Mediterranean world who directly cared for the sick in charity hospitals and home visits. Though it was not a cure-all for

---

13. This is not a religious studies textbook and I lack the space to cover these religions in greater detail than a few paragraphs. I do, however, encourage you to learn more on your own about the interconnected histories of these traditions. For a start, read Amir Hussain, Roy C. Amore, and Willard Oxtoby, *World Religions: Western Traditions*, 5th ed. (Oxford: Oxford University Press, 2019): Judaism, see 80–159, Christianity, see 160–241, Islam, see 242–311.

the economic and health woes of the poor. Flagrant inequalities persisted. Still, the emphasis on charity in these communities helped mitigate some of the plight of the most destitute.[14]

Plague's arrival put charitable beliefs to the test. As the outbreaks worsened from 1348 to the seventeenth century, some of the social structures supporting care for the poor broke down, particularly in Christian societies in Europe. In France, the Byzantine Empire, the Holy Roman Empire, the Italian principalities, England, and Spain the wealthy fled in fear of the disease, along with some higher-ranking clergy. Local governments issued orders and hired mercenaries to protect the properties of the rich from "looting" by the poor while they were away. The ruling elite, both governmental and ecclesiastical, now saw the poor as a threat to their own health and wealth rather than as a community for which they had responsibility. Physicians fled, knowing the full risk of the disease and leaving the sick to their fate. Meanwhile, many priests and nuns remained and tended the sick, seeing it as their religious duty to care for the poor and ill, and died alongside those to whom they ministered. The death toll among lower-ranking clergy meant a reduction in opportunities for assistance, and it whittled away one of the last foundations upon which the poor depended for support.

Though there was not the same level of flight and fear of the poor among Muslim elites, the Plague nonetheless damaged structures aiding the poor. In Mamluk-controlled Egypt and the Ottoman Empire, Islamic dictums encouraging charity and compassion for the sick ironically facilitated the spread of the disease in the large metropolises. Hopes for assistance drew rural Plague victims to the more densely populated cities. As Plague ravaged the urban spaces they congregated in, aid became increasingly scarce. Even accommodations for a proper burial became less tenable as the body count increased, and there are documented cases of masses of corpses being dumped in the Nile River due to the expense and health risk of so many funerals.[15]

Part of the reason these support structures faltered were differences in how practitioners and leaders of Christianity and Islam viewed the disease itself: whether they considered it a punishment or martyrdom, the appropriateness of flight from Plague regions, and popular perceptions of Jews in times of Plague. Many European Christians tended to view the Plague as a punishment from God for individual sins or the sins of the community. God demanded reckoning, they

---

14. James William Brodman, *Charity and Religion in Medieval Europe* (Washington, DC: Catholic University of America Press, 2009), 1–88, 245–66; Ann G. Carmichael, *Plague and the Poor in Renaissance Florence* (Cambridge: Cambridge University Press, 1986), 90–107; Dols, *The Black Death*, 236–54.

15. Carmichael, *Plague and the Poor*, 59–86, 108–26; Dols, *The Black Death*, 236–54.

thought, and the response to Plague embraced by many members of Christian societies and their religious and local leaders was to seek purification to avoid God's wrath. This took many forms, ranging from donations to the Catholic Church, mortification of the flesh, flight from the "sinful" community to maintain one's spiritual purity, expulsion of "sinful" members of the community such as prostitutes or thieves, and persecution of strangers and minorities perceived as having brought "sin" into the community.[16]

Many Muslim religious explanations for Plague did not view it as a punishment. There were three basic components of Muslim religious interpretations of Plague: 1) Plague was a martyrdom and mercy from God for a Muslim; 2) because it was a mercy from God, a Muslim should not enter nor flee a Plague-stricken region; and 3) many Islamic religious leaders believed it could not be passed from person to person, so flight from a region or persecution of the ill was irrelevant. Both faiths were clearly trying to reconcile the theological problem of Plague: How could God, they pondered, let an evil in the world? The most common Christian explanation blamed Plague not on God but on the flawed morality of the community that invited divine retribution. This provoked fear, which led to the spread of the disease through expulsions and mass evacuations. The most common Muslim interpretation portrayed the illness as a gift rather than a curse—an opportunity to die and join Allah in heaven as a martyr. The latter interpretation encouraged more assistance to the sick and insisted the disease was not spreading, which increased infection rates even as officials discouraging flight created limited quarantines.

Michael Dols, who wrote the first major work on the history of Plague responses in Medieval Muslim societies, suggested the reason for disagreement on flight and disease as punishment stemmed from the fact the Bible has an apocalyptic narrative in the Book of Revelations and the Qu'ran does not.[17] Paul Slack, an historian specializing in medieval and early-modern England, agreed on the differences in the two responses. Slack, however, argued that Islamic "fatalism" about the disease as a mercy from God not to be resisted led to one response of partial inaction, whereas the Christian emphasis on sin in the community provoked active, persecutory measures as a form of penance because sin could be atoned for in Christian belief.[18] Both religions' interpretations had, as we saw earlier, detrimental impacts on societal structures to support the poor.

---

16. Dols, *The Black Death*, 286–91.

17. Dols, *The Black Death*, 84–142, 281–96.

18. Paul Slack, "Responses to Plague in Early Modern Europe: The Implications of Public Health," *Social Research* 55, no. 3 (Autumn 1988), 433–53, 438.

The more frantic Christian response, however, had dire consequences for minorities, particularly Jews. Such a response did not occur in Muslim-dominated communities. In Muslim societies, Jews fleeing communities during times of Plague went against Muhammed's teachings in the Hadith not to leave a Plague-ridden area, but this alone did not warrant punishment. Ottoman officials' concerns were less religious and more economic in the fourteenth to sixteenth centuries. They feared Jews leaving would hurt local economies. Jewish craftsmen were the primary artisans engaged in broadcloth weaving. Broadcloth was one of the principle exports of the Ottoman Empire and quotas were expected of each locality. Yet despite threats of reprisal, no actual measures appear to have been taken against Jews leaving Plague-afflicted Muslim-dominated urban centers.[19]

The reason some Jews fled Muslim-controlled urban centers such as Salonica, a broadcloth-manufacturing Greek city controlled by the Ottoman Empire, stemmed from previous experiences with Christian responses to Plague. Many Jews living in large urban centers in the Ottoman Empire in the fifteenth and sixteenth centuries had fled Christian Europe after the fourteenth century. Despite Pope Clement VI (r. 1342–1352), the leader of the Catholic Church, issuing a decree stating Jews were also God's people and should not be blamed for Plague, local religious interpretations and mob mentalities encouraged the slaughter and torment of Jews during the Black Death.[20]

Slack, Dols, and Stuart Borsch, another historian of Medieval Muslim societies, contended the reason for this difference was that Christians frequently interpreted their religious texts as blaming Jews for Christ's crucifixion.[21] Regardless of the supposed theological grounding for persecuting Jews, anti-Semitism (hatred of people of Jewish faith and descent) was commonplace in many European Christian communities. During the Plague, Flagellants, members of a series of Christian religious movements in the fourteenth century, wandered across Europe preaching the disease was a punishment from God heralding the End Times. The remedies, leaders of these groups preached, were "mortification of sinful flesh" through self-mutilation (or "flagellation," hence the name of the movement) and attacking the wealthy, the organized Church, and Jews. Flagellants viewed these groups as having "corrupted" God's people. Sometimes during the Black Death, the approach of a group of flagellants was enough to drive a community into an

---

19. Nükhet Varlik, "Plague, Conflict, and Negotiation: The Jewish Broadcloth Weavers of Salonica and the Ottoman Central Administration in the Late Sixteenth Century," *Jewish History* 28, no. 3/4 (2014): 261–88.

20. Dols, *The Black Death*, 281–302; Watts, *Epidemics and History*, 10.

21. Slack, "Responses to Plague," 439; Dols, *The Black Death*, 281–302; Borsch, *Black Death*, 1–9.

FIGURE 1.2 Thousands of Jews across Europe over several centuries were persecuted and murdered, blamed by anti-Semitic Christian neighbors and local leaders for the spread of disease, kidnapping, and any other crimes or unexplained phenomena.
Source: Burning of Jews during the Black Death epidemic, 1349. Credit: Brussels, Bibliothèque royale de Belgique, MS 13076–77, f. 12v. Public Domain.

anti-Semitic frenzy, killing or expelling Jews in the city or village before the flagellants arrived, to prevent further destruction (see Figure 1.2).[22]

In other instances, anti-Semitism and persecution of Jews occurred without the flagellants. Medieval European Christians frequently entertained conspiracy theories about Jews. Some Christians called Jews the "Killers of Christ," claimed Jews hated all Christians, and said Jews had elaborate networks to kidnap and sacrifice Christian children or poison wells. These paranoid notions were false, born of hatred of a minority population, but they had dire consequences. Take for example the case of Châtel in modern-day Switzerland. In 1348, Christians around Lake Geneva began circulating the idea that the leaders of a predominantly Jewish metropolis, Toledo in Spain, had plans to poison Christendom. "Poison conspiracies" asserted Plague was the result of Jewish poisoning schemes across Europe, and therefore the way to contain the disease was to eliminate Jews.

---

22. For more on the Flagellants and their origins in Italy and Germany, see Norma Cohn, *The Pursuit of the Millennium: Revised and Expanded Edition* (New York: Oxford University Press, 1970), 127–47.

The following text is a perfect example of how thoroughly convinced many medieval European Christians were about the existence of poison conspiracies. What follows is a confession made under torture by Agimet, a Jew who was arrested as a result of these hate-filled claims:

> Agimet the Jew, who lived at Geneva and was arrested at Châtel, was there put to the torture a little and then he was released from it. And after a long time, having been subjected again to torture a little, he confessed in the presence of a great many trustworthy persons, who are later mentioned . . . Rabbi Peyret, a Jew of Chambéry, . . . sent for this Agimet . . . [and] he said: "We have been informed that you are going to Venice to buy silk and other wares. Here I am giving you a little package of half a span in size which contains some prepared poison and venom in a thin, sewed leather-bag. Distribute it among the wells, cisterns, and springs about Venice and the other places to which you go, in order to poison the people who use the water of the aforesaid wells that will have been poisoned by you, namely, the wells in which the poison will have been placed."
>
> Agimet took this package full of poison and carried it with him to Venice, and when he came there he threw and scattered a portion of it into the well or cistern of fresh water which was there near the German House, in order to poison the people who use the water of that cistern . . . Agimet confessed further that after this had been done he left at once in order that he should not be captured by the citizens or others, and that he went personally to Calabria and Apulia and threw the above mentioned poison into many wells.[23]

Although there was no truth to this poison conspiracy, a number of Jews who lived on the shores of Lake Geneva were arrested like Agimet. Jews were tortured and records of their coerced confessions were sent from one town to another in Switzerland and down the Rhine River into Germany.

The pattern repeated itself and thousands of Jews in the Alps and Rhineland, in at least two hundred towns and hamlets, were butchered or immolated. In 1349 Strasbourg, now in France, nine hundred Jews were burned alive on St. Valentine's Day on similar charges and there are countless other examples of such events across Europe over the next five hundred years.[24] Many European

---

23. "The Confession of Agimet of Geneva," Châtel, October 20, 1348 as quoted and translated in *The Jew in the Medieval World: A Source Book, 315–1791*," edited by Jacob R. Marcus (New York: Atheneum, 1969), 44–45.

24. Watts, *Epidemics and History*." 10.

Jews who survived the fourteenth-century pogroms fled to the more tolerant Mamluk-Egypt or Ottoman Empire, but Jewish communities continued to live with a fear of such mob-driven mass murders for centuries.

Alongside religious explanations for Plague, physicians and academics in Islamic and Christian communities alike tried to find more direct physical explanations for the disease's origin and spread. Planetary alignments, astrological signs, and the weather all played their roles in some of these explanations, but two dominant notions emerged among physicians in Europe, Southwest Asia, and North Africa: miasma and contagion.

Miasma, described by the ancient Greek physicians Hippocrates (c. 460–370 BCE) and Galen of Pergamon (129–210 CE), held that a corruption of the air, water, or soil made a community sick. The corruptive spirit, or *pneuma,* according to Galen, polluted the atmosphere and imbalanced a victim's internal "humors."[25] This ancient idea, including copies of Hippocrates's and Galen's works in translation, frequently appeared in medical texts on the bookshelves of Christian, Jewish, and Muslim physicians across the Mediterranean world and influenced them to believe the disease was environmentally driven and one could escape it.

Contagion theory was new. Proposed by Muslim physicians and a few French and Italian Christian doctors, contagion theory held it was not the environment, but contact with a sick person that spread illness. Both theories necessitated very different approaches to manage the health of the community. Debates over these causal factors, though contested by some Christian and Islamic theologians at the time, led to changes in how city officials and doctors reacted to Plague.[26] In the next two sections, we will explore how these emerging notions of health shaped and transformed urban responses in Mamluk-controlled Cairo and in the Italian principality of Florence.

Cairo: Mamluks, Ottomans, and Contagion

Egypt had taken on a very different cultural character after centuries of conquest by Macedonians, Romans, and the Islamic dynasties of the Fatimids and Ayyubids. No longer the land of the Pharaohs of the antiquity, Cairo, Egypt was the capital of Mamluk-Sultanate of Egypt and Syria, which lasted from 1250 to 1517 when the Ottomans conquered the region. The Mamluks were not a distinct family, ethnic, or religious group, but a multiethnic group in a meritocratic

25. Hippocrates, "Epidemics I and III," in W. H. S. Jones, trans., *Hippocrates, Vol. 1* (Cambridge, MA: Harvard University Press, 2014); R. E. Siegel, *Galen's System of Physiology and Medicine* (Basel: S. Karger, 1968), 196–359.

26. Dols, *The Black Death,*" 84–95.

society comprised of "slave soldiers." In the centuries before the formation of the Mamluk-Sultanate, and even during, a Mamluk (an Arabic word translating to "property") typically started out as a child prisoner of war from conflicts in Eastern Europe and Central and Southwest Asia, coming from a range of religious and ethnic backgrounds. These children were sold by Italian merchants to ruling elite in what is now modern Iraq, Syria, and Egypt. Once purchased, they were then trained as soldiers and converted to Islam, but rarely did they learn to speak Arabic. After their training was complete, they were granted their freedom in exchange for fealty to an emir or sultan. Once freed, a Mamluk could rise in rank according to merit, even becoming an emir (a type of feudal lord who held considerable property and commanded soldiers).[27]

In 1250, the Ayyubid Sultanate—the precursor to the Mamluk Sultanate—collapsed after ten years of conflict with European kingdoms, the Seventh Crusade, and a revolt of Mamluks in Egypt. Mamluks from Syria joined forces with the Mamluks in Egypt in 1250. The year before, the Ayyubid sultan, as-Salih Ayyub (r. 1240–1249), died and his widow, Shajar al-Durr (r. 1250–1257), became the Sultana of Egypt. As the law at the time required male leadership, however, Shajar al-Durr married the freed Mamluk, Emir Aybak (r. 1250–1257), who became the first Mamluk Sultan of Egypt, founding the Bahri Dynasty (1250–1382). Afterward, freed Mamluks could aspire to rise to the rank of sultan, without any familial ties to the ruling family, if they had the leverage and martial ability to do so. The system of merit-based promotion for freed Mamluks expanded during the Bahri Dynasty and Burji Dynasty (1382–1517) of the Mamluk-Sultanate. The Mamluks of Egypt also ruled Syria, with a regional capital in Damascus.[28]

Under Mamluk rule, Cairo flourished as a cultural and commercial hub in the Mediterranean world. Mamluk emirs and sultans routinely patronized the arts, like other rulers in Southwest Asia, North Africa, and Europe during what is called the Renaissance Era or Islamic Golden Age. Cairo attracted travelers, merchants, artists, and migrants from the Mongolian steppes to Spain, from Italy and France to the Barbary Coast. Its success made it a prime target for Plague outbreaks, which came with regularity from the thirteenth to sixteenth centuries, and the Black Death/Great Mortality of 1347 to 1350 was one of the core events destabilizing the Bahri Dynasty and led to factional struggles among Mamluk emirs ending with the rise of the Burji Dynasty (also Mamluk-based) in 1382.[29] The impact of recurrent Plague outbreaks ultimately broke down military and economic structures in Egypt. In 1517 the region was conquered by the Ottoman

---

27. André Raymond, *Cairo* (Cambridge, MA.: Harvard University Press, 2000), 7–118.

28. Borsch, *Black Death*." 25–34.

29. Raymond, *Cairo*, 118–48.

Empire. Plague did not abate with the transition of power and outbreaks remained a threat for generations, with one of the most potent arriving in 1791 during Ottoman rule.[30]

The Plague controls of the Mamluks in Cairo laid a foundation for the later Ottoman responses, primarily wedded to the religious interpretations of Plague we analyzed earlier in the chapter. Mamluk emirs and sultans continued to pay for physicians for the poor, providing funeral expenses for the destitute, and some maintained the practice of inviting the poor into their own homes to reside for a time. New ideas on disease, modifying the religious interpretations, began to emerge as early as the 1350s. An early variant of contagion theory advocated by Lisān Al-Dīn Ibn Al-Khatīb (1313–1374), from whom we saw a quote at the start of this chapter, is one example. Although the theory was widely diffused, there was resistance to this new interpretation of Plague and so the impact on controls was limited.

The Islamic World, spanning from Spain to Southeast Asia, maintained a rich and regular transmission of ideas by scholars. Lisān Al-Dīn Ibn Al-Khatīb was a physician and poet who lived in the Emirate of Grenada, which is now part of southern Spain. At the time, this kingdom was dominated by adherents of Islam known as the Nasrid Kings. In the late 1340s, Al-Khatīb wrote a treatise in which he argued for a modification of miasma theory and religious interpretations of the spread of Plague. Based on empirical evidence, he asserted Plague was a "contagion" that could spread from person to person, the infected could bring the "bad air" with them, and measures needed to be put in place to prevent outbreaks.

Al-Khatīb even argued flight from a Plague-stricken region was justified for one's safety, provided the infected themselves did not flee. This contradicted generally accepted Islamic beliefs about Plague as a form of martyrdom not to be avoided. This idea gradually disseminated around the Mediterranean and even spread to Christian-dominated societies, like the Italian principalities and France, throughout the fourteenth to sixteenth centuries. Though not credited, Al-Khatīb's work even played a role in the formulation of a cohesive "theory of contagion" for all disease in *De Contagione*, a manuscript produced in 1526 by the Italian physician Giralamo Francastor (1476–1553).[31]

Lisān Al-Dīn Ibn Al-Khatīb's ideas met with resistance from religious authorities. He was executed as a heretic in 1374, though this was likely the result of his

30. Michael W. Dols, "The Second Plague Pandemic and Its Recurrences in the Middle East: 1347–1894," *Journal of the Economic and Social History of the Orient* 22, no. 2 (May 1979): 162–89, 175–77.

31. Dols, *The Black Death.*" 91–95.

regular criticism of the Nasrid Kings—for which he had been exiled twice. As notions of contagion as the source of disease entered Mamluk society, governing elites and religious authorities opposed the new interpretation. We can, however, see some evidence of contagion theory in newly implemented controls in Cairo.

During waves of Plague in the 1400s, Mamluk rulers transformed the traditional urban communal activities around death and religious celebration. During times of Plague, restrictions were introduced on how many individuals could attend a funeral and on the number of attendees to common prayer, as well as bans on mass street gatherings during important religious festivals. The Mamluk sultans even placed travel restrictions on the Hajj.[32] The Hajj is a religious duty of Muslims to make pilgrimage to Mecca, a city in modern-day Saudi Arabia.[33] Such drastic restrictions indicate a heightened fear of the disease being transmitted from person to person. In general, however, the Mamluk and later Ottoman self-quarantine practices of encouraging Plague victims to remain in their own homes and have physicians come to them appear to be a continuation of older religious policies.

Plague disproportionately impacted the poor, according to the best records historians have examined regarding the demographics of infection.[34] Historians' arguments as to why this may have been the case point to interaction with animals, as the poorer strata of society were directly involved in agricultural labor. Unlike what we see in Italian city-states like Florence in the next section, however, there were no punitive measures against the poor because of this association. Urban spaces were feared, but not the poor themselves. Despite the Islamic proscriptions against it, flight from Plague was common among the elite. During the Great Mortality in the 1340s, the Mamluk sultan fled Cairo for an island in the Nile River, hoping to escape Plague. The primary concern was long-term depopulation, which for both the Mamluks and the Ottomans meant economic decline in the capital of their Egyptian holding.

Efforts to maintain strict barriers did not come with major punitive actions. Borsch argues this is because of the massive losses suffered by the Mamluk army, which was hard hit by Plague fatalities and too weak to enforce actions against

---

32. Dols, *The Black Death*, 91–109.

33. According to Islamic tradition, Muhammed had journeyed to Mecca to visit the site where Abraham's son Ishmael—thought to be the father of all Muslims—and his mother had been housed by Abraham next to the Kaaba—a giant black stone held to have been brought by the Archangel Gabriel for part of the construction of this home. For more on the *Hajj*," see the anthology edited by Eric Tagliacozzo and Shawkat M. Toorawa, *The Hajj: Pilgrimage in Islam* (Cambridge: Cambridge University Press, 2016).

34. Borsch, *Black Death*," 24–39; Dols, *The Black Death*," 143–68.

large portions of the population.[35] Alan Mikhail, by contrast, argues that the environmental contexts of Cairo, both under the Mamluks and the Ottomans and even to present day, are a better explanation for the lack of Plague controls and lack of persecution of the poor. Mikhail insists Egyptians and their Mamluk and Ottoman rulers put Plague in the context of frequent famines, floods, droughts, and other natural disasters and therefore viewed Plague with less frenetic fear than European counterparts, considering the regular recurrence of disease a common aspect of everyday life in Egypt.[36] Whatever the reason, the Plague controls implemented in Cairo from 1347 to 1791 did not directly target the poor as a cause of disease. Though these controls may not have benefitted the poor in any measurable way, the policies did not specifically single them out for negative action against them or worsen their situation. This stands in contrast to the Republic of Florence, where a blend of morality and contagion evolved into rigid sanitary policies and legislation against the poor.

Florence: *Publica Utilitas*, Sanitary Policies, and Persecution of the Poor

The Florentine Republic was a state in Italy centered around the powerful Tuscan city of Florence from 1115 to 1512. The Republic was ruled by a coalition of wealthy families. These great families often indulged in factional rivalries for rotating dominance in Florence, the capital of the Republic. The Republic was governed as a constitutional republic starting in 1293, heavily influenced by the objectives and goals of whichever families held the reins of government or its funds. The 1293 Ordinances of Justice divided Florentine holdings into administrative districts and provided structure for local and regional governance, with the city of Florence at the top of the administrative hierarchy. This system persisted mostly intact until 1533 when Pope Clement VII (r. 1523–1534), a member of the Medici family from Florence, used his influence as leader of the powerful Papal States and leader of the Catholic Church to force a restructuring of the Florentine Republic. He created in its place the Duchy of Florence, which became a hereditary Dukedom held by members of the Medici until the family died out in 1737.[37]

---

35. Borsch, *Black Death*, 40–54.

36. Alan Mikhail, "The Nature of Plague in Late Eighteenth-Century Egypt," *Bulletin of the History of Medicine* 82, no. 2 (Summer 2008): 249–75.

37. Kenneth R. Bartlett, *A Short History of the Italian Renaissance* (Toronto: University of Toronto Press, 2013), 93–113. See also John M. Najemy, *A History of Florence, 1200–1575* (Malden, MA: Blackwell, 2008), 5–35, 63–187.

Like Cairo, Florence was a wealthy city in the fourteenth and fifteenth centuries. After 1298, Florence had become the most prominent banking center in Europe. Three wealthy banking families—the Bardis, the Peruzzis, the Acciaolis, and later the Medicis—were the key beneficiaries of this shift in economic fortune. Wealth generated by financial sector growth spurred patronage of the arts, ushering in what historians have traditionally referred to as the Italian Renaissance—a "rebirth" of the arts and scholarship contemporaries and some historians claimed Italy and Europe had not seen since the ancient Roman Empire.[38] Wealthy families competed with each other for governmental and economic power and in displays of prestige. Influential families commissioned great sculptures, paintings, architectural wonders, poetry, and music as symbols of their status. Writings in the Tuscan dialect, funded through such support, were important to Italian culture in this era and beyond and helped cement the Tuscan dialect's grammar, structure, and vocabulary as the standard Italian language.[39] Dante Alighieri (who you may know as the author of *The Divine Comedy*), Petrarch (a great scholar poet), and Giovanni Boccaccio were some of the famous authors who benefitted from Florentine patronage.

Plague was more than the subject for Boccaccio's literary masterpiece, *The Decameron*. The Republic of Florence was hit hard by the Black Death from 1347–1352 and faced recurrent bouts of Plague nearly every twenty years for the next three centuries.[40] The impact of the Black Death on societal structures and economic prosperity was so great it nearly bankrupted Florence in the 1350s. Leaders of the Florentine Republic were influenced by experiences of Plague outbreaks, new contagion theories of disease, and fears of economic decline. Building upon the authority given to Florence and the hierarchy of local officials outlined in the Ordinances of Justice, the government of the Republic crafted a codified response to Plague in subsequent outbreaks to prevent such detrimental outcomes. It is important to remember even as Florentines shifted from a miasma to a contagion theory on the spread of disease, they were unaware of microbes and still did not know infected fleas transferred the disease to humans from infected animals.

The Florentine system of health as a *publica utilitas*—a public utility or benefit—and sanitary policies for response to disease influenced many European governments' policies in the pursuit of a healthy society for centuries to come.

---

38. For more on debates over the label "Renaissance" for this period of history, see William Caferro, *Contesting the Renaissance* (Malden, MA: Wiley-Blackwell, 2011).

39. Najemy, *A History of Florence*." 307–40.

40. Carmichael, *Plague and the Poor in Renaissance Florence*." 59–107.

Viewing health as a public utility necessitated the creation of elaborate bureaucracies to craft and enforce Plague controls. This task was entrusted to local boards of health and, in the case of Florence, these bodies derived their authority over municipal and rural jurisdictions from the Ordinances of Justice. These special health commissions emerged as a crisis measure in 1348 and became a standing body in the fifteenth century.

The health commission typically comprised eight to ten prominent citizens from wealthy or aristocratic backgrounds. These individuals determined what measures could be taken to prevent and contain Plague with a minimal amount of social disruption, which in their perspective usually meant minimal disruption of commercial activity. The transformation in the fifteenth century of now having a body of officials to effectively enforce those policies gave more potency to Plague controls as policies evolved. The main areas of focus were sanitary policies for city management, property protections for those who fled, and modifications to quarantine. The newer legislation, much like some of the more extreme cultural religious reactions to Plague, reinforced societal inequalities based on one's wealth and place in the economy—or "class"—through assumptions made about the poor as a source of contagion and therefore a threat to public health and the local economy. Now, however, inequality was enforced through a bureaucratic structure as Plague controls morphed into social controls.[41]

The first shifts were the introduction of stricter sanitary policies. New legislation outlined Plague controls starting in 1348, but the body of laws continued to grow well into the seventeenth century. These measures aimed to remove both miasma and contagion from the city. Used clothing and linens were barred from sale in markets to prevent the spread of possible contagion. Dead bodies had to be placed in wooden caskets, rather than laid in family tombs or wrapped in sackcloth, to prevent the "spread of *fetor*." No dead bodies could be transported to the city for burial. Commerce and transit were suspended. There were bans on the sale of fresh meat and hides. Waste needed to be cleaned from the streets, including offal from butchering animals and tanning hides. Warnings were issued to citizens urging them not to associate with the sick. All of these sanitary measures were rigidly enforced as legislation outlined strict punishments for violation of any of these decrees. Penalties included seizure of property, burning of property and homes of violators "to remove contagion," and even execution. The laws were designed to protect the community.[42]

---

41. Carmichael, *Plague and the Poor*, 90–126.

42. Carmichael, *Plague and the Poor*, 108–10.

You can see the pride with which Florentine officials viewed new sanitary policies in a statement from Leonardo Bruni, who was the chancellor of Florence from 1406 to 1444:

> Indeed, it seems to me that Florence is so clean and neat that no other city could be cleaner. Surely this city is unique and singular in all the world, because you will find there nothing that is disgusting to the eye, offensive to the nose, or filthy under foot. There the great diligence of all inhabitants ensures and provides that all filth is immediately removed from the streets, so you see only what brings pleasure and joy to the senses. Therefore, in its splendor, Florence probably excels all the cities of the world.[43]

In this quote you see traces of miasma theory's influence here, but we also see in the applauding of the "great diligence of all inhabitants" a communal responsibility of the individual to prevent contagion by maintaining sanitary conditions in the city.

Removing filth was key. Fifteenth-century Florentine health commissioners, however, defined offal and waste as filth. The positive of community action, of each denizen contributing to the public health, had a negative side in the condemnation of those inhabitants perceived as a detriment to Florence's shining streets. Even as the reasoning behind these laws shifted to contagion theory, policies maintained an emphasis on the morality of the individual by placing culpability for the spread of illness on victims and practitioners of specific professions—prostitutes, butchers, cloth merchants, and tanners—as "violators." Categorizing the spread or potential spread as a failing in their actions warranted individual condemnation, sentencing, and punishment.[44]

There was a disproportionate impact on the poorer strata of Florentine society as they depended upon several of the banned industries for piecework. Barred from earnings in textiles, tanning, and slaughterhouse work, some resorted to begging, vagrancy, or even prostitution to earn a living—activities also banned by Florentine sanitary policy as a threat to the morality, cleanliness, and health of the city-state. Arguments about morality were seamlessly blended with new sanitary policies, seemingly adhering to the idea "cleanliness was next Godliness"—a dictum the variants of which we will explore again and again in public health responses in the nineteenth and twentieth centuries in later chapters of this textbook.

Controls against prostitution and "sodomy"—an archaic pejorative term for homosexuality—were implemented to "rout out evil and crime that can befall

---

43. Leonardo Bruni, *Laudatio Florentinae Urbis.*" as translated in Benjamin Kohl and R. Witt, eds., *The Earthy Republic of the Italian Humanists* (Philadelphia: University of Pennsylvania Press, 1978), 138.

44. Carmichael, *Plague and the Poor*, 108–10.

the city of Florence from the dishonesty of these women, living and working everyday in the city, because in their shamelessness they commit many sins offensive to God and to the honor of the said city, and in their lasciviousness they form a bad example to others" and might, legislators argued, lead to a breakdown of obedience to other sanitary measures for street-cleanliness.[45] Other options for poor men included offering their services in cleaning the filth from the city streets and/or the burial of Plague dead—undesirable jobs leaving them open to infection and further exclusion from society.[46]

The health commissions also constructed bureaucracies that provided rigid protections of property of the wealthy who fled Florence's outbreaks of Plague and transformations to quarantine policy. The poor, who lacked the resources to flee, often remained behind as the only inhabitants of Plague-afflicted cities. Florence was no exception to this pattern. The flight of the wealthy from urban areas led to two associations between poverty, disorder, and disease. The first, associating the poor with disorder, arose from a primary concern about the breakdown of social order. Elites who owned land, manors, and businesses in Florence feared the poor would take advantage of Plague to steal and occupy property.

This fear was heightened after socioeconomic inequalities resulted in the Ciompi Revolt of 1378–1382. The Revolt was a rebellion of craftsmen, laborers, and artisans who were not members of guilds and therefore were not allowed to participate in the governance of the Republic of Florence. They demanded greater involvement. The uprising was brutally suppressed by mercenaries and soldiers hired by the elite of Florence. Plague, the fleeing elite feared, might spark another such uprising. The city government employed guards to protect property while the elite were away. These guards were authorized to use deadly force at the slightest indication of revolt from within by the poor and to expel "roving bands of migrants," feared to bring more contagion and revolutionary ideas.[47] The second, an association of poverty with disease, was essentially a self-fulfilling prophecy. Since the poor remained in Plague-infected urban areas, a growing perception emerged associating the poor with filth and contagion. Plague appeared worse in urban centers and the poor remained in urban centers, so clearly, Florentine elite citizens and legislators thought, the poor were the source of illness. We now

---

45. Florentine State Archives, *Provv. Reg.* 16, Folder 9 (Jan. 9, 1319) as translated in Carmichael, *Plague and the Poor*, 98, where Carmichael states in the text and footnote on page 157 that this exact language, first appearing in 1319 in this initial statute was preserved in later sanitary legislation well into the fifteenth century.

46. Carmichael, *Plague and the Poor*, 93–107.

47. Lantschner, Patrick. "The Ciompi Revolution Constructed: Modern Historians and the Nineteenth-Century Paradigm of Revolution," *Annali di Storia di Firenze* 4 (2011): 277–97; Carmichael, *Plague and the Poor*, 116–21; Watts, *Epidemics and History*." 15–25.

know this to be erroneous, but this view connecting poverty and Plague impacted Florentine reforms to quarantine policy.

Fifteenth-century sanitary legislation modified quarantine procedures, turning the charity hospitals of the fourteenth century into *lazarettos* (pest houses) in the fifteenth century and beyond. Quarantine, or containing and isolating the sick, had existed prior to the emergence of contagion theory, as those adhering to miasma also thought bad air could spread. The difference, however, was in the implementation. Rather than a passive system of quarantine, where communities would avoid certain areas until the "bad air" where Plague was identified had dissipated, more activist measures were taken to stop Plague before it started. Unlike the poor hospitals providing charity and shelter for the sick we saw earlier in this chapter, the new *lazarettos* often functioned more like prisons.

During outbreaks of Plague in the fifteenth and sixteenth centuries, Florentine officials preemptively ordered the roundup of vagrants, beggars, prostitutes, and migrants living on the streets. Whether they were exhibiting symptoms of Plague or not, these disenfranchised people were thrown into the pest houses to be isolated from the community. Viewed as "human filth" and treated as such by local officials, they were removed from the streets to keep the city "clean" of contagion and amoral influences. There, they were exposed to pestilence as they were held in the *lazarettos* for the duration of a Plague outbreak, sharing residency with other individuals who exhibited symptoms of Plague who were also placed in the *lazarettos* for quarantine. Although the Florentine state did pay for the healthcare of those placed in the *lazarettos*, the stigma associated with these buildings, the flight of physicians and some clergy in fifteenth- to seventeenth-century outbreaks, and forcing asymptomatic individuals into these pest-houses led to their occupants being forgotten there, exposed to disease and left to die.[48]

Conclusion

In this chapter, we explored religious and early local governance responses to Plague from the thirteenth to sixteenth centuries. What we might term some of the earliest public health measures were profoundly local responses to a global disease outbreak. The debates over immorality, miasma, or contagion as the primary source of disease we saw in this chapter persisted well into the nineteenth and twentieth centuries, when bacteriology and virology at least put an end to the miasma/contagion dispute if not the question of morality's link to disease. While some of the policies and outlooks around the Mediterranean world emphasized

---

48. Carmichael, *Plague and the Poor*, 108, 116–26; Watts, *Epidemics and History*, 21–25.

care and charity toward the sick and the poor, others persecuted religious minorities. The emergence of sanitary policies in the Republic of Florence emphasized assigning blame for disease as a component of "cleaning the city." Assigning blame for illness, unfortunately, has remained a common feature of both cultural and medical responses to public health crises to the present.

We can even see this with Plague itself. During the Third Pandemic of Plague across Europe, Asia, Africa, and North America at the turn of the twentieth century, specific ethnic groups—such as Chinese migrants to the United States—and the poor were singled out in government Plague controls.[49] Even today, many who live in wealthier countries in North America and Europe tend to assume Plague is a "medieval" disease, impacting poorer "developing countries" such as India or Madagascar. In reality, there are yearly cases of Plague in the Southwestern United States. In an outbreak of typhus—another disease spread by infected fleas—in Los Angeles in 2019, the homeless were blamed for "horrendous hygiene" fostering populations of rodents and fleas. The media linked "poverty" with diseases from the "Middle Ages" many erroneously assume are long gone.[50] The ongoing association with race or socioeconomic status with disease is one of the chief ways public health responses can intentionally and unintentionally exacerbate societal inequalities. In the next chapter, we will examine how racism and classism were part of the context in which new sanitary policies were created in response to outbreaks of cholera in the nineteenth and twentieth centuries.

FURTHER READING

Bigon, Liora. "Bubonic Plague, Colonial Ideologies, and Urban Planning Policies: Dakar, Lagos, and Kumasi." *Planning Perspectives* 31, no. 2 (2016): 205–26.

Echenberg, Myron J. *Plague Ports: The Global Impact of Bubonic Plague, 1894–1901.* New York: New York University Press, 2007.

Stearns, Justin K. "New Directions in the Study of Religious Responses to the Black Death." *History Compass* 7, no. 5 (2009): 1363–75.

Vann, Michael G., and Liz Clarke. *The Great Hanoi Rat Hunt: Empire, Disease, and Modernity in French Colonial Vietnam.* New York: Oxford University Press, 2019.

Winter, Michael, and Amalia Levanoni, eds. *The Mamluks in Egyptian and Syrian Politics and Society.* Leiden: Brill, 2004.

---

49. James C. Mohr, *Plague and Fire: Battling Black Death and the 1900 Burning of Honolulu's Chinatown* (Oxford: Oxford University Press, 2004), 7–16, 41–68, 83–110.

50. "Plague," https://www.cdc.gov/plague/index.html; Anna Gorman, "Medieval Diseases Are Infecting California's Homeless," *The Atlantic,* last updated March 11, 2019, https://www.theatlantic.com/health/archive/2019/03/typhus-tuberculosis-medieval-diseases-spreading-homeless/584380/.

2 CHOLERA, COLONIALISM, AND CLASS

Hundreds of people were racked with violent spells of vomiting and diarrhea. Death came swiftly. Bodily tissues and blood vessels collapsed under extreme dehydration. Victims left behind a torrent of excrement as a result of their explosive symptoms, which in turn helped to spread the disease. This was what the town of Jessore in Bengal, India experienced in 1817, setting off a regional outbreak and then an epidemic of a sickness then called *cholera morbus*. The illness spread across South Asia as a result of increased trade and a conflict now known as the Third Anglo-Maratha War. In central India a detachment of the private army of the East India Company (EIC) under the leadership of Lord Moira the Marquis of Hastings encountered the disease during a military campaign to subjugate India to British rule and EIC control.[1] He kept a daily log of his troops' engagements with Muslim Pindari and Hindu Maratha resistance fighters and, as it turns out, the beginnings of a massive cholera epidemic in India in the early nineteenth century. Hastings noted the following in his diary from November 13–15, 1817:

> 13th November. Camp Talgong. The dreadful epidemic disorder which has been causing such ravages in Calcutta and in the southern provinces, has broken out in camp. It is a species of *cholera morbus*, which appears to seize the individual without his having had any previous sensations of the malady. If immediate relief is not at hand, the person to a certainty dies within four or five hours.
>
> 14th November. Ninety-Seven deaths are reported to me as having occurred during yesterday forenoon. There is an opinion that the water of the tanks, the only water which we have at this place, may be unwholesome and add to the disease . . .
>
> 15th November . . . It is evident that this is the same pestilence as has been raging in the lower provinces. We have information of its gradually ascending the river to Patna, Ghareepore, Benares, and Cawnore.[2]

---

1. Sheldon Watts, *Epidemics and History: Disease, Power and Imperialism* (New Haven, CT: Yale University Press, 1997), 178.

2. *The Private Journal of the Marquis of Hastings*, Vol. II, Published by the Marchioness of Bute (London, 1858), 2.

As the EIC army marched across India in search of clean water and continued their mission to conquer India, the disease followed them. Governor General Hastings recorded in his diary that by November 15, five hundred of the men under his command had died from the illness. The outbreak in Jessore soon became a full-fledged epidemic raging from 1817 to 1825 as it spread across the whole of India in large part by groups of private soldiers like Hastings and his men.[3] By July 1818 alone, when the first short-lived respite from the epidemic came, tens of thousands in India had already died from the disease.[4]

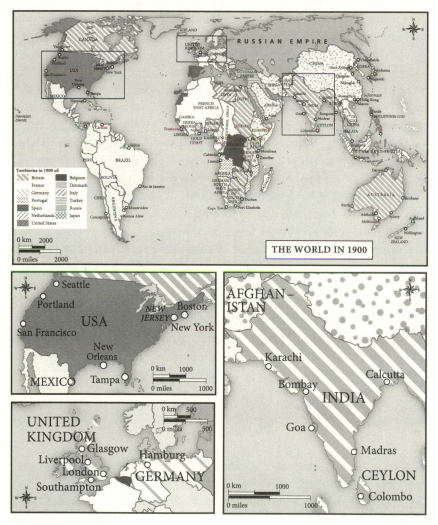

MAP 2.1 Map of World

3. Watts, *Epidemics and History*, 178–80.

4. C. Macnamara, *A History of Asiatic Cholera* (London: Macmillan and Co., 1876), 46–63.

The example of cholera during the Third Anglo-Maratha War in India is one of many demonstrating how the expansion of European empires in the eighteenth and nineteenth centuries brought with it globalized commerce, conflict, and disease. Although pandemics were not new, European imperialism heralded increased frequency of outbreaks and epidemics of disease on a global scale. Thanks to the growing power of the British East India Company and other avenues of maritime and overland trade, the same cholera epidemics in India turned into a wave of outbreaks north of the Himalayas. Cholera spread to Tsarist Russia and the Habsburg Empire in the late 1820s, and then, most famously, resulted in massive epidemics in Great Britain, Imperial Germany, and the United States from the 1830s to the early 1900s (see Figure 2.1).[5]

Initial public health responses in Britain, Imperial Germany, and the United States were guided by the internationally popular sanitary movement. Starting in the 1830s and 1840s in Britain, the sanitary movement operated on the "filth theory" of disease. Sanitarians like Edwin Chadwick insisted the key to combating disease in the new heavily industrializing and increasingly urbanizing Europe was to quite literally "clean up" the city. Street cleaning campaigns, infrastructure projects, and new urban planning techniques were all integral to this process.[6] Older historical scholarship on the sanitarians portrayed them as heroic individuals transforming European and American society to combat illness.[7] The sanitary movement was indeed a step forward for public health and international cooperation in some areas, such as emphasizing the importance of hygiene and associating a decrease in pollution and waste in public places with better community health. More recent scholars, however, such as the Richard Evans, Sheldon Watts, and J. N. Hays, have criticized presenting the sanitarians in solely a positive light. These historians complicate the picture by pointing out early responses to cholera and other diseases in the industrial, urban world were based in social Darwinism and moralization campaigns.[8] Sanitarians assumed supposedly amoral lower classes and immigrant groups from South Asia and the Ottoman

---

5. Watts, *Epidemics and History*, 178–83; J. N. Hays, *The Burdens of Disease: Epidemics and Human Response in Western History* (New Brunswick, NJ: Rutgers University Press, 2009), 135–55.

6. Hays, *The Burdens of Disease*, 142–50; Martin Gorsky, "Public Health in the West since 1800: The Response," in *Public Health in History*, ed. Virginia Berridge, Martin Gorsky, and Alex Mold (New York: McGraw Hill, 2011), 42–57, 51–57.

7. Traces of this approach persisted into the early 1980s, such as in Anthony S. Wohl, *Endangered Lives: Public Health in Victorian Britain* (London: Littlehampton Book Services, 1983).

8. Richard J. Evans, *Death in Hamburg: Society and Politics in the Cholera Years* (Oxford: Oxford University Press, 41, 109–10, 209, 474–76, 562–63; Watts, *Epidemics and History*, 197, 209–10, 251, 263–70; Hays, *The Burdens of Disease*, 142–55.

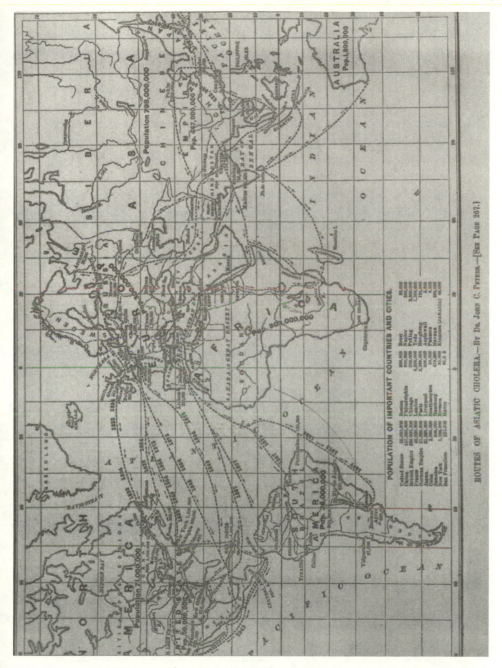

Figure 2.1 This map, from *Harper's Weekly*, a popular American political magazine in the nineteenth century, depicts the spread of cholera across the globe at in the decades preceding its publication. Note how maritime and land routes related to trade in the Atlantic, Indian, and Pacific Oceans, as well as increased European imperialism and military activity in Asia and Africa, convey the disease.

Source: Courtesy of the Collections of the National Library of Medicine

Empire were predisposed for the illness.[9] As part of the effort to cleanse the city, sanitary movement advocates influenced urban planning. Planners divided the city by class, concentrating the supposedly "filthy" poor and working classes into sectors of the city with higher levels of industrial and biological waste and less access to clean water and resources in metropolises like London, Hamburg, Paris, and New York.[10] As we will see later in this chapter, sanitarian initiatives to combat outbreaks of disease often reinforced class and racial inequalities and actually increased the disproportionate rate of mortality from cholera among members of these disenfranchised groups.

In this chapter, we will learn about key changes to public health management resulting from the 1854 Broad Street cholera outbreak in London, the 1892 to 1893 epidemic in Hamburg, and a host of waterborne illnesses in the water supply of New Jersey from 1901 to 1908. In all three instances, greater governmental control and regulation of infrastructure, utilities, response mechanisms, and policy helped to challenge some of the disparities in health among the poorer and immigrant communities of British, German, and American society. The work of John Snow led to increased government centralization and regulation of the infrastructure for sewers and running water in Britain. Robert Koch's success with, and advocacy for, a bacteriology-based response ultimately led to legislation empowering national over local government during public health crises in Imperial Germany. John L. Leal's experimentation with and defense in court over water chlorination led to new federal policies and regulations for water treatment in the United States. Though not the intent per se, all of these efforts by physicians and governments to centralize infrastructure, response, and policy regarding water ultimately led to uniformity of water quality which in turn decreased the disproportionate number of cases of waterborne illness among poorer residents of all three countries (see Map 2.1).

Even as these policies were becoming increasingly effective in the West, British colonial administrators continued to make decisions based on older policies and assumptions of predisposition for the disease among "colonial subjects" in South Asia, the point of origin for cholera. We will end this chapter by exploring how colonial governments in India refused to adopt the costlier approaches of quarantine, infrastructural improvements, and water treatment routine in Europe and the United States. British colonial administrators claimed the measures would disrupt trade, expressed false concern about violating the "traditional culture" of their colonial subjects, and insisted such programs would be ineffective among "unhygienic natives." These racial associations with a lack of cleanliness had

---

9. Gorsky, "Public Health in the West since 1800: The Response," 50–52.

10. Evans, *Death in Hamburg*, 470–568; Hays, *The Burdens of Disease*, 135–55.

persisted—despite the new scientific knowledge acquired by individuals such as Snow, Koch, and Leal—since the time of Governor General Hastings, whose diary entries you read here. In addition to chronicling the spread of cholera in India in his diary he also placed blame on the Pindari horsemen and Indian camp followers for spreading the disease among his men in 1817 and referred to these groups and lower-class soldiers as "creatures falling under sudden attacks of this dreadful infection."[11] The end result of British administrative decisions to block and/or selectively apply new public health protocols in India was a growing imbalance in the quality of public health responses between Britain and its colony from 1857 to 1935, as cholera outbreaks decreased in Europe while becoming deadlier and more frequent in India across the late nineteenth and early twentieth centuries (see Map 2.1).

Sanitarians and Sewers: Cholera in Britain, 1830s–1850s

Waterborne cholera broke out in Britain several times in the nineteenth century, but the two most consequential were the 1831 to 1832 outbreak starting in Sunderland, England and the 1854 Broad Street cholera outbreak in London.[12] Both of these outbreaks shaped British domestic public health policy, ultimately leading to changes in infrastructure and a centralization of authority and regulation. To understand the causes for these outbreaks and the impact responses to them had on health and class inequality, we first must understand the context in which outbreaks of disease and reactions to them occurred. Britain, like much of western and central Europe, underwent rapid societal, demographic, and physical transformation, enabling the disease to spread and accentuated disparities in living conditions among different socioeconomic classes.

The ongoing Industrial Revolution initiated at the end of the eighteenth century, dependent on importation of raw materials from exploited colonies, fostered a demand to increase global connections and brought epidemics and pandemics of disease alongside trade and conquest. Industrialization also created new urban centers of production with swift and unprecedented growth. Urban areas in Britain and other parts of Europe increased from both increasing birth rates and migration to the city centers. Urbanization was far from a new process, and by this point cities had been growing since antiquity, but the shift from rural to higher urban population densities was now more exponential. Both Paris and London, for example, doubled in size between 1801 and 1850. Paris increased from half a million residents to a million and London grew from a population of

---

11. Watts, *Epidemics and History*, 178–79.

12. Watts, *Epidemics and History*, 186, 198.

over one million to over two million in this period.[13] Can you imagine the impact such astronomical growth would have on your own community—its infrastructural, housing, and health conditions?

This population growth strained cities. Pollution increased, amplified the volume of human and animal waste, and placed people in cramped and crowded lodgings. The negative health impacts of these developments were largely borne by the lower classes. In addition to increasing the size of cities, industrialization brought with it new social classes. German philosopher Karl Marx, in his 1867 work *Capital*, dubbed these new classes of capitalist societies the proletariat, or working class, and the bourgeoisie, and the middle class.[14] Although class frequently mapped onto income level, the European conception of class more often defined members of social strata based on their roles in the industrial economy. For example, those who worked and did manual labor in domestic service, factories, mills, mines, railways, and dockyards of industrializing Europe were part of the working class. Their supervisors, accountants, and most importantly the owners and financiers of these industries and sites of production and shipping made up the middle class.

With the new classes came distinct class cultures distancing themselves from one another in their forms of entertainment, value systems, and attitudes toward parenting and family structure. Industrial urbanization also divorced the classes from one another geographically within the cities in which they now resided.[15] Nineteenth-century urban planners in Britain, France, Germany, and elsewhere in Europe molded and reshaped the city to keep these distinct groups and the economic roles with which they were associated separate. Tanneries, glue factories, dead animal products, chemical industry, gas factories, madhouses, hospitals, and even prisons and public executions were eventually relegated to the city outskirts.[16] Developers and city planners located shipping industries, railyards, and those production sites dependent on these forms of transit for raw materials and distribution of their wares near rivers and ports.[17] Across Europe and the

13. Hays, *The Burdens of Disease*, 142; Martin Gorsky, "Public Health in the West since 1800: The Context," in *Public Health in History*, ed. Virginia Berridge, Martin Gorsky, and Alex Mold (New York: McGraw Hill, 2011), 23–41, 28.

14. John Merriman, *A History of Modern Europe From the Renaissance to the Present* (New York: Norton, 2010), 567–627; If you would like to read more of Marx's own philosophy, see the following edited translation of his major: Karl Marx, *Capital: An Abridged Edition*, ed. David McLellan (Oxford: Oxford University Press, 2008).

15. Merriman, *A History of Modern Europe*; Robin W. Winks and Joan Neuberger, *Europe and the Making of Modernity, 1815–1914* (New York: Oxford University Press, 2005), 65, 237.

16. John H. Merriman, *The Margins of City Life: Explorations on the French Urban Frontier, 1815–1851* (New York: Oxford University Press, 1991), 3–30, 59–83.

17. Evans, *Death in Hamburg*, 50–77, 109–43.

United States, homes for middle- and upper-class families were placed near city parks, shopping centers, museums, and sites of culture and tourism.[18] Industrial workers, on the other hand, lived near the sites where they labored.[19] Often, these working-class dwellings in British cities housed several families, were exposed to nearby industrial pollution, and had poor insulation and ventilation.

Imagine for a moment you are a member of the working class in this era. You lack running water in your home and you spend part of your day gathering drinking and cooking water from shared community pumps, often maintained by church parishes, tapped into the ground water or a nearby river. More often than not in nineteenth-century London and other cities across Great Britain, you would share a single toilet with all of the denizens of a single, multistory apartment building or sometimes you might have to share that toilet with all the residents of an entire city block.[20] Those toilets were not fitted with plumbing to drain to the sewers, but instead dumped into unlined holes in the ground— night-soil pits—and needed to be regularly emptied. Those pits also leaked their contents into the same ground water from which the community pumps drew their supply.[21] It is little wonder mortality rates from disease were higher among the lower classes, and it is in this context in which the 1831 to 1832 cholera outbreak and the sanitary movement emerged.

The 1831 to 1832 outbreak arrived first in Sunderland, but quickly spread to all of England, Wales, and Scotland. The best figures available to historians suggest over 31,000 died of cholera across Great Britain in the span of a year.[22] Victims fell ill suddenly like they had in India in 1817. Death often came swiftly as the heart and kidneys in many victims failed within hours of the presentation of symptoms.[23] Although cholera, like many diseases, cares little for the social rank of its victims and killed across age, class, and race, the poor faced disproportionate levels of infection, concentrated in districts like those described earlier. The diarrhea from those stricken with the disease filled the streets, the night-soil pits, and leached into the ground water, spreading the illness further.

The insight that cholera could be spread person to person was not yet commonplace. Knowledge of germ theory was still not available until later in the

---

18. Andrew Lees and Lynn Hollen Lees, *Cities and the Making of Modern Europe, 1750–1914* (Cambridge: Cambridge University Press, 2007), 13–69, 99–128.

19. Winks and Neuberger, *Europe and the Making of Modernity*, 106–108, 224–25, 295–99, 324–35.

20. Gorsky, "Public Health in the West since 1800: The Context," 36–38.

21. Hays, *The Burdens of Disease*, 143.

22. Watts, *Epidemics and History*, 195.

23. Hays, *The Burdens of Disease*, 136.

century. Early efforts to combat the disease, headed by members of the afore-mentioned sanitary movement, focused on environmental factors. Sanitarians adhered to the miasma theory of disease rather than the older contagion theory discussed in relation to bubonic plague in chapter 1. Miasma theory held that disease was spread not person to person, but by the environment. Sanitarians in Britain associated "filth" with disease and therefore called for numerous in-frastructural improvements to remove pollution, both industrial and biologi-cal, from segments of cities. In response to the outbreak, sanitarians like Edwin Chadwick called for redesigned sewers, rather than the simple tunnels in which excrement sat and formed stagnant pools, complete with regular flushings with water to force the sewers to drain at a site outside of towns and cities. They de-manded fresh water be piped into each dwelling and the installation of flushing toilets to replace the night-soil pits currently in use. They called for streets to be cleaned.[24]

None of these reforms happened overnight. The cost of such large-scale ven-tures, which sanitarians suggested be shouldered by the government, stagnated development. There was a great deal of resistance from politicians seeking to reduce government spending. None of the sanitary reforms, however, associ-ated the problem of cholera with contaminated water. Sanitarians, adhering to miasma theory, thought the disease was caused by the smell. The sanitarians advo-cated draining the cesspools, creating sewers, removing stagnant water collection pools, and replacing them with plumbing to eliminate and or contain foul odors thought to cause disease. As a result, no one gave any thought to the possible impact of the construction of large, government run sewers draining directly into the Thames River. They were focused on the removal of odorous waste from the city space.[25] Some of these measures were implemented quickly and the problem abated as removal of the excrement did lessen the incidence of cholera. This mea-sure of success gave sanitarians more sway in British politics to pursue other items on their agenda.

Earlier in the chapter, I mentioned how scholars have started to challenge the older view the sanitarians helped to decrease inequality in their societies. Historian J. N. Hays has argued that British association of the disease with its Indian origins combined with racist stereotypes of Asia then held by Europeans. Europeans believed India was a place of extreme overpopulation, crowding, filth, and poverty. This in turn, he states, reinforced the sanitarians' views of the causes and proper response to the disease: namely, combating environmental factors and

---

24. Watts, *Epidemics and History*, 191–200; Hays, *The Burdens of Disease*, 145–47.

25. Steven Johnson, *The Ghost Map: The Story of London's Most Terrifying Epidemic and How It Changed Science, Cities, and the Modern World* (New York: Riverhead Books, 2006), 116–21.

the problem of the poor.[26] Sheldon Watts, another historian, goes further. He argues that sanitarians used the 1831 to 1832 outbreak and their partial success in response as political ammunition to advance a program of welfare reform against the poor, whom they viewed as sources of "filth" and illness. As evidence, Watts points to Edwin Chadwick's involvement in both the Poor Law Amendment Act of 1834 and the *Report on the Sanitary Condition of the Labouring Population of Great Britain* in 1842.

Let's take a moment to look at Watts's argument and assess his claim by looking at Chadwick and the key pieces of evidence to which Watts points. Edwin Chadwick, one of the primary leaders of the sanitary movement in Britain, was not a medical professional, but a politician. Examine this excerpt of Chadwick's 1842 *Report on the Sanitary Condition of the Labouring Population of Great Britain*:

> After as careful an examination of the evidence collected . . . I beg leave to recapitulate the chief conclusions . . . First . . . that the various forms of epidemic, endemic and other disease caused, or aggravated, or propagated chiefly among the laboring classes by atmospheric impurities produced by decomposing animal and vegetable substances, by damp and filth, and close and overcrowded dwellings prevail amongst [this] population . . . That the population so exposed is less susceptible of moral influences, and the effects of education are more transient than with a healthy population. That these adverse circumstances tend to produce an adult population short-lived, improvident, reckless, intemperate, and with habitual avidity for sensual gratification.
>
> . . . And that the removal of noxious physical circumstances, and the promotion of civic, household, and personal cleanliness are necessary to the improvement of the moral condition of the population.[27]

Having looked at part of this piece, we can see Chadwick's concern about environmental factors and disease. What about Watts's claim Chadwick had classist attitudes toward the poor as a source of illness? There are hints of it. The reference to "damp and filth" prevailing amongst "this population," the poor, is one example. Chadwick also ties in morality here, claiming the poor were "short-lived, improvident, reckless, intemperate, and with habitual avidity for sensual gratification." Words and their meanings, like value systems and fashions, change over time

---

26. Hays, *The Burdens of Disease*, 142.

27. Edwin Chadwick, *Reprinting of "Report on the Sanitary Condition of the Labouring Population of Great Britain, 1842,"* ed. M. W. Flinn (Edinburgh: Edinburgh University Press, 1965), 422–25.

and we need to consider context when looking at a document from the past. In the nineteenth century, "intemperate" was often a synonym for "alcoholic" and "habitual avidity for sensual gratification" implied impropriety with regards to frequency of sexual encounters and number of partners. Both were traits a nineteenth-century sanitarian associated with immorality. On the opposite side, Chadwick paired "personal cleanliness," and therefore health, with morality later on in the quote. Still, a good historian would look for more evidence to corroborate. Let's continue looking at Chadwick's record, then, by considering another piece of evidence from Watts: the role the sanitarians played in the Poor Law Amendment of 1834.

Alongside the demands Chadwick and other sanitarians made concerning changes to sewers, water supplies, and general cleanliness in the city, he called for local boards of health to supervise the construction and management of poor houses.[28] In an effort to curtail central government spending as a result of the massive infrastructural improvements demanded by the sanitarians, during the summer of 1833 Parliament declared the response to all future outbreaks of cholera and should "be left to the prudence and good feelings of those communities where it may occasionally show itself," essentially relegating immediate response to localities.[29] The burden for dealing with the poor, deemed by most elites to be the epicenter for the illness, shifted to townships and cities in a new structure for poverty assistance. The system and guidelines for these poor houses, to be managed by "Guardians" elected by local tax-payers, were set down in the Poor Law Amendment Act of 1834, which gained momentum in Parliament after the 1831 to 1832 cholera outbreaks. The conditions for admission to and residency within one of these poorhouses, as set down by Chadwick and other proponents of the law, can be summarized as follows:

1. All residents were to be dressed in a standard uniform.
2. Food and sustenance were rationed to the minimum to discourage dependency and comfort.
3. Alcohol and tobacco were forbidden as they were seen as moral impediments.
4. The only reading material allowed in the poorhouses were copies of the Bible. All other materials were prohibited.
5. Residents were required to listen to sermons by lay preachers during meals.
6. "Inmates," regardless of marital status, were segregated by gender to prevent lascivious behavior and to stem the "increase" in the poor population. This resulted in husbands and wives, parents and children, being separated.

---

28. Watts, *Epidemics and History*, 196–97.

29. Watts, *Epidemics and History*, 196.

This is much clearer proof Chadwick and the other sanitarians saw the poor as amoral and thought their immorality needed to be curbed before it led to societal problems, such as overpopulation and disease. The guiding logic behind these policies, which read more like prison regulations than those of an aid organization, was the concept of "less eligibility."[30] Chadwick and others like him had two goals in drafting these policies this way. The policies aimed to reduce welfare costs in order to free up funds for infrastructural improvements. Yet these policies also sought to make conditions in the poor houses so undesirable the "idle, able-bodied poor" would find them undesirable and seek gainful and moral employment, thereby "eliminating" poverty.[31] Chadwick, like many sanitarians, associated poverty with disease. Much like responses to bubonic plague covered in chapter 1, associating poverty with disease in the nineteenth century still went hand-in-hand with an assumption poverty was the result of the sinful life of an individual or community. The general argument ran that poverty was the result of immoral behavior, which in turn led to more immoral behavior such as the vices of alcoholism and licentiousness, and poverty therefore fostered "unclean living" leading to disease.

The sanitarians endorsed the Poor Law of 1834, which was intended to reduce disease by "solving" the problem of poverty. The majority of the poor and destitute were not amoral nor were they all unemployed, but rather underpaid. Yet those who drafted the law chose to operate on stereotypes and assumptions. Far from eliminating disease, the horrid conditions of these poor houses increased the occurrence over the next two decades. Malnourishment, cramped housing conditions in these local facilities, and a lack of things ironically deemed "luxuries" by these activists, such as indoor plumbing and flushing toilets, ensured higher rates of disease among those seeking aid in these facilities.[32] Despite evidence of the deplorable environments in poor houses, politicians viewed flight from these sites of supposed aid as proof they were solving the problem of poverty.

Fellow politicians gave Chadwick more authority in 1848, when through the Public Health Act he and other sanitarians created a central nationwide three-person Board of Health to oversee the local management of boards of health and the removal of odiferous excrement from communities.[33] As "inmates" exited these poor houses or were expelled for violating one or more of the rules, homelessness and housing density increased again. Even though the government became more heavily involved in sewer construction and maintenance thanks to the sanitarians, infrastructural improvements were faster in wealthier parts of

---

30. Watts, *Epidemics and History*, 196.

31. Watts, *Epidemics and History*, 196–97.

32. Watts, *Epidemics and History*, 197.

33. Johnson, *The Ghost Map*, 118.

the cities and towns of Great Britain that could supplement the cost via private investment, often to the detriment of those down-stream in the socioeconomic hierarchy. For example, upper-class neighborhoods in London built sewers draining into the Thames River. Their sewage and waste flowed away from their homes and dumped instead in proximity to the "foul air of working-class neighborhoods" located along the river's banks.[34] A resulting second epidemic of cholera in 1848 to 1849 killed 50,000 in England and Wales, with the death tolls heavily concentrated in the poorer districts of major cities.[35]

Removing the Pump Handle: The 1854 Broad Street Cholera Outbreak in London

The problem of urban poverty persisted in Britain. Unevenly distributed public works improvements fostered a breeding ground for the next outbreak of cholera in 1854. Amidst a series of outbreaks in London in 1854, the most significant was in the district of Soho, located a mile from the now filthy River Thames. Throughout the seventeenth and part of the eighteenth centuries, Soho had been a wealthy district of London, frequented by artists and aristocrats, and with luxurious homes. By the nineteenth century, however, those luxurious homes had been subdivided into cramped tenements for working-class families and the neighborhood. Soho looked very much like the working-class neighborhoods described earlier, with few toilets between tenants, no indoor plumbing, and drinking and cooking water pumps drawing from the River Thames. The district was crowded with slaughterhouses and cowsheds, lacked sewer structures, and had acquired the reputation as one of London's red-light districts thanks to the brothels and street prostitutes located there. On August 28, 1854, an outbreak of cholera began in a working-class home when Thomas and Sarah Lewis's infant daughter began vomiting and passing watery, green stools.[36] Within three days, 127 people had died in the neighborhood. As cesspools overflowed during the outbreak, London officials had them emptied and dumped into the Thames: the source of water for the pumps in the neighborhood. By the end of the outbreak, 616 people in this neighborhood alone had perished.[37]

The significance of this outbreak is partly the result of the work of a physician named John Snow. He made a series of observations about the 1848 to 1849

---

34. Johnson, *The Ghost Map*, 69–70.

35. Johnson, *The Ghost Map*, 34.

36. Johnson, *The Ghost Map*, 16–22.

37. John M. Eyler, "The Changing Assessments of John Snow's and William Farr's Cholera Studies," *Sozial-Und Präventivmedizin* 46, no. 4 (July 2001): 225–32.

outbreak confirmed in his more thorough analysis in 1854. During the 1848 to 1849 outbreak, Snow had speculated fecal matter, not the environment alone, was the means by which the disease was transmitted. The return of cholera in 1854 offered an opportunity to confirm this hypothesis through a skill-set now called "analytic epidemiology." Snow conducted a thorough study of water quality—chiefly the presence of fecal matter—across various sources and compared his findings to information from his interviews of cholera victims or their surviving relatives. He then constructed what is often called his "Ghost Map" of Soho, charting the location of water pumps, cesspools, and homes where cholera was present. He concluded it was not odor, but water contaminated with feces spreading the illness. He traced many of the victims' water usage to the Broad Street Pump, managed by St. Luke's parish, which drew water from ground water leaching from the River Thames. The same river London officials had used as the dump site for the cesspools filled with cholera victims' excrement and the same river into which sewers from wealthier districts emptied. With this evidence, Snow was able to convince the vicar of St. Luke's, Henry Whitehead, to remove the handle from the Broad Street Pump to prevent the usage of the contaminated water.[38]

However, when Snow presented his findings to other physicians, Chadwick and other sanitarians denounced Snow's argument as ludicrous.[39] Later in the century germ theory, which we'll explore in the next section, unquestionably confirmed Snow's hypothesis about cholera's link to contaminated water. Even beforehand, though, other physicians, such as William Budd in Bristol, drew similar conclusions as Snow and pushed for changes to water management. Under a decade later, after Snow himself had died, his work and that of other physicians had convinced the government to modify the sewer designs of the sanitarians. Public outcry over the "Great Stink"—the sewage in the River Thames—as well as the works of physicians like Snow resulted in a redesign of London's sewers by Joseph Bazalgette, an English engineer. The overhaul cost the British government around four million English pounds, roughly $250,000,000 in today's US dollars, and was completed by 1865. The new system arranged pipes conveying London's sewage to dump into the River Thames only during high tide. The subsequent low tide would pull waste out toward the ocean, flushing it away from groundwater supplies.[40] Cholera struck Britain again, but the death tolls dropped each time. Though not intended to do so, this government-led infrastructural development contributed to a decline in the gross disparity of occurrence of water-borne illnesses like cholera in the lower classes.

---

38. Gorsky, "Public Health in the West since 1800: The Response," 48.

39. Hays, *The Burdens of Disease*, 147–50.

40. Johnson, *The Ghost Map*, 207–208.

Cholera, Containment, and Centralization:
Imperial Germany and the United States

The 1854 outbreak in London was not the last visitation of cholera, nor were India and Great Britain the only countries affected. Britain's experiences with cholera in the 1830s and 1850s were both part of global pandemics of the disease that would occur again in the 1860s, the 1890s, and the early twentieth century. The sanitary movement, which became popular globally, played a role in the response to these outbreaks in other countries in Europe and the Americas. In both Germany and the United States, the political strength of sanitarians meant governments responded to illnesses like cholera and typhoid by using older strategies based on miasma theory. Such Chadwick-like models continued to negatively impact immigrant groups and the poor.

Nevertheless, new discoveries about the cause of water-borne illnesses like cholera and typhoid shifted the discussion on how best to prevent outbreaks and the role of government in prevention. Sanitarians attempted to silence these challenges to their dominant position in public health during major public health crises like the 1892 outbreak of cholera in Hamburg Germany and a series of outbreaks of cholera and typhoid in the United States in the later half of the nineteenth century. The failure of sanitarian policies in these moments led to reevaluation of newer models of disease prevention and changes in policy, infrastructure, and water treatment ultimately easing the socioeconomic inequality of disease in Europe and the United States.

The outbreak of cholera in Hamburg, Germany in 1892 presented new challenges to the now international sanitary movement. German sanitarians had made major strides in Imperial Germany toward fulfilling the goal of eliminating waste from the city through infrastructure projects and waste disposal programs. Hamburg, like London, was a major port city in the nineteenth century with a major river, the Elbe, into which the city's sewers emptied. Hamburg's sewer system in the 1890s was far more sophisticated than London's in 1854. Although not perfect at eliminating waterborne illnesses, Hamburg's fully articulated sewers were better equipped to handle the volume of waste and prevent backflow into drinking water supplies, lessening the incidence of disease.[41]

In addition to more advanced sewers, the German physician Robert Koch, one of the founding fathers of germ theory, had discovered the true cause of cholera. On an 1883 expedition including trips to India and Egypt, he had isolated the bacteria *Vibrio cholerae* as the microbe responsible for cholera. (see Figure 2.2)[42]

---

41. Evans, *Death in Hamburg*, 109–43.

42. Christoph Gradmann, *Laboratory Disease: Robert Koch's Medical Bacteriology*, trans. Elborg Forster (Baltimore: John Hopkins University Press, 2009), 181–201.

voraussetzen, daß gerade in dem Kampf gegen Seuchen von ganz festen und wissen-
schaftlich durchgearbeiteten Grundlagen ausgegangen wird; aber leider ist das noch
nicht überall der Fall und namentlich der Cholera gegenüber fehlt es an einer solchen
festen Basis. Man hat allerdings eine Menge von Ansichten über das Wesen, die

Figur 1.

Vom Epithel entblößte
Schleimhautoberfläche.

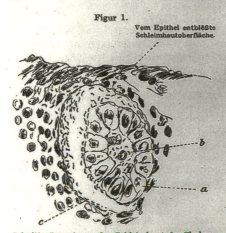

Figur 2.

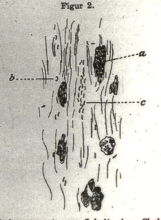

Schnittpräparat von der Schleimhaut des Cholera-
darms. Eine schlauchförmige Drüse (a) ist schräg
durchschnitten. Im Innern (b) derselben und
zwischen Epithel und Basalmembran (c) zahlreiche
Kommabazillen. 600 mal.

Deckglaspräparat vom Inhalt eines Cholera-
darms. Kerne der abgestorbenen Epithelien (a).
Halbkreisförmiger Kommabazillus (b). Beson-
ders charakteristische Gruppierung der Kommabazillen (c). 600 mal.

Figur 3.

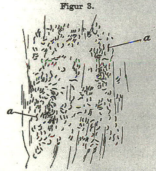

Figur 4.

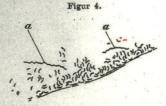

Deckglaspräparat. Choleradejektion auf feuchter
Leinwand (2 Tage lang). Starke Vermehrung der
Kommabazillen, darunter S-förmige (a). 600 mal.

Deckglaspräparat. Vom Rande eines Tropfens
Fleischbrühe mit Reinkultur der Kommabazillen. Lange schraubenförmige Fäden (a).
600 mal.

Verbreitungs- und Infektionsweise der Cholera bereits geäußert, und es sind verschiedene
Theorien darüber aufgestellt; aber die Meinungen gehen doch noch soweit auseinander,
sie stehen sich noch so schroff gegenüber, daß wir sie als Stützen, als Ausgangspunkte
für unsere Maßnahmen zur Bekämpfung dieser Seuche nicht ohne weiteres annehmen
können.

FIGURE 2.2 This image from Koch's collected works depicts and medically describes
the effects of *Vibrio cholera*, the bacterium Robert Koch identified as being the cause of
the disease.
Source: Robert Koch

Koch, building on the work of John Snow and others, determined the disease was spread when food or water supplies were contaminated by fecal matter containing the bacteria. He recommended several policies to the German government to prevent outbreaks of the disease: 1) embargo of shipping from areas afflicted with cholera; 2) a quarantine of the infected in hospitals where they could be treated and kept hydrated; 3) regular testing of water supplies and rivers for the bacteria; and 4) disinfection squads using caustic chemicals to kill the bacteria in areas where infection was rampant.[43] Why, then, did the 1892 outbreak result in the death of over eight thousand people in Hamburg?

Historians have pointed to several variables that made Hamburg susceptible to cholera. Some scholars argue the primary reason Hamburg was the only city on continental Europe to be hit so hard by the disease in the 1890s lay in the federal structure of Imperial Germany. Following German Unification in 1871, the new German parliament approved a constitution similar to the US structure with varying degrees of governmental power given to local, state, and national authorities. These scholars argue the intense favoritism for local authority among government officials in the new state contributed to the severity of Hamburg's outbreaks.[44] Even though Germany had started blocking British shipping in the 1880s and threatened a full embargo in 1884 ostensibly over concerns of the spread of cholera, but in actuality as part of a tariff dispute between the two countries, this federal structure of government allowed Hamburg to strike its own course.[45] While the rest of Germany enforced this cordon sanitaire on shipping, Hamburg continued to admit British vessels at port, thereby allowing cholera to enter the city.

The historian Richard Evans agrees with these scholars: Germany's federalism played a role. Evans, however, argues that the more important factors contributing to the lethality of the 1892 outbreak were economic interests and social stratification.[46] The political fortunes of sanitarians and merchants in Hamburg were linked, he argues, which added incentive to prevent the embargo of British ships. Furthermore, Hamburg had engaged in similar urban planning to London. The poor lived in cramped accommodations, with little access to running water or flushable toilets, in the districts of the city situated along the highly trafficked, dirty commercial waterways, constantly exposed to the profitable transit along

---

43. Evans, *Death in Hamburg,* 267–90, 303–304, 373–74; Gradmann, *Laboratory Disease,* 11–17.

44. Evans, *Death in Hamburg,* 1–27. Here in his work, Evans outlines and debates numerous German, British, and American historians on this issue.

45. Evans, *Death in Hamburg,* 118–20, 133–34, 145–46; Hays, *The Burdens of Disease,* 151.

46. Evans, *Death in Hamburg,* 27–109, 126–79, 403–69, 508–38.

which the communicable disease was introduced. This was particularly true in the older, denser city districts of Altstadt Nord and Altstadt Süd, where not all flushable toilets in densely populated tenements were properly connected to sewer lines and where seasonal flood waters from the River Elbe often created standing pools of wastewater.[47] These factors in turn made quarantine procedures more difficult to enforce in these parts of the city without completely shutting down trade as the rest of Germany already had.

Sanitary movement adherents and sympathizers in Germany latched onto the fact the disease was more concentrated in the poorer parts of the city. Many German sanitarians, like their British counterparts, blamed cholera on the poor and their proclivity to "drink," by which they meant alcoholism.[48] Sanitarians, wedded to the "miasma theory" of disease, also disapproved of Koch's bacteriological approach and used the disproportionate infection rate among the poor as evidence in their efforts to try to discredit Koch and his findings.[49] The dominant view of the disease in Hamburg was advocated by Bavarian scientist Max von Pettenkofer, who suggested that "meterological events" and changes to the water table in a locale caused cholera, not a bacterial agent.[50] Pettenkofer's rivalry with Koch was so intense Pettenkofer ingested a sample of *Vibrio cholerae* to prove his point. When Pettenkoffer became "mildly ill," he and other German sanitarians tried to use the stunt as evidence to discredit Koch's work.[51] The scholar J. N. Hays, who we looked at earlier, agrees with Evans and further argues that merchants in Hamburg, fearful quarantine and embargo policies would hurt their profit margins, lent financial and political support to sanitarians in their effort to dismiss Koch's bacterial discovery and germ theory.[52]

During the height of the outbreak in 1892, Koch and other bacteriologists proposed an Epidemics Bill to the German parliament to confer more power to the Imperial State in times of health crises. In Altona, a city neighboring Hamburg, Koch ultimately managed to compel local officials to follow his proscriptions to prevent the spread of cholera after the death toll in Hamburg reached the thousands. Sanitarians in 1892 fought against the bill, defeated it, and fought it again in court when it was reintroduced in 1899. In civil proceedings, German sanitarians tried to use expert testimony and examples to prove miasmic theories

---

47. Evans, *Death in Hamburg*, 138–41, 431–35.

48. Evans, *Death in Hamburg*, 234, 355.

49. Hays, *The Burdens of Disease*, 149–54.

50. Evans, *Death in Hamburg*, 237–46.

51. Gradmann, *Laboratory Disease*, 14–17.

52. Evans, *Death in Hamburg*, 246–51; Hays, *The Burdens of Disease*, 148–54.

explained cholera and Koch's bacteriological explanation did not hold water. This time, however, when one of Pettenkofer's students, Rudolf Emmerich, tried the same demonstration as his mentor to discredit Koch, it failed. Emmerich, who claimed bacteria in "drinking water" played no role in the spread of the disease, died after ingesting water he intentionally contaminated with cholera.[53] The sanitarians lost, but not because of Emmerich's demise.

Bubonic plague, oddly enough, helped solidify bacteriology's place as integral to a centralized cholera response. Cholera was no longer the most feared disease as the outbreak faded into the past, but there was renewed concern of the return of bubonic plague in Asia in the 1890s. Scientists proved in 1894 and 1898 the bubonic plague was caused by a bacterial agent through a chain of contagion from fleas and rodents to humans. Fears of the plague spreading to Europe gave Koch and other bacteriologists the support they needed in their fight for legislation. In 1900, the German Epidemics Law passed. Now the government could compel localities to engage in quarantine, force the embargo of vessels from afflicted areas, centralize policies for the maintenance of sewer infrastructure to certain standards, and demand regular screening of water and food supplies for bacterial agents responsible for disease. Building on the infrastructure reforms their sanitarian rivals had established, bacteriologists like Koch were able to supplement advances in waste-water engineering with water testing and chemical disinfectants to eliminate disease-causing bacteria.[54] The result of centralizing these policy directives was a drastic decline in cholera, typhoid, and dysentery deaths in Europe as these methods spread to other countries. These policies indirectly addressed the problem of class inequality in terms of disproportionate deaths from water-borne diseases because the reforms benefited all members of the population.

"King Cholera" was a yearly visitor in the United States for much of the nineteenth century and followed Americans along the course of Westward expansion, but cholera was a less lethal killer in the United States than other waterborne illnesses like typhoid or dysentery. There were larger outbreaks in 1832, 1849, and 1866 in New York, some densely populated cities in the American South following the Civil War, and smaller outbreaks in Los Angeles and San Francisco. Still, the death tolls from cholera in the United States were lower than those in Europe, South America, or Asia in the same period.

The rarity of lethal outbreaks of the illness, however, made cholera more fearful for Americans in the nineteenth century as they heard of mounting fatalities in Europe and Asia and triggered preemptive public health responses. Sanitarians

---

53. Evans, *Death in Hamburg*, 499–508.

54. Hays, *The Burdens of Disease*, 152–54.

in the United States engaged in similar classist responses as their British and German counterparts in the early half of the 1800s.[55] Unlike Chadwick's response or that of German sanitarians, the American perception of the disease, like the British in India, also contained a racialized component. The notion cholera was an "Old World" problem that should remain on the other side of the Atlantic and the assumption of the disease's "Asiatic" origin sparked a range of anti-immigrant policies dovetailing with mounting American nativism during the late nineteenth century.[56]

Consider the image in Figure 2.3. This political cartoon appeared in a popular American magazine called *Puck* in 1883. We know little about the artist, Friedrich Graetz. He was an Austrian immigrant to the United States. We also

THE KIND OF "ASSISTED EMIGRANT" WE CAN NOT AFFORD TO ADMIT.

FIGURE 2.3 This image by Friedrich Graetz, depicting cholera sailing into the Port of New York on a British ship, was published in the American periodical *Puck* on July 18, 1883. Beneath it was a caption that read: "The kind of 'assisted immigrant' we cannot afford to admit."
Source: Courtesy of Yale University, Harvey Cushing/John Hay Whitney Medical Library

---

55. Charles E. Rosenberg, *The Cholera Years: The United States in 1832, 1849, and 1866* (Chicago: University of Chicago Press, 1987), 1–12, 133–50, 192–234.

56. For more on nativism, racism, and the emergence of anti-immigrant sentiments in various periods in American History, see Natalia Molina, *How Race Is Made in America: Immigration, Citizenship, and the Historical Power of Racial Scripts* (Berkeley: University of California Press, 2014).

know the founder of the magazine *Puck*, Joseph Keppler, was also an Austrian immigrant and the periodical was originally published in German.[57] In the image, the vessel is pulling into the New York harbor. We can see it bears a British flag, indicating the creator of this image associates Britain's global shipping network with the spread of cholera. The ship itself is being met by a force of officials from the New York Board of Health, armed with "cannons" bearing the names of various chemical disinfectants. The imagery might be referencing an American policy requiring some limited forms of chemical disinfectant as a health crisis response since the 1860s or it could be Graetz was aware of Koch's more recent research on the topic.

The anthropomorphic depiction of cholera and the caption of the photo, however, indicate a less than objective scientific view of disease. Graetz portrayed cholera as death personified, which is common for many diseases represented in art throughout history. The image of death here, however, is clad in a caricature of an array of South and Southwest Asian clothing. This again, might indicate his awareness of Koch's work, especially his 1883 voyage in which he determined strains of the disease emanated from India and Egypt. When tied with the caption, however, it combines to express a deep-seated racism. The caption read "The kind of 'assisted immigrant' we cannot afford to admit." American anti-immigrant sentiments ran very high in the nineteenth century, even among recent immigrants themselves. Although Keppler and Graetz were pro-immigrant and saw the United States as a haven for refugees, they primarily viewed it as a haven solely for European migrants like themselves. Western and Central Europeans and Americans often shared a negative view of the Ottoman Empire, India, and China as sources of Asiatic diseases, which would explain Graetz's antagonism and racism. It was also common in the United States to make incorrect arguments against admitting immigrants by claiming immigrants were carriers of these diseases.

Public Boards of Health in the United States subjected arriving immigrants to densely packed quarantine wards and screenings of immigrants. Politicians campaigned and legislated against the admission of various groups due to inflated fears they would introduce Asiatic diseases like cholera to America's shores.[58] American governmental policies concerning disease were especially harsh toward Jewish, Chinese, and Mexican immigrants in the nineteenth and twentieth centuries. The 1892 Immigration Law reduced the number of Eastern European Jews

---

57. Tom Culbertson, "The Golden Age of American Political Cartoons," *Journal of the Gilded Age and Progressive Era* 7, no. 3 (July 2008): 277–95.

58. John Raymond McKiernan-González, *Fevered Measures: Public Health and Race at the Texas-Mexico Border, 1848–1942* (Durham, NC: Duke University Press, 2012), 29–30, 76–77, 278, 283.

allowed to enter the United States because of racial assumptions Jewish families in New York had introduced typhus and other illnesses.[59]

Anti-immigration activists targeted Chinese immigrants in the 1882 Chinese Exclusion Act because of false arguments Chinese communities were the source of bubonic plague, cholera, and venereal diseases in California.[60] In 1917 the US Public Health Service, the precursor to the Centers for Disease Control, began subjecting Mexican immigrants at the border to forced baths in kerosene and vinegar to "prevent the presence of lice—and typhus—in the United States."[61] These attitudes did not fade with the rise of bacteriology and a better scientific understanding of disease in the twentieth century and continued to be reinforced by public health officials discussing disease prevalence in populations with little nuance. Even today in the twenty-first century you have likely heard many of these anti-immigrant attitudes and a faulty, racist association of certain groups with certain diseases. Can you think of any examples in your own life when public health policies or educational material reinforced racial stigmas and inequalities?

Living in poor, isolated districts within major cities in the United States, immigrants, much like their American and European lower-class counterparts, did experience higher rates of disease. The sanitary movement in the United States had, like in Britain, reinforced these disparities with stereotyping and victim blaming. Yet sewer reforms were beginning to benefit these groups as cities transformed their infrastructure, improving the quality of life for all. A definitive shift came with the advent of preventative water treatment. Here, the story of New Jersey physician John Leal is needed for us to understand how something deemed objectionable at the time—chemical disinfectant in the water supply—became centralized policy and therefore reduced the death toll from waterborne diseases.

John L. Leal was a physician who began working for the Jersey City Water Supply Company in 1899 as its sanitary advisor. He was responsible for maintaining the seven-billion-gallon Boontown Reservoir, which opened in 1904, and preventing sewage from contaminating this water supply. A trained bacteriologist, Leal was familiar with the works of Robert Koch and Louis Pasteur and routinely tested the water supply's bacteria count. Finding unusually high levels of bacteria, he began experimenting with preventative chemical disinfectant, a tactic he knew was then being tested in Lincoln, England. He began experimenting with doses of calcium hypochlorite, colloquially known as chlorine,

59. McKiernan-González, *Fevered Measures*, 282–83.

60. Nayan Shah, *Contagious Divides: Epidemics and Race in San Francisco's Chinatown* (Berkeley: University of California Press, 2001), 1–16, 17–76, 120–57; McKiernan-González, *Fevered Measures*, 283.

61. McKiernan-González, *Fevered Measures*, 283.

to samples of the water to see its effect. Chlorine had been used in Maidstone, England after a Typhoid outbreak in 1897, but as a high-dose, one-time effort meant to respond to the crisis after the fact. Convinced of the efficacy of regular, low-dose treatment of water supplies to prevent bacteria from entering the water supply, in 1908 Leal ordered the construction of a chlorination plant at the Boontown Reservoir as a test for other plans or devices.

What immediately followed was a lawsuit by citizens of Jersey City against the Jersey City Water Supply Company. The idea of water treatment was not popular and customers were worried about "poison" in their water. They alleged the company had violated its contract to deliver "pure and wholesome water" to the community. Leal was brought before the New Jersey Chancery Court, then the highest court in the state's legal system. Over the course of two years, Leal defended his stance and successfully convinced Chancellor William J. Magie of the safety of chlorine for water purification.[62]

The 1910 verdict, which found the water delivery system was "pure and wholesome … and is effective in removing in removing from the water those dangerous germs which were deemed by decree to possibly exist therin," set a precedent.[63] Chlorination programs were implemented by private water companies across the United States, with backing from and often required by the state and federal governments who were their clients. The result was a drastic drop in the number of deaths from all water-borne illnesses, such as typhoid, dysentery, and cholera, in areas implementing the new system of water treatment. Soon, other countries followed suit with preventative water treatment, able to point to the Boontown Reservoir case to prove efficacy and safety.[64] Though not the intention, the introduction of chlorination of communal water supplies remedied the disproportionate death toll from waterborne illnesses among the poor and immigrant groups in every region in which water treatment was introduced.

Reinforcing Inequalities: Cholera in British-Controlled India into the Twentieth Century

As new methods in sewer construction, public health laws and policies, and water treatment systems spread over the course of the nineteenth and twentieth centuries, death tolls from cholera and other waterborne illnesses went down

---

62. Michael J. McGuire, *The Chlorine Revolution: Water Disinfection and the Fight to Save Lives* (Denver, CO: American Water Works Association, 2013), 111–256.

63. See the records of the trial: Between the Mayor and Aldermen of Jersey City, Complainant, and Patrick H. Flynn and Jersey City Water Supply Company, Defendants: On Bill, etc (In Chancery of New Jersey) 12 vols., 1908–10, 1–6987.

64. McGuire, *The Chlorine Revolution*, 257–318.

in several European countries, the United States, and the British Dominions of Canada, New Zealand, Australia, and South Africa. Yet these effective public health initiatives and responses were not distributed equally across the globe. They were not even distributed equally across a single political entity, the British Empire. Even as British officials rolled out these reforms at home and in several of Britain's colonies, colonial officials denied India much needed improvements to infrastructure, quarantine, and water supply policies. As a result, deadly outbreaks of cholera raged in India well into the mid-twentieth century while the disease seemingly vanished from other parts of the globe. So why didn't British colonial officials in India implement the changes in the nineteenth and twentieth centuries needed to prevent these fatal epidemics? Lack of knowledge cannot be used as an excuse, since the British government was rolling out these reforms in Great Britain itself.

Watts argues British colonial officials grounded their rejection of these policies on commercial interest. Watts lays out his argument by pointing to the period between 1860 and 1921. As we saw earlier in this chapter, this period was when the greatest transformations in cholera policy were occurring around the world. India was the most heavily populated area in the British Empire, with 200 million inhabitants—ten times the population of the United Kingdom. Due to the economic significance of India to the empire, some British officials in India in the 1850s and 1860s imposed new policies of quarantine, shipping bans, and new thoughts on water and sewage controls. This intervention fit nicely with the British imperial narrative, which described the conquest of India as a humanitarian endeavor, bringing the "gifts" of Western medicine and "civilization" to the subcontinent.

Watts argues, however, in 1868 there was a "policy reversal." Despite criticism from members of the Royal Army Medical College in Netley, England who favored ongoing intervention, colonial officials in 1868 proclaimed "cholera in India was a disease of locality, never spread by human agency, and against which direct intervention was useless."[65] Even after Koch's research expedition of 1883, the British colonial government in India continued to pursue this new policy of nonintervention and actively tried to silence opposition. Watts points to Michael Cudmore Furnell (1829–1888), a British doctor working as sanitary commissioner in Madras, India. Furnell implored the authorities in India to adopt Koch's methods and even met with Koch in person in 1884 seeking advice. In response, the provincial governor removed Furnell from his post in an effort to silence

---

65. Sheldon Watts, "From Rapid Change to Stasis: Official Responses to Cholera in British-Ruled India and Egypt, 1860 to c. 1921," *Journal of World History* 12, no. 2 (Fall 2001): 321–74, 324.

him. Furnell continued to speak out until his sudden death in 1888, but his cries against the 1868 policy reversal went unheeded.[66]

Watts contends British medical officials in India and the United Kingdom were influenced by their own financial investments. Three of the London-based medical societies influential to medical policy in the empire were dominated and managed by Sir Joseph Fayrer (1824–1907). Fayrer was also the leading member of the Army Sanitation commission and the Medical Board of the India Office, overseeing the official reports about the colony delivered to Parliament. Fayrer was closely tied to Prime Minister William Gladstone (1809–1898), who held four terms as prime minister between 1868 and 1898. Gladstone's government oversaw major expansions of the British Empire and emphasized the importance of trade. To preserve economic growth, the prime minister himself took the position it was irrational to quarantine ships coming to Britain from India due to cholera since the disease had already come to Britain and was being dealt with effectively there. Fayrer and Gladstone, Watts argues, had similar "investment portfolios." Instituting quarantine procedures in India and vessels coming from the colony would, they worried, might lead to severe financial losses if trading partners in Europe and the United States learned of disease outbreaks via such quarantines and then placed embargos on British shipping. The Istanbul Conference of 1866, an international meeting of sanitation experts from several west and central European countries, the United States, and the Ottoman Empire, had already threatened as much if Britain failed to adhere to agreed-upon international health policies.[67] To avoid commercial losses, Fayrer used his post to support Gladstone's economic position and to silence any concerns about cholera in India. He hired "experts" who claimed to disprove Koch's findings in 1883. Fayrer drafted numerous government memos emphasizing cholera was "localized" and could not be spread by human agency. He repeatedly and publicly claimed cholera was "unique to India" and England had little to fear from repeated outbreaks easily and effectively handled on Britain's shores. When medical officials pointed to earlier outbreaks of cholera in India in 1867, which had left over 100,000 Indians dead, and insisted on a proactive intervention, Fayrer argued the expense on India would be a waste and again had the critics removed from their posts.[68]

This stance continued to blend with racist attitudes toward Indians and outbreaks continued to rage across the turn of the century. The worst came in 1900, during what is known as the Great Famine. Much-needed rains from monsoon

---

66. Watts, "From Rapid Change to Stasis," 327–28.

67. Watts, "From Rapid Change to Stasis," 344–46.

68. Watts, "From Rapid Change to Stasis," 335–40, 347–50.

season never arrived in western, central, and southern India. As a result of the drought, severe food shortages occurred impacting millions of Indians who were displaced into relief areas run by the British military in the colony. These relief camps, densely populated and lacking in basic water reforms for pumps and sewage then common in Britain, became breeding grounds for cholera. By some estimates, more than 900,000 Indians died from cholera in these camps as the British authorities refused to engage in quarantine procedures or water reform even during the crisis of the Great Famine.

British officials haughtily denied responsibility, claiming outbreaks of cholera were common for India, "visiting the population with a rhythmic intensity," and were convinced the lack of personal hygiene among the indigenous population was to blame.[69] Even an early attempted experiment with chlorination in 1903 developed independently of Leal's work, conducted by Vincent B. Nesfield of the Indian Medical Service, was systematically and bureaucratically forgotten to preserve this view.[70] A similar crisis occurred again in 1905, leaving nearly half-a-million Indians dead as the British government continued to insist funds were not available for intervention and the expense would be wasted on the unhygienic Indian population.[71]

Cholera relief for India came in the wake of these tragedies and growing anti-colonial movements. After a series of reforms in the early 1900s, Indians started training as hospital assistants in Indian schools tied to medical colleges back in Britain. The Montagu-Chelmsford Reforms of 1920 came a few months after the Amritsar Massacre in which British authorities had murdered 379 Indians who were peacefully protesting against British rule. The measure was Britain's attempt to address backlash from the massacre by loosening some of Britain's stranglehold over Indian civic affairs. It included clauses ceding public health policy decisions to local Indian authorities. Indian doctors and medical officials pushed for increased intervention along the lines of then-commonplace standards for hygiene and sanitation in Europe and the United States.

The Indian death toll from cholera dropped from 3.8 million in the 1910s to 1.7 million in the 1930s to 380,100 in the early 1950s. In the United States, the invention of a glucose-electrolyte solution for victims reduced the mortality rate of cholera to under 1 percent. Distribution of the solution started in India after

---

69. Watts, "From Rapid Change to Stasis," 366–69; Aidan Forth, *Barbed Wire Imperialism: Britain's Empire of Camps, 1876–1903* (Berkeley: University of California Press, 2017), 109–12. Bubonic plague also ran rampant in British-controlled famine camps (see pp. 112–16 in Forth, *Barbed Wire Imperialism*).

70. V. B. Nesfield, "A Chemical Method of Sterilizing Water without Affecting Its Potability," *Public Health* 15 (July 1903): 601–3.

71. Watts, "From Rapid Change to Stasis," 368–70.

the Second World War, reducing cholera's impact on Indians.[72] In the years after India's 1947 independence from Britain, the affordable Mark II and Mark III water pumps invented by Indian engineer Cyrus Gaikwad helped continue the downward trend in cholera deaths as the pumps were disseminated across numerous urban and rural Indian communities by the 1980s.[73] Though British officials had for centuries claimed to be the medical "saviors" of India in their imperial civilizing mission, British policy had actually hindered advancements in public health. Greater autonomy and ultimately independence removed these obstacles and allowed Indian medical professionals to finally intervene and begin rectifying the gross disparity in cholera deaths between the United Kingdom and India.

Conclusion

In this chapter, we looked at how outbreaks of the disease cholera disproportionately impacted the poor in the nineteenth century. We examined how initial responses to these outbreaks in British India, Great Britain, the United States, and Germany exacerbated class inequality due to assumptions about the poor held by the multinational sanitary movement. Racial stereotypes about migrants and disease in Europe and the United States during the nineteenth and twentieth centuries led to horrid policies worsening the predicaments of minorities and colonized peoples. Alternatively, more scientific responses and an increasing centralized role of the state improved conditions, minimizing inequality. Sewer infrastructure reform, bacteriological methods, epidemiological laws, and developments in water treatment decreased class inequality in waterborne illnesses by lowering the overall incidence in societies. Global disparities, however, continued. Attempts to spread this system internationally failed, due to commercial interests, competing scientific claims, and colonial bigotry. This led to greater disparity between Europe and Asia during cholera outbreaks due to British colonial policy in India. Even today, the geographical and economic prejudices held by governing officials of supposedly more advanced states and international bodies stymy the application of global water and sanitation measures. Parts of the world, such as Haiti, Yemen, and Syria, remain susceptible to cholera as natural disasters, conflict, and diplomatic sanctions by other governments hinder public health interventions. In chapter 3, which covers the control and management of sexually transmitted diseases, we will continue to examine how imperialism, race, and especially gender stereotypes continue to impact policy and how public health systems selectively replicate themselves.

---

72. Watts, *Epidemics and History*, 210–12.

73. Arun Kumar Mudgal, "India Handpump Revolution: Challenge and Change" (Swiss Centre for Development Cooperation in Technology and Management/UNICEF/UNDP, September 1997), 1–12.

FURTHER READING

Anderson, Warwick. "Excremental Colonialism: Public Health and the Poetics of Pollution." *Critical Inquiry* 21, no. 3 (Spring 1995): 640–69.

Echenberg, Myron J. *Africa in the Time of Cholera: A History of Pandemics from 1817 to the Present*. Cambridge: Cambridge University Press, 2011.

Hamlin, Christopher. *Cholera: The Biography*. Oxford: Oxford University Press, 2009.

McGuire, Michael J. *The Chlorine Revolution: Water Disinfection and the Fight to Save Lives*. Denver, CO: American Water Works Association, 2013.

McKiernan-González, John Raymond. *Fevered Measures: Public Health and Race at the Texas Mexico Border, 1848–1942*. Durham, NC: Duke University Press, 2012.

3

CONTROLLING THE COLONIZED AND FEMALE BODIES

VD CONTAINMENT, EUGENICS, AND EXPERIMENTATION IN METROPOLE AND COLONY

Millions of specialized lice infesting pubic hairs and leaving behind welts in the skin from their bites; flaking, dry, itching, and burning skin; swollen, painful genitals covered in blisters and pus; madness; death: these are examples of symptoms of some of the sexually transmitted diseases (STDs) humans encounter. These intimate illnesses, also known as venereal diseases (VD), are as old as sexual intercourse, and have been well-documented since the fifteenth century. In 1494 syphilis spread among French soldiers laying siege to the Italian city of Naples. From the battlefields of the Italian War of 1494–1498, syphilis, a.k.a. the "French disease," grew to a Europe-wide epidemic. An estimated five million people died in the year following the war of the secondary complications of necrosis of the flesh, neurological damage, and organ failure associated with the disease.[1] By the eighteenth century, Chinese doctors postulated syphilis, increasing in frequency because of more regular contact with Europeans, was spread through semen and might contaminate a fetus if exposed to infected ejaculate, suggesting additional threats to society from the disease.[2]

Initially, these diseases were thought to be hereditary or a punishment from a divine entity. Later, European states focused on promiscuity and a lack of morality as the cause. As Europeans fixated on the social nature of these ailments, they crafted mechanisms of societal control to limit the spread of STDs. In European and American communities, social controls initially targeted prostitutes. Eventually

1. J. D. Oriel, *The Scars of Venus: A History of Venereology* (London: Springer-Verlag, 1994), 11–24.

2. Frank Dikotter, "A History of Sexually Transmitted Diseases in China," in *Sex, Disease, and Society: A Comparative History of Sexually Transmitted Diseases and HIV/AIDS in Asia and the Pacific*, ed. Michael Lewis, Scott Bamber, and Michael Waugh, Contributions in Medical Studies 43 (Westport, CT: Greenwood Press, 1997), 67–83.

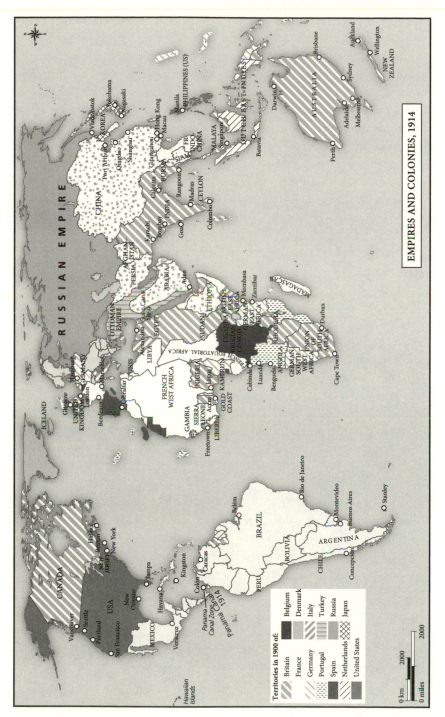

MAP 3.1 Map of World

attitudes and policies laid a foundation for a general outlook of women simultaneously as victims of STDs but also as reservoirs through which the diseases spread to men. These controls developed and grew alongside European imperial expansion and racism. In empires that spanned the globe from the eighteenth to twentieth centuries, French, German, British, and American colonial officials developed a similar logic toward colonized subjects as vectors for illness. European and American medical professionals argued STDs were "tropical illnesses" to which nonwhite populations were more susceptible due to their perceived inferiority, morally and physically, as viewed by supposedly civilized Europeans.

We can see these racialized and gendered perceptions of STDs enduring well into the twentieth century and beyond. Take a moment to reflect on the following two quotes. The first comes from Captain W. M. B. Sparkes, the British head of the detachment of the Royal Army Medical Corps, writing a report on the spread of syphilis among the indigenous population in British-controlled Uganda from 1910:

> In large centres like Kampala special legislative measures should be taken to deal with the number of loose [African] women who are wandering about prostituting. Many of these women are to be found living with the servants of Europeans, therefore no woman except the recognized wife of an [African] servant should be allowed in the compounds, as I am certain that these women are a source of danger to the community.[3]

Now examine a statement from Emillio Settimelli, one of the founders of an early-twentieth- century artistic and social movement known as Italian Futurism, from 1918:

> Gonorrhea—I can't deny it—is annoying, it hurts and it's slightly embarrassing, yet—due to the funny mechanisms of mortality—it is also what makes a man a man . . . To be forced to treat our most delicate parts roughly, to clean yourself like a rusty rifle . . . all this gives a new aplomb to a man and eliminates forever the down of boyhood.[4]

---

3. Capt. W. M. B. Sparkes, RAMC, "Report on the treatment of venereal diseases from January 27th 1909 to March 31st 1910," included in Uganda Protectorate, *Annual Medical and Sanitary Report for the year 1909* (Entebbe: Government Printer, 1910), 12.

4. Emillio Settimelli, *Nuovo modo d'amare*, Rocca S. Casciano, Capelli, 1918, 92–93, as quoted and translated in Bruno P. F. Wanrooij, "'The Thorns of Love': Sexuality, Syphillis and Social Control in Modern Italy," in *Sex, Sin and Suffering: Venereal Disease and European Society since 1870*, ed. Roger Davidson and Lesley A. Hall (New York: Routledge, 2001), 137–59. For more on Italian Futurism, see Walter L. Adamson and Ernest Ialongo, "Introduction: Reconsidering Futurism," *Journal of Modern Italian Studies* 18, no. 4 (2013): 389–92.

After a quick read of these passages, does anything stand out to you when comparing these two statements? Sparkes and Settimelli, both white, European men from the 1910s, are part of the same worldview of STDs and sex in the twentieth century. In Sparkes's statement we see how a British medical officer viewed women, specifically colonized women, in the colony as the source of VD. He made assumptions about their morality and their sexual promiscuity to explain the spread of syphilis, described these women as a "danger to the community," and suggested controls on their behavior to curb the outbreak. In Settimelli's statement, we see a more permissive attitude about male sexual promiscuity and a jocular tone about the shame of gonorrhea. For Settimelli, STDs represented a man's "virility," displayed as a bizarre, and painful, badge of honor recounting his sexual conquests. A clear double standard existed in European countries and their colonies regarding whose activities needed to be controlled to prevent the spread of VD. We also see a double standard as to which groups of the population were branded with the societal stigma of these ailments. So how were these gendered and racially guided views created and then made transnational at the dawn of the twentieth century?

This chapter argues that European and American imperial powers crafted racist and misogynist public health to contain STD controls and merged those policies with aggressive intervention by governments to control women's and colonized subjects' bodies. Geographically, this chapter focuses on the British, German, French, and US empires of the nineteenth and twentieth centuries, which spanned much of Africa, Asia, Polynesia, and the Caribbean. Imperial health structures, regardless of which Western empire implemented them, were designed to halt the spread of disease while simultaneously reinforcing colonial subjugation and gender hierarchies (see Map 3.1). Europeans and white Americans regarded some STDs, such as syphilis, as a threat to unborn children and therefore a threat to the racial "health of the nation" due to the physical deformities and disabilities such maladies caused during fetal development. As such, policies against STDs, when wedded with eugenicist laws, also robbed some men and women, but especially colonized women, of their reproductive rights. Together, we will chart the overlapping histories of venereal disease perception, containment, racial segregation of sex, and attempts by governments to control female and colonized bodies.

The chapter is broken into five sections. First, we look at the history of how colonized women came to be regarded as the "vectors" of STDs and why white Euro-Americans came to believe diseases like syphilis had a "tropical origin." Second, we'll explore the history of Euro-American STD and prostitution controls from the metropole, such as the British Contagious Diseases Act of 1864, which were subsequently applied in these societies' colonial holdings. Third, we'll assess how these controls morphed into attempts by Euro-American empires to manage miscegenation—racial mixing—which white Europeans and Americans viewed with the same disdain as STDs. Fourth, we'll outline the related history of the then growing field of eugenics and how it incorporated concerns about STDs to advocate for even greater levels of state control over the bodies of women and racial others. Finally, we will see how these four threads came together with a longer history of imperial medical experimentation on oppressed groups with the examples of the Tuskegee Syphilis Experiment (1932–1972) and Guatemala Syphilis Experiments (1946–1948) conducted by the United States Public Health Service (USPHS).

Mosquito Women: Tropical Medicine and Racism in STD Perception

"Medically speaking, [the prostitute] can be thought of as the intermediate host or carrier of *Spirochaeta pallida* [an older name for the bacteria thought to cause syphilis], just as the mosquito is host for the malarial parasite."[5] This statement, written by a VD specialist at the Mayo Clinic in 1919, indicates how American and European medical and government officials viewed STDs. Male doctors and policymakers labeled women both as the primary vectors and as defenseless victims of STDs in a hierarchy dependent on the race and class of the women involved (see Figure 3.1). In the nineteenth and twentieth centuries, medical professionals in European countries and the United States portrayed STDs themselves as having "tropical origins." As we saw in the previous chapter on cholera, Europeans and Americans were quick to associate outbreaks of disease with Asian and African populations, blaming these groups and their perceived lack of civilization for epidemics and pandemics in the nineteenth century. Studies tracing the point of origin for the bacteria causing diseases like cholera and bubonic plague to South or East Asia reinforced these views, as if the evolutionary emergence of a disease-causing agent was the fault of the societies existing in those regions. The explanation for how something as global and universally human as STDs, especially syphilis, were regarded as tropical diseases lies in the history of imperialism and the creation of a public health field called "tropical medicine."

As we discussed in the previous chapter, one of the goals of European empires, Japan in the twentieth century, and the United States in its westward conquest and acquisition of overseas territories after the Spanish-American War in the 1890s was the "civilizing mission." These empires believed they had a duty to "uplift" other societies to a European-style of government and culture. They often coupled economic and cultural goals with another objective: to tame the landscape. To

---

5. John H. Stokes, *Today's World Problem in Disease Prevention* (Washington, DC: US Public Health Service, 1919), 105.

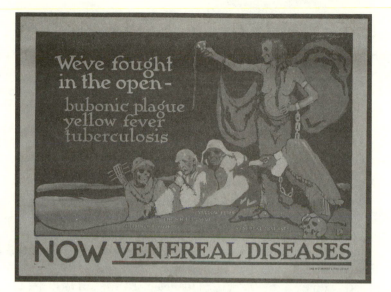

FIGURE 3.1 This image is from an educational postage stamp produced by the American Social Hygiene Association in 1918 to raise funds for campaigns to fight STDs at home and abroad. Much like the Puck cholera image we saw in the last chapter, diseases are personified here, with racialized and gendered stereotypes. Venereal disease, the only one anthropomorphized as a woman, is displayed here as a clichéd colonial prostitute, topless and clothed only in a billowing red dancing-skirt and golden bangles and chains.
Source: Digitized image used courtesy of the Library of Congress. LC-USZC4-4257: "We've fought in the open-bubonic plague, yellow fever, tuberculosis—now venereal diseases," designed by H. Dewitt Welsh in conjunction with the U.S. Committee on Public Information, Division of Pictorial Publicity, 1918. Copyright not renewed.

urbanize regions in Africa, Asia, the Pacific, and the Americas and make them more profitable, governmental officials and colonial advocates from imperial powers believed they needed settlers from their own countries to occupy the colonies and guide their development. In several instances, European and American imperial governments made plans for white settlers to ultimately "replace" local populations, thereby achieving the goal of cultivating the wilderness by eradicating entire societies and populations.[6] We can see this worldview expressed by Americans sympathetic to Europe's brutal imperialism in a quote from the the *Atlanta Constitution* in 1896: "The different governments of Europe are all repeating in Africa the work of colonization which has made America populous [here meaning full of white settlers], and before them the negro must go, as did the Indian in America."[7]

---

6. Laura Briggs, *Reproducing Empire: Race, Sex, Science, and U.S. Imperialism in Puerto Rico* (Berkeley: University of California Press, 2002), 34.

7. "The Misfortune of a Race," in *The Atlanta Constitution*, March 2, 1896 as quoted Raymond Jonas, *The Battle for Adwa: African Victory in the Age of Empire* (Cambridge, MA: Belknap Press, 2011), 5.

European and white American settlers in the eighteenth and nineteenth centuries met with resistance from indigenous populations and were frequently unprepared or ill-adapted to face the unique natural settings in areas like the Congo or Zambezi River Basins, the Amazon Delta, the Caribbean, or the Malay Archipelago. Disease proved to a hindrance to conquest. White Europeans and Americans had little or no resistance to yellow fever, malaria, or the various hemorrhagic fevers in the interior of Africa. Diseases like Rinderpest decimated livestock populations upon which Europeanized settlers depended. Europeans in the eighteenth century dubbed Africa "the White Man's Grave."[8] Entire conquering armies were laid down by disease and whole settlements disappeared.

Colonizers answered resistance from colonized subjects with brutal military force. Similarly, imperialists sought to eliminate parasites, viruses, and bacteria obstructing their mission to remake the world in their own image. Governments in the United States, Great Britain, France, Germany, and a host of other countries formed offices to research and propose solutions to these barriers to colonial settlement—the new discipline of tropical medicine.[9] Tropical medicine became a collaborative endeavor between empires. French, British, German, American, and Italian colonial medical officers exchanged information on combating malaria by draining swamps, handing out mosquito nets, and developing the first variations of the prophylactic drug quinine.[10] German and British medical officers located the causal agent for and coordinated a response to an outbreak of trypanosomiasis (sleeping sickness) in the region around Lake Victoria, which bordered the colonies of both empires in East Africa.[11] The US-based Rockefeller Foundation formed the International Health Commission in 1913, which collaborated with the British Colonial Office in efforts to eradicate hookworm in the Caribbean, sub-Saharan Africa, and South Asia.[12] The same group unsuccessfully sought to eradicate yellow fever across Latin America and the US South through forced vaccination and drastic environmental alteration.[13]

---

8. Philip D. Curtin, "'The White Man's Grave:' Image and Reality, 1780–1850," *Journal of British Studies*, 1, no. 1 (November 1961): 94–110.

9. Briggs, *Reproducing Empire*, 33–35.

10. Randall M. Packard, *The Making of a Tropical Disease: A Short History of Malaria* (Baltimore: John Hopkins University Press, 2007) 1–18, 84–149.

11. Mari Webel, "Medical Auxiliaries and the Negotiation of Public Health in Colonial Northwestern Tanzania," *Journal of African History* 54, no. 3 (November 2013): 393–416.

12. Randall M. Packard, *A History of Global Health: Interventions into the Lives of Other Peoples* (Baltimore: John Hopkins University Press, 2016), 32–39.

13. Nancy Leys Stepan, *Eradication: Ridding the World of Diseases Forever?* (Ithaca, NY: Cornell University Press, 2011), 50–103.

At times colonizers indirectly aided colonized subjects through their medical research and policies, reducing death tolls from these maladies, but colonial health officials were not generally motivated by humanitarian concerns. Tropical medicine aimed to preserve white settler populations and economic interests, to prevent disastrous reductions the populations of colonized subjects used for coerced labor in the colonies, to maintain the strength of European and American military forces in occupied regions, and to block illnesses from spreading to Europe or the United States.[14]

The racialized worldviews of specialists in tropical medicine influenced their "scientific findings" on the origin of STDs. They believed falsely syphilis originated among and was spread by people of color around the world. Syphilis posed a grave threat to the civilizing mission espoused by the US and European powers. Syphilis also caused birth deformities and miscarriages if contracted by pregnant women. At points in the nineteenth and twentieth centuries, doctors also believed syphilis caused sterility in white men. Medical officers were concerned over what they called "tropical sterility"—European men and women contracting STDs such as syphilis and gonorrhea would hinder their ability to reproduce, which would in turn hinder efforts to build self-sustaining white settler communities. Such illnesses threatened reproduction in white settler colonies and also provoked fear these STDs would "spread back" to Europe and the United States, endangering the "white race" on a global scale.

The rise of laboratory medicine and testing for microbial causal agents, building on the work of Robert Koch and Louis Pasteur, allayed some of the extreme fears about sterility, but bad science continued to place the blame on colonized subjects. In 1905, a German dermatologist named Erich Hoffmann and a German tropical medical researcher for the Imperial Colonial Office in Berlin named Fritz Schaudinn, working at Charité Hospital in Berlin, argued they had discovered the microbe responsible for syphilis: *Spriochaeta pallida*. *S. pallida,* now known as *Treponema pallidum pallidum*, bears a superficial similarity to the protozoans responsible for African sleeping sickness. For this reason, German researchers, American biologists, and French scientists at the Institut Pasteur proposed "tropical origins" for syphilis, suggesting it had come from the Congo River Basin to the Great Lakes Region of East Africa or arguing it had emerged in the Caribbean and spread to Europeans by the Columbian Exchange.[15]

White European and American medical researchers and biologists further argued evolution had made Africans more promiscuous. Authors in the *Journal*

---

14. Briggs, *Reproducing Empire*, 33–35; Jessica Lynne Pearson, *The Colonial Politics of Global Health: France and the United Nations in Postwar Africa* (Cambridge, MA: Harvard University Press, 2018), 24–26, 113–40.

15. Briggs, *Reproducing Empire*, 34–64.

of the American Medical Association asserted that "the negro springs from a southern race, and as such his sexual appetite is strong," which they claimed was proven by "the size of the negro's penis," the "peculiar shape of the female's external sex organs," and the "diminished gray matter of the negro brain."[16] These supposed medical facts at the time were never proven and never satisfied even the barest minimum of evidence from well-constructed, well-reasoned experimentation or examination.

Public health officials, however, acted on these theories based on pure conjecture and centuries of racism to craft policy. Given the frequency of sexual encounters between European and American troops and women who were colonized subjects in these empires, African, Polynesia, Asian, and Hispanic women in their colonies were branded as the "back doors of our homes . . . the places where the germs come in," posed a threat to public hygiene and safety of "fair-haired young sailors . . . come into these tropical ports."[17] As we will explore in the next section, the same imperial collaboration exhibited in response to health threats like malaria existed in the creation of policies to regulate the spread of "tropical disease" in the form of STDs.

Politics of Prostitution: Imperial STD Controls

> If a man saw me and liked me, then he would come to my door and knock and ask to come in . . . The best way to find men was for them to come to your room and you talk, you make tea for them, you keep your house clean, you keep your bed clean, you have sex with him, and then he gives you money . . . I didn't go openly looking for men and men came to my house with respect.[18]

This quote comes from a Kenyan woman named Kayaya Thababu speaking of her experience as a prostitute in 1920s Nairobi in an interview with historian Luis White. She indicates prostitution in the then-British colony was not a secretive profession, nor was it viewed entirely with disdain by local populations or

---

16. Briggs, *Reproducing Empire*, 60–65; Allan M. Brandt, "Racism and Research: The Case of The Tuskegee Syphilis Experiment," in *Tuskegee's Truths: Rethinking the Tuskegee Syphilis Study*, ed. Susan M. Reverby (Chapel Hill: University of North Carolina Press, 2000), 16–17.

17. The partial quote is from Gavin Payne of the Red Cross for the Attorney General of US Puerto Rico, *Special Report of the Attorney General of Porto Rico to the Governor of Porto Rico*, 48–51, as quoted in Briggs, *Reproducing Empire*, 59–61.

18. Interview with Kayaya Thababu as quoted in Luis White, "Prostitution, Identity, and Class Consciousness in Nairobi during World War II," *Signs* 11, no. 2 (Winter 1986): 255–73, 259–60.

the European clientele. Nor was prostitution as widespread as the quote at the beginning of this chapter from Sparkes in nearby British-controlled Uganda in 1910 claimed, when he said there were a large number of "loose women wandering around prostituting themselves."[19] Though several European communities viewed prostitution as morally questionable, it was still openly practiced in European nations and their colonial empires.

Heightened concerns over STDs and mixed-race births, as we will look at later in this chapter, lent a new sense of urgency to moralistic, Victorian campaigns against prostitution in the nineteenth and twentieth centuries. European and American governments, as well as their colonial branches, opted to control the sexual behavior of their citizens through legislation and regulation as part of public health programs.

Officials rejected the obvious solution—restricting the sexual liaisons of European and American men at home and in the colonies to prevent the spread of STDs from partner to partner, from continent to continent. Educational efforts to mitigate the spread of STDs via male promiscuity with campaigns warning of the risk and the distribution of condoms failed. European and American men ignored the flyers and refused to use prophylactics. Medical professionals from the nineteenth century onward also claimed that men denied sexual release risked "hydraulic" dysfunction from spermatic buildup. European and American doctors took as a given the need for women to be made sexually available to European and American soldiers stationed in colonies and in overseas conflicts to prevent such damage. Condoning or ignoring the horrors of rape, granting shore leave for informal romantic liaisons, or allowing visits to brothels and hired prostitutes, military officers and government officials dared not prohibit sexual encounters—and in many instances actively encouraged them despite medical concerns—for fear of mutiny.[20]

Since limiting the sexual activity of European and American men failed through haphazard enforcement and limited compliance, legislators, officers, doctors, and moralization societies chose instead to focus their efforts on controlling women's bodies by regulating the world's oldest profession. These campaigns in the metropoles and colonies of empires depicted women, particularly indigenous women in the colonies, as prostitutes regardless of whether they sold sex or not, and targeted women for social controls in the various anti-STD programs.

The collective imperial toolkit for VD control included regulatory licensing of "commercialized vice" (a.k.a. prostitution), forced screenings, quarantine, and

19. Sparkes, "Report on the treatment of venereal diseases," 12.

20. White, "Prostitution" 255–60; Briggs, *Reproducing Empire*, 24–73; Daniel J. Walther, *Sex and Control: Venereal Disease, Colonial Physicians, and Indigenous Agency in German Colonialism, 1884–1914* (New York: Berghahn Books, 2015), 13–52.

compulsory treatment for STDs. These controls, first introduced in Britain, addressed morality concerns over prostitution and venereal disease outbreaks in the armed forces. In 1864, after two years of Parliamentary inquiry, legislators passed the first of a series of Contagious Diseases Acts (CDA). The legislation gave British police the right to arrest any woman in Britain suspected of commercial vice. The officer would have to swear under oath before a magistrate the woman was a common prostitute. The suspected prostitute then faced compulsory gynecological screening for STDs, specifically gonorrhea and syphilis. If found to be infected, she was then placed in what was called a "lock hospital" to undergo forced treatment for the disease. Later Contagious Disease Acts modified this system, adding registration with the state and regular screenings of sex workers to receive and renew licenses to ply their trade.

In the colonial sphere, the CDA and laws they inspired added additional regulations and restrictions on women. Such policies became commonplace in the British, French, and German empires. In British-controlled India and Uganda, Germany's African colonies, and many of France's imperial territories, officials suspected all indigenous woman of prostitution and removed the requirement for the arresting officer to swear as much in a court of law. These European colonial regimes also added curfews, limiting when all indigenous women could be out on city streets, supposedly prostituting themselves, and they would be arrested on the spot if out past a proscribed hour.[21] In many instances, indigenous women did not speak the same language as the arresting officer or the male European doctors who conducted the forced screenings, adding another layer of terror to these state-sanctioned invasions of their bodies and sexual rights.

Indigenous women licensed as prostitutes by colonial administrations had to limit their clientele. Registered women in the German, British, and French empires, for example, could only serve British/French/German clients and could not engage in any sexual liaisons with African or Asian men under penalty of law. This limitation was supposedly to prevent screened, clean prostitutes from being "contaminated" with STDs by indigenous men. By segregating the customer base of registered prostitutes, colonial governments also reinforced racial purity and heteronormativity. White men serviced by a subset of registered sex workers would not have to fear indirect sexual contact with black- or brown-skinned men who were their colonized subjects since they, in theory, were not having sex with the same women.[22]

---

21. Lesley A. Hall, "Venereal Diseases and Society in Britain, from the Contagious Disease Acts to the National Health Service," in *Sex, Sin and Suffering*, ed. Davidson and Hall, 120–36; Philippa Levine, "Public Health, Venereal Disease, and Colonial Medicine in the Later Nineteenth Century," in *Sex, Sin and Suffering*, ed. Davidson and Hall, 160–72; Briggs, *Reproducing Empire*, 23–30, Walther, *Sex and Control*, 91–131.

22. Briggs, *Reproducing Empire*, 25.

The CDA and others like them elicited controversy. In Britain, moral and religious movements pushed for outright bans of prostitution instead, fearing regulation and licensing "legitimized" prostitution. Additionally, women's advocacy groups, like the Ladies National Association for the Repeal of the Contagious Disease Acts, argued that the acts violated basic civil liberties of women at a time when British women fought for equality before the law.[23]

In the United States, these social campaigns, frequently led by religious figures and middle-class white women, strongly influenced legislation. The majority of US cities and states tolerated prostitution for a time and later banned it, but the US federal and state governments never licensed and regulated prostitution due to fears that "European" policies led to moral decline. US territories not yet formally states, however, tolerated and licensed prostitution. During US imperial expansion westward places like the Dakota territories allowed prostitution. Once the federal government granted these regions were granted statehood, however, western territorial legislatures made a show of banning the sex trade. In US overseas territories like the Philippines or Puerto Rico, however, public health officials adopted policies like the British CDA, complete with licensure and screening.[24] The differences in how the United States handled STD controls in the United States proper versus its overseas holdings is an exemplar of how empires practiced a system of double standards, with one set of rules and policies for the center of the empire and another set for its colonies.

Though colonized peoples often protested measures like the CDA, in some instances, such as in British-controlled Uganda, local men supported policies regulating or controlling prostitution in the service of STD prevention. In the region of Buganda, which was granted a degree of autonomy in British-controlled Uganda, indigenous chiefs showed their support of the colonial administration's named the Townships (Venereal Diseases) Rules of 1913 by passing their own laws against STDs in 1913 and the Adultery and Fornication Law in 1918.[25] Concerned about syphilis's threat to unborn babies, these laws forced Bugandan women to accept random genital inspections for illness by both Bugandan men and European doctors. Of both laws, the nominal King of Buganda, Duadi Chwa, told British officials "it is proper to pass a Law to prevent fornication ... because it greatly diminishes the increase of the nation: the women do not bear properly and they are very much infected by diseases through excessive fornication."[26]

23. Judith R. Walkowitz, *Prostitution and Victorian Society: Women, Class, and the State* (Cambridge: Cambridge University Press, 1980), 67–148.

24. Briggs, *Reproducing Empire*, 30–73.

25. Michael W. Tuck, "Venereal Disease, Sexuality and Society in Uganda," in *Sex, Sin and Suffering*, ed. Davidson and Hall, 191–204.

26. As quoted in Tuck, "Venereal Disease," 201.

Clause 18 of the 1913 law sought to protect "innocent women" who could bear children. It established fines for "any infected person who shall have sexual intercourse with an unmarried girl who is *not a* prostitute," thus permitting men to freely infect women deemed prostitutes which were considered undeserving of societal protection.[27]

We may be surprised by what looks like African complicity in colonization by a European power, but we need to consider this in another light. These laws, jointly enforced by Bugandan men and British colonial officials, were designed by colonized Bugandan men to maintain their own social hierarchies and controls over Bugandan women. To the men in the Lukiko—the Bugandan Parliament—there were only two types of women who could be exposed to STDs: immoral, adulterous women and "innocents" infected by men who had been previously seduced by immoral, adulterous women. The aim was to control those women who supposedly posed a sexual threat to the society and its reproduction, limit the sexual autonomy of all women, and simultaneously preserve men's rights to sexual access to women in any context with prostitutes for infected men and "pure girls" for uninfected men. Bugandan men saw in British colonial policy a common interest: the prioritization of male interests in, rights to, and control of women's bodies.

Parliament repealed the CDA in Britain in 1886, thanks in part to the efforts of British women's rights activists. The Acts, however, persisted in Britain's colonies and variants remained in the colonial empires of Germany, France, and the United States, to name a few.[28] Colonial administration regulations pertaining to prostitution and STDs often went hand-in-hand with other forms of reproductive control by the state. Permissive attitudes toward white male promiscuity in the colonies, coupled with the refusal of men to wear condoms, had another inevitable biological result: pregnancies.

Pregnancy as "STD": Racial Mixing and State Control of Sex

As empires expanded from 1884 to 1918, fears of miscegenation—a.k.a. "racial mixing"—blended with simultaneous campaigns against STDs and their association with indigenous Africans and Asians by European doctors. This was particularly true in the German and French empires. Even as women were increasingly advocating for greater control over their own bodies through legal recognitions and the right to vote, competing understandings of what it meant to be ethnically German or French forced a renegotiation of national inclusion and citizenship. European governments and social activists steeped in imperial racial

---

27. Tuck, "Venereal Disease," 201.

28. Walkowitz, *Prostitution*, 233–45.

hierarchies started to view mixed-race pregnancies as a kind of STD—a threat to the health of the nation. Acting upon their own volition in the early years of the twentieth century, three German colonies—Southwest Africa (1905), Tanganyika (1906), and Samoa (1912)—outlawed mixed marriages and, in some cases, denied citizenship to the children of such unions. The laws sparked a huge debate in Germany and its colonies over the legality and morality of these moves. German men in the colonies asserted their paternal right to confer citizenship on their children, forcing an evaluation of citizenship by blood. Imperialist and nationalist social organizations back in Germany, which had previously backed citizenship by blood, now advocated a narrower definition of citizenship based on an imagined "national purity."[29] In the French empire, a debate over paternity suits, at home and in the colonies, showed that women, lower classes, and non-Europeans were marginalized as the state tried to control definitions of citizenship and sexual intercourse among its subjects around the globe.[30]

Gender was intertwined with racial definitions in the colonies of European empires. The women's movement in Germany and France, already active far before official colonialism, was initially hindered, then aided, and ultimately transformed by the colonial experience. Along with the challenge to male citizenship rights, the antimiscegenation laws passed in colonies enabled the inclusion of women in discussions of national citizenship, albeit in a twisted fashion. Women in Germany and France were exalted as guardians of racial purity and bearers of culture. In this role, though, European women found their rights limited through increased state surveillance and restrictions on their choice of sexual partners and reproductive rights. Simultaneously, indigenous women were stripped of legal rights. Despite some social movements and legislative attempts to expand European citizenship laws and paternity suit procedures to include colonized subjects, many Europeans continued to demonize and "prostitutionalize" indigenous women and occasionally indigenous men. European colonial governments and European women's movements portrayed African and Asian colonized subjects as cunning and vicious enemies of racial purity and the work of civilization. By tempting Europeans into liaisons, nationalist groups and governments

---

29. Birthe Kundrus, *Moderne Imperialisten: Das Kaiserreich im Spiegel der Kolonien* (Köln: Böhlau, 2003), 230–32, 259–64; Krista O'Donnell, "The First *Besatzungskinder*: Afro-German Children, Colonial Childrearing Practices, and Racial Policy in German Southwest Africa, 1890–1914," in *Not So Plain as Black and White: Afro-German Culture and History, 1890–2010* (Rochester, NY: University of Rochester Press, 2005), 61–82.

30. Jean Elizabeth Pederson, "Special Customs: Paternity Suits and Citizenship in France and the Colonies: 1870–1912," in *Domesticating the Empire: Race, Gender, and Family Life in French and Dutch Colonialism*, ed. Julia Clancy-Smith and Frances Gouda (Charlottesville: University Press of Virginia, 1998), 44–64.

claimed, colonized subjects threatened to drain resources for "European children" through claims for support of their own mixed-race children.

European lawmakers defined the rights of European women in a limited fashion based on the ability of those women to produce "pure" Frenchmen, Germans, Dutchmen, and so on, and nothing more. Cultural taboos and legislation placed further limitations on European women's ability to freely choose whom she had sex with, regardless of race. Debates raged across Europe on the issue of whether European women could still be called European or maintain the citizenship rights of their respective nations if they had partaken in sexual relationships with non-Europeans.[31] In some instances, unlike European men, European women were "summarily disenfranchised from their national community on the basis of their conjugal choice."[32] This double standard in sexual morality and racial purity is similar to what we saw in the quote from Settimelli earlier in this chapter. While European men were given a great deal of latitude in their sexual activities, regardless of consequences such as the spread of VD or the production of at the time taboo mixed-raced children, women were condemned and punished for the same actions.

Such laws were not unique to European empires. As many of you reading may well know, the United States had bans on interracial marriages passed and enforced by numerous state governments until 1967, when the Supreme Court declared such antimiscegenation laws unconstitutional in *Loving v. Virginia.* The US Congress never passed a national law against mixed marriage, but from the late nineteenth century on, various state laws from Louisiana to Maryland, from Virginia to California, had banned marriage between persons of African, Native American, Filipino, and Asian descent and "whites." Some laws against intermarriage between South Asians and Native Americans and those of European descent dated back to the seventeenth century when the United States was still a mix of British, French, and Spanish colonies. The goal of many of these laws, especially after the American Civil War, was to maintain the strict racial hierarchies and oppression of racial minorities, specifically those of African descent, that had existed in American society for centuries. Those convicted of violating these laws were charged with a felony and faced jail time and fines or, worse, lynch mobs committing murder to enforce rigid racist societal structures outside courts of law.[33] From the nineteenth century on, these concerns about racial mixing and

---

31. Ann Laura Stoler, *Carnal Knowledge and Imperial Power: Race and the Intimate in Colonial Rule,* (Berkley: University of California Press, 2010), 105.; Wildenthal, *German Women,* 105–21.

32. Stoler, *Carnal Knowledge,* 104-111..

33. For more on miscegenation law in the US across the centuries, see Peggy Pascoe, *What Comes Naturally: Miscegenation Law and the Making of Race in America* (Oxford: Oxford University Press, 2009), 1–16, 77–130, 205–306.

desire for racial purity both in European empires and in the United States also took on a "scientific" appeal as a public health debate and a new field of study branching from a misguided understanding of the theory of evolution: eugenics.

The Eugenicists: Race Hygiene, STDs, and Reproductive Rights

"Eugenics," "racial hygiene": some people in the nineteenth and twentieth centuries invoked these terms to describe a set of ideas societies should use science to carefully engineer a perfect, ideally adapted, superior race for the good of public health and welfare—the ultimate state control of the body. We tend to associate programs of racial purity in systems of public health with the Nazis and the horrors of the T4 program and the Holocaust. Germany's supposedly unique history of *Rassenhygiene* (racial hygiene) dominated much of the literature on the topic after World War II.[34] Historians Stefan Kühl, Philippa Levine, and Alison Bashford argue against the excessive focus on Germany. They contend that while it is important to address the Holocaust as part of the history of eugenics, as we will later in this chapter, there is a larger historical context to be explored.[35] These scholars successfully demonstrate how eugenicist movements have an older, transnational, and complex set of rationalizations tied to other aspects of reproductive health, the community, and systems of welfare. It is this larger set of connections between eugenics its relationship to debates over social welfare, sexual health, and reproduction that are of interest to us as we explore the societal inequalities reinforced by the seemingly unrelated issue of STD controls. Before going too much further, however, we need to address the historical origins and basic tenants of eugenics.

The supposed science of eugenics, a word derived from Greek words *eu* meaning "well" or "good" and *genos* meaning "people of common or shared descent," began in the United Kingdom, despite its ancient etymology. It emerged in the wake of the 1859 publication of *On the Origin of Species*, in which British biologist Charles Darwin outlined theories on evolution and variation in animals and

34. For example, Bernard Semmel, "Karl Pearson: Socialist and Darwinist," *British Journal of Sociology*, 9 (1958), 111–25; Shelia Faith Weiss, *Race Hygiene and National Efficiency: The Eugenics of Wilhelm Schallmayer* (Berkeley: University of California Press, 1987); Sören Niemann-Findeisen, *Weeding the Garden: Die Eugenik—Rezeption der frühen Fabian Society* (Münster: Westfälisches Dampfboot, 2004).

35. Stefan Kühl, *For the Betterment of the Race: The Rise and Fall of the International Movement for Eugenics and Racial Hygiene* (New York: Palgrave MacMillan, 2013), 1–10; Philippa Levine and Alison Bashford, eds., *The Oxford Handbook of the History of Eugenics* (New York: Oxford University Press, 2010), 3–26.

plants, arguing natural selection guided the development and transformation of all organisms on earth over time. He also included a small section on artificial selection, showing how through selective breeding humans had domesticated animals like cows, pigs, and dogs into forms different from their wild forebears.[36] Francis Galton—British statistician, armchair psychologist and anthropologist, and Darwin's cousin—read this work and started trying to apply these theories to humanity in a science he dubbed eugenics, the focus of which he claimed was the "study of agencies under social control that may improve or impair the racial qualities of future generations, either physically or mentally."[37]

In *Hereditary Genius*, first published in 1869, Galton concluded humans had disrupted their own natural selection. He insisted civilizations and societies passing laws to protect the underprivileged, the mentally ill or "feeble-minded," and the physically weak hindered human evolution. The "unfit" being allowed to survive and reproduce, he and later eugenicists contended, had created poverty, disease, sexual infections and deviance, crime, and mental deficiencies. Galton advocated humans should rectify this by abandoning natural selection altogether and engaging in carefully calculated population controls.

Eugenicists throughout the 1870s and beyond, building on Galton, crafted plans for a variant of artificial selection, whereby governments would regulate fertility, encouraging and monetarily supporting birth rates among those with desirable traits while simultaneously hindering reproduction among members of society deemed "unfit" through birth control, marriage bans, fines, and forced sterilization. To identify the fit versus the unfit, Galton, a statistician, advocated testing the population and careful compiling the collected data on health and mental capacities to determine the best couples to selectively breed and identify those to exclude for the betterment of the race.[38] By the 1920s the eugenics movement was an international crusade, with organizations in several countries, including but not limited to Britain, the United States, Germany, France, Poland, Brazil, and various European settler colonies across Africa and the Pacific. There were even international conferences to exchange ideas on medical experimentation, best medical practices and testing to advance "racial hygiene," and strategies for eugenicists for how best to lobby their respective governments for legislation eugenicists believed would protect racial health (see Figure 3.2).[39]

---

36. Charles Darwin, *The Origin of Species* (London: John Murray, Albemarle Street, 1859).

37. Levine and Alison Bashford, *History of Eugenics*, 4–5.

38. Francis Galton, *Hereditary Genius: An Inquiry into Its Laws and Consquences*, 2nd ed. (London: Macmillan and Co., 1892), 1–49, 336–83.

39. Kühl, *Betterment of the Race*, 11–28, 47–70.

FIGURE 3.2 The United States frequently played host to such events in the 1920s and 1930s, including the Second and Third International Congresses of Eugenics. Events were held scheduled prestigious venues like Universities or the American Museum of Natural History to add a sense of credibility to the proceedings.

Source: Wall panel showing "The Relation of Eugenics to Other Sciences," based on a paper by Dr. Harry H. Laughlin. 'A decade of progress in Eugenics. Scientific' *Papers of the Third International Congress of Eugenics held at American Museum of Natural History*, New York, August 21–23, 1932. Reprinted in Baltimore by The Williams & Watkins company, 1934. Credit: Wellcome Collection. CC BY

Eugenics never gained wholesale acceptance and did face significant criticism even in the nineteenth and early twentieth centuries. Notable biologists and paleontologists argued eugenicists misunderstood evolution in their quest for a more limited "breeding stock," while religious leaders from the Catholic Church, Judaism, and some branches of Protestantism objected to attempts at birth control, euthanasia, and the disruption of "natural life."[40] Despite such resistance, however, eugenicist-inspired policies did become law in several countries as a result of lobbying or government officials who subscribed to racial hygiene ideologies. In the United States, for example, Congress passed the 1924 Immigration Act, limiting immigration to the country to "old, Nordic stock races" after the

40. Levine and Alison Bashford, *History of Eugenics*, 18–20.

eugenicist Immigration Restriction League lobbied the legislature and convinced representatives other migrant groups from Asia, Eastern or Southern Europe, and a host of other regions were contaminating the mental and physical health of the country and draining resources for desirable populations.[41] In the 1927 *Buck v. Bell*, the Supreme Court of the United States upheld as constitutional state laws requiring compulsory sterilization of epileptics and the intellectually disabled; Chief Justice Oliver Wendell Holmes Jr. famously told Carrie Buck and her defense "three generations of imbeciles are enough" before sending her back to Virginia for the surgery, taking away her ability to reproduce.[42]

Meanwhile in Germany in 1939, Hitler signed and had his personal physician, Karl Brandt, oversee the infamous *Aktion* T-4 program. This order went beyond the existing sterilization laws and required doctors to report patients' hereditary and acquired mental and physical disabilities to the government. Once registered with the Interior Ministry, these individuals, children and adults alike, were targeted to be "euthanized"—murdered—by Nazi doctors, police, or army officials, depending on location.[43] Propaganda issued by the Nazis before implementation of the program argued citizens with hereditary "defects" and even soldiers who had sustained injuries were a drain on resources needed for the betterment of the "Aryan race," claiming someone with a hereditary defect "costs the nation 60,000 Reichsmarks during his lifetime. Fellow citizen, that is *your* money too."[44] Throughout the first half of the twentieth century, even *after* the horrors of World War II and the atrocities of the Nazi Regime became known to the world, several provinces and states in multiple countries, including Canada, Britain, France, Brazil, Cuba, Mexico, India, and the United States, also passed laws 1) permitting compulsory sterilization of the mentally ill or disabled; 2) prohibiting marriage to individuals with mental illness or a known hereditary illness; 3) banning mixed-race marriages in legislation that looked eerily like the antimiscegenation laws of the nineteenth-century empires; and 4) requiring testing for syphilis before marriage, as the disease was thought to be hereditary and was known to be a danger to the fetus during pregnancy.[45]

41. Ian Robert Dowbiggin, *Keeping America Sane: Psychiatry and Eugenics in the United States and Canada 1880–1940* (Ithaca, NY: Cornell University Press, 2003), 192–227.

42. Paul A. Lombardo, *Three Generations, No Imbeciles* (Baltimore: John Hopkins University Press, 2008).

43. Michael Burleigh and Wolfgang Wippermann, *The Racial State: Germany 1933–1945* (Cambridge: Cambridge University Press, 1991), 59, 101–04, 136–68.

44. Quote, translated by this book's author, from a poster advertising the Magazine, "*Neues Volk*, the Monthly Magazine of Bureau of Race Politics of the National Socialist Party of Germany," circa 1938. The poster is part of the collections of and is frequently on display at the *Deutsches Historisches Museum* in Berlin, Germany.

45. Kühl, *For the Betterment of the Race*, 19, 47–90, 157–80.

That last point brings us back to our discussion of STDs. It may seem odd to include a discussion of eugenics, racial hygiene, and birth control debates in a chapter on the history of STD controls, but these historical narratives are interwoven throughout the nineteenth and twentieth centuries. Consider the following quote from Dr. Marie Carmichael Stopes, an early twentieth-century British paleobotanist known for her active advocacy of women's rights and family planning, but also infamous for her embrace and advancement of Galton's theories on racial health:

> The power of parenthood ought no longer to be exercised by *all*, however inferior, as an "individual right." ... That the community should allow syphilitic parents to bring forth a sequence of blind syphilitic infants is a state of affairs so monstrous that it would be hardly credible were it not a fact. Yet I have by me a letter sent to me by race-conscious parents who were infected innocently and after the birth of three successive syphilitic children, *the mother was refused by her doctor all information in answer to her enquiries as to how she could prevent the crime of bringing such lives into existence.*[46]

This quote is from Stopes's book *Radiant Motherhood*, intended as a manual for expectant parents, particularly mothers, published first in 1920 and reprinted in 1932. Fascism was on the rise across Europe and eugenics was experiencing a heyday of sorts. Rather than detailing what challenges or biological changes a mother could expect while expecting, however, Stopes used the book to forward the concept of eugenics. Look at the text provided. Stopes regarded syphilis as a concern for the health of the race because of a common side effect of syphilis during pregnancy—developmental issues for the fetus causing blindness and other disabilities. Stopes viewed such children as a societal burden and condemned parents bringing such children into the world as perpetuating a "monstrous" act. Her solution was to prevent the "inferior"—meaning the poor, the ill-formed, or the infected—from having the "power of parenthood." Stopes associated amorality with STDs and viewed both as a threat to racial well-being. Stopes described the couple as "infected innocently" in order to distance these two from the moral stain of an STD, as they sought to do what Stopes argued was the moral and just thing: prevent the "racial-crime of bringing such lives into existence." The duty of pursuing methods of birth control, however, Stopes placed on the woman, who asked her doctor but was denied access to any method of birth control, which was illegal at the time in many countries including Britain and the United States. True

---

46. Marie Carmichael Stopes, *Radiant Motherhood: A Book for Those Who Are Creating the Future* (New York: G. P. Putnam's Sons, 1932), 237–38. Emphasis in original.

to form for the period, Stopes did not expect nor ask men to wear condoms—by far the simplest means of birth control and STD prevention available.

Stopes's position was a complex one. On the one hand, she advocated for women's rights to choose whether or not to pursue pregnancy and to do so responsibly, which is an admirable goal. Yet Stopes's motives were eugenicist and she viewed the disabled, the infected, and a host of other groups as inferior "degenerates" unfit to reproduce. Her classist and even misogynist tendencies are clear in other parts of the book. In some sections, she advocates pronatalism—policies to encourage women to have more children—for the middle class. She believed the British government should finance middle-class families so fit individuals could produce more offspring and not be held back by fiscal responsibility. Conversely, Stopes insisted that working-class women needed to curb their promiscuity, stop spreading STDs, and make use of birth control to prevent overpopulation in the form of what she deemed undesirable children.[47] In 1920, Stopes tried to get Prime Minister Lloyd George to read *Radiant Motherhood* and in 1922 attempted to get members of Parliament to signal opposition to increasing birthrates by the "C3 population" (working-class, in Stopes's eugenicist parlance) in a survey she sent them.[48]

Stopes also funded a number of what she called "Mother's Clinics" that provided free medical care for working-class women, encouraging them to avoid pregnancy to preserve resources for more "fit" children from the middle class. Again, there was on the one hand a benefit for working-class women—free and reduced-cost care and birth control to prevent unwanted pregnancies. At the same time, Stopes and her clinics also labeled working-class women who chose to have more children as criminals doing irreparable damage to the health of the racial community.[49] We even see this in the branding of some of the clinic's products. Birth control devices like the cervical plug shown in Figure 3.3 were distributed at Stopes's clinics and trademarked as "Racial" or "Pro-Racial," indicating their purpose.

Eugenicist attitudes about who has the right and/or responsibility to reproduce have persisted well into the twentieth and twenty-first centuries. As late as 1995, forty-seven countries still had pronatalist policies encouraging desirable couples to have children.[50] Several Western and European countries still offer welfare programs, like the German *Mutterschaftsgeld* (Motherhood Money) and *Kindergeld* (Child Money) systems and France's various pronatalist programs since the 1920s, with one of the key goals being to increase the number of

---

47. Carmichael Stopes, *Radiant Motherhood*, 162–252.

48. June Rose, *Marie Stopes and the Sexual Revolution* (Boston: Faber and Faber, 1992), 138, 161.

49. Claire Debenham, *Marie Stopes' Sexual Revolution and the Birth Control Movement* (New York: Palgrave MacMillan, 2018), 75–99, 121–31.

50. Leslie King, "'France Needs Children': Pronatalism, Nationalism and Women's Equity," *Sociological Quarterly* 39, no. 1 (Winter 1998): 33, 33-52.

FIGURE 3.3 This image is of a contraceptive device for women known as a cervical plug or cap. Manufactured for Dr. Marie Stopes's free women's clinics, these devices were given away or sold at a low price to working-class women. Along with spermicidal candies, Stopes had these manufactured under the brand names "Racial" and "Pro-Racial" to emphasize her view that contraception aided in the "creation of a new and irradiated race." *Source:* Rubber vault cap, London, England, 1915–1925. Credit: Science Museum, London. Attribution 4.0 International (CC BY 4.0)

children born of white European women who are citizens of the states in which they live.[51] As we will see in the next section, narratives about certain groups as unfit or doomed to extinction led to racist medical policies permitted and justified experimentation on those defined as "inferior others" by US and European scientists, including experimentation on the effects and treatment of STDs.

The "Doomed Race": Eugenics and Experimentation on Oppressed Racial Groups

Nineteenth- and early twentieth-century European and American anthropologists, however, extrapolated eugenicist views of "fitness" onto all the populations of the world. Looking at various societies in Africa, Asia, the Pacific, and

---

51. King, "'France Needs Children,'" 33–52; Ivonne Honekamp, "Family Policy in Germany: Appraisal and Assessment," *Journal of Family History* 33, no. 4 (October 2008): 452–64.

South America, white Europeans and Americans concluded some groups were "doomed races" fated for extinction. Not surprisingly, the justification given was these races had not attained European-style civilizations and were therefore considered "less advanced." Eugenicists and their sympathizers wedded to this view forwarded anti-immigration measures, expanded European settler colonies to make "better use" of the land, and, notoriously, committed genocides around the globe.[52]

Medical experimentation on groups Europeans and US doctors deemed doomed races in the service of improving pharmaceuticals or even medical knowledge for the treatment, care, and successful reproduction of "desirable" white Europeans and Americans was commonplace in empires. After being informed by the League of Nations Health Organizations that his limited human trials in France for a tuberculosis vaccine were inadequate proof of its success, the French doctor Albert Calmette proceeded to experiment on 40,000 colonized test subjects in the poorest district of the city of Algiers, the capital of French-controlled Algeria. He conducted these trials between 1930 and 1956 knowing he would not receive such approval for massive human testing anywhere in Europe.[53] From the 1890s to the 1910s, German physicians experimented with blood transfusions, testing both techniques and the ability to develop immune sera, on their colonial subjects in Cameroon and German East Africa. These Africans were treated in similar fashion to animal test subjects, with doctors even going so far as to intentionally infect "strong Negros" with malaria and blood samples from monkeys and pigs to see what immune response was generated or demonstrate parasite transmission.[54] US physicians and pharmaceutical companies experimented on Puerto Rican women, without informed consent, in the 1950s to develop an effective birth control and test methods of state-sanctioned forced sterilization.[55] These are only a few examples of racially prejudiced medical attitudes from the past that have influenced

52. Peter J. Bowler, "From 'Savage' to 'Primitive': Victorian Evolutionism and the Interpretation of Marginalized Peoples," *Antiquity* 66, no. 252 (1992): 721–29; Patrick Brantlinger, *Dark Vanishings: Discourse on the Extinction of Primitive Races, 1800–1930* (Ithaca, NY: Cornell University Press, 2003), 1–44, 164–88.

53. Clifford Rosenberg, "The International Politics of Vaccine Testing in Interwar Algiers," *American Historical Review* 117, no. 3 (June 2012): 671–97.

54. Thaddeus Sunseri, "Blood Trials: Transfusions, Injections, and Experiments in Africa, 1890–1920," *Journal of the History of Medicine and Allied Sciences* 71, no. 3 (October 2015): 293–321.

55. Briggs, *Reproducing Empire* covers the eugenicist and racist history of US pharmaceutical experimentation on Puerto Rican women in drug trials of the birth control pill in the 1940s and 1950s (see pp. 74–141); Matthew Connelly, *Fatal Misconception: The Struggle to Control World Population* (Cambridge, MA: Belknap Press, 2008), 11, 155–94.

ongoing pharmaceutical experimentation in the now former colonies of the European empires.[56]

Empires also experimented on oppressed groups within the boundaries of their own countries and during times of war and genocide. An infamous example of the latter is Josef Mengele conducting a series of horrifying experiments on Jews in Nazi extermination camps, some the data from which has disturbingly been used for decades by doctors around the world despite its unethical and murderous origins.[57] The cases we will explore in depth in this section, however, are ones you may not be as familiar with: the Tuskegee syphilis experiment in Alabama (1932–1972) and the Guatemala syphilis experiments (1948–1946), both directed by the United States Public Health Service (USPHS).

In 1932 the USPHS, the precursor to the Centers for Disease Control, proposed a study on the effects of untreated syphilis on the human body. The experiment was supposedly building on a previous one conducted in Oslo, Norway between 1890 and 1910 stated conventional treatments, which included mercury and arsenic, were of no value and found "27.9 percent of patients" underwent "spontaneous cure" of the disease without any treatment. The study called into question the available treatments, but still advocated administration of mercurial ointments, given the extreme risks of cardiovascular disease, insanity, and early death if syphilis went untreated.[58] Doctors at the USPHS claimed they were repeating this study and would complete their research in six to eight months. Funding was secured from the Rosenwald Foundation and a site in the United States was chosen for the selection of human test subjects: Macon County, Alabama—which at the time had a supposedly 35 percent prevalence of the disease in the population.

Macon County was selected by the USPHS because of its large African American population. The city of Tuskegee, Alabama in Macon County had been a site for an educational experiment advocated by African American civil rights activist Booker T. Washington in 1900. The Rosenwald Foundation had backed this endeavor to "uplift" former slaves in the American South through education

---

56. For more on medical experimentation before and after colonization, see Melissa Graboyes, *The Experiment Must Continue: Medical Research and Ethics in East Africa, 1940–2014* (Athens: Ohio University Press, 2015). See also Julie Livingston, *Improvising Medicine: An African Oncology Ward in an Emerging Cancer Epidemic* (Durham, NC: Duke University Press, 2012).

57. For more on Mengele and his horrid work, see Paul Weindling, *Victims and Survivors of Nazi Human Experiments: Science and Suffering in the Holocaust* (London: Bloomsbury Academic, 2015); Tuskegee was not the only instance of medical experimentation by the US during and after WWII.

58. Brandt, "Racism and Research," 19.

and vocational training and already had a well-established presence in the area, having funded the construction of schools and hospitals. The Great Depression of 1929 had caused the Rosenwald Foundation to withdraw its funding to the educational endeavors and left the area impoverished, even as the Foundation promised funding to the USPHS for the syphilis experiment in the same year. As such, medical care was increasingly unavailable for African Americans suffering from a host of maladies, including syphilis, making the site "ideal" for a case study. Scientific theories about the prevalence of syphilis among individuals of African descent we explored earlier in the section on the history of tropical medicine also encouraged white American doctors to pick the site. These USPHS officials saw the African American citizens of Macon County, particularly the men with their "oversized genitalia" and supposedly "lustful ways," as ideal test subjects more likely to have the disease and less likely to seek treatment due to lack of availability and education.[59]

Since doctors knew untreated syphilis lead to death, the selection of communities for study needed to avoid the possible destruction of what white medical officials deemed "desirable populations" as the disease was allowed to run its course. The doctors, subscribing to eugenicist notions of evolution, believed African Americans and Africans generally were a doomed race fated for extinction and therefore syphilis would hasten this end. Dr. Thomas W. Murrell, a lecturer and medical staff member at the University College of Medicine in Richmond, Virginia, stated in 1906: "The scourge [syphilis] sweeps among them . . . Perhaps here, in conjunction with tuberculosis, will be the end of the negro problem. Disease will accomplish what man cannot do"—indicating the eradication of African Americans.[60] The doomed race therefore, white American doctors argued, could be studied and prodded by the USPHS, sacrificed to the horrible effects of a fatal disease supposedly to acquire beneficial medical knowledge.

The experiment, which used uninfected individuals as a control group rather than those receiving treatment, had no uniformity in its selection of test subjects across age or when they had acquired syphilis, and no informed consent from the subjects themselves. The study lasted not six to eight months as projected, but forty years. The researchers lured African American men into the study with promises of free treatment for syphilis. Doctors and nurses gave these men placebos as medical officials documented the ravages of the disease. Other subjects were not even told they had the disease as researchers added new men to the rolls for the study. Over the course of forty years these men, uninformed of their

59. Brandt, "Racism and Research," 15–19.

60. Thomas W. Murrell, "Syphilis in the Negro: Its Bearing on the Race Problem," *American Journal of Dermatology & Genito-Urinary Disorders* 10 (August 1906): 307.

diagnosis, unwittingly exposed their wives, sexual partners, and, in many cases their unborn children to syphilis.

For four decades, the USPHS went to great lengths to prevent the men who were subjects of the study from seeking treatment elsewhere, providing lists of names to doctors across Alabama and even US Army medical officers when subjects were drafted urging these doctors not to treat the patients and participate in the deception in order to preserve the "integrity of the study." When penicillin became available as a treatment for syphilis in the 1950s, at the time much more effective than mercury or arsenic, efforts were also taken to block hospitals and physicians from administering the antibiotic to the men in the study. Even in the wake of the civil rights movement in the 1960s, doctors at the CDC, which had taken over the study after it replaced USPHS, rationalized the inherent racism of the experiment. Dr. J. Lawson Smith remarked in a 1969 ad hoc meeting about the study at the CDC, "You will never have another study like this; take advantage of it," referring to the changing racial dynamics in the United States as African Americans were increasingly able to assert their legal rights.[61]

The study ended in 1972 in response to criticism from the press and an order from the US Department of Health, Education, and Welfare (HEW). News of the study was hardly a surprise to the American public, even though presented as such, since the researchers involved had been publishing their findings in journals and medical papers for decades. Even after the HEW report on the study condemned the doctors for not providing penicillin when it was available, the ongoing notion was, though founded in racism, the study had produced "good science." It had not. No useable data was ever attained by this research outside of what was already known: syphilis should not be left untreated. Those who ran the study still tried to defend their work, arguing it was a well-grounded study even though it lacked the basic requirements of a high-school science fair project by failing to have a valid control group. It would be two more years before the US government would settle a class-action lawsuit, agreeing to pay reparations of survivors of the study, their spouses, and descendants, maxing out at a paltry $37,500 per individual. In 1997 the United States finally issued a formal apology to the survivors via President Bill Clinton at a White House Ceremony.[62]

While denying treatment to African Americans in the Tuskegee Experiment, the USPHS also experimented with penicillin as a treatment and prophylactic against syphilis, gonorrhea, and chancroid among other oppressed groups in

---

61. Brandt, "Racism and Research," 19–26.

62. Brandt, "Racism and Research," 26–29; Susan E. Bell, "Events in the Tuskegee Syphilis Project: A Timeline," in *Tuskegee's Truths: Rethinking the Tuskegee Syphilis Study*, ed. Susan M. Reverby (Chapel Hill: University of North Carolina Press, 2000), 34–40.

Guatemala from 1946–1948. Though not a formal colony of the United States, much of the country's land was owned by the US-based United Fruit Company, which had enormous influence over Guatemala's government. Combined with aid influence from the US government and the Pan American Sanitary Bureau, these factors gave the USPHS leverage over the Guatemalan government to allow experimentation in their country. The experiment was run by Dr. John C. Cutter, who would later participate in the Tuskegee experiment and be its staunchest defender. To test if penicillin could be used as an effective prophylactic and treatment for the three STDs under observation, Cutter reached agreements with the Guatemalan government to experiment on prisoners, soldiers, and residents of mental health asylums in Guatemala. As his test subjects did not already have syphilis, gonorrhea, or chancroid—and since the purpose of the study was to determine if penicillin could be used preventatively—Cutter and his team intentionally infected test subjects. In the ultimate control of women's bodies, Cutter forced women infected with one or more of the STDs to lie about their condition and have sex with inmates in Guatemala's prisons and Guatemalan soldiers to mimic normal exposure. When no women with the STDs were available, the team developed a inoculum (a sample) of the diseases to insert into the women's vaginas before they had sex with soldiers and inmates. The men were injected with penicillin or forced to apply it as a cream to their penises before intercourse. Predictably, penicillin did not work as a preventative. Imitating his previous Terre Haute Prison experiments with gonorrhea in 1943–1944, Cutter also intentionally injected syphilis and gonorrhea into mental health patients—who could not, due to their disability, give informed consent—to test the effectiveness of treatment and the nature of transmission. The unethical nature of these studies was even recognized at the time, as similar studies in the United States had already been critiqued. The experiment was quietly shut down in 1948. It was exposed decades later in the twenty-first century, prompting a presidential inquiry into the unethical study in 2011. No reparations have ever been paid to the victims.[63]

Conclusion

In this chapter, we examined the interconnected histories of tropical medicine, STD controls, antimiscegenation laws, and eugenics. Public health efforts to contain STDs in the ninteenth and twentieth centuries, influenced by racial hierarchies and legal inequalities between the sexes, transformed into more aggressive intervention by governments into all aspects of sex and reproduction. Imperial

---

63. Susan M. Reverby, "'Normal Exposure' and Inoculation Syphilis: A PHS 'Tuskegee' Doctor in Guatemala, 1946–1948," *Journal of Policy History* 23, no. 1 (2011): 6–28.

health structures replicated systems of containment designed to halt the spread of disease while simultaneously reinforcing colonial subjugation. Social movements and governments increasingly controlled sexual encounters and women's bodies through legislation and policies, sometimes with eugenicist aims. Laura Briggs, an historian who works on US-controlled Puerto Rico, asserts empire was an "international economic, political, and cultural system that shared common assumptions, strategies and rules." This was particularly true, she claims, in the case of science, medicine, and the regulation of social interactions, where "methods of managing women, disease, and armies moved from place to place" were shared between empires, as we have seen in this chapter. [64] European and American imperial powers that held common views of racial hierarchies and gender norms collaborated to internationalize public health strategies. Though these policies alone did not result in a formal internationalist structure of public health, empire laid the groundwork for a form of global health governance heavily influenced by European and American interests and values and, at times, faulty science founded on those views. In chapter 4, we will take a more focused look at how local controls evolved into imperial controls and, finally, explore demands for international law on health and social controls related to the drug trade and addiction.

FURTHER READING

Briggs, Laura. *Reproducing Empire: Race, Sex, Science, and U.S. Imperialism in Puerto Rico*. Berkeley: University of California Press, 2002.

Davidson, Roger, and Lesley A. Hall, eds. *Sex, Sin and Suffering: Venereal Disease and European Society Since 1870*. New York: Routledge, 2001.

Levine, Philippa, and Alison Bashford, eds. *The Oxford Handbook of the History of Eugenics*. New York: Oxford University Press, 2010.

Walther, Daniel J. "Sex, Race and Empire: White Male Sexuality and the 'Other' in Germany's Colonies, 1894–1914." *German Studies Review* 33, no. 1 (2010): 45–72.

Weindling, Paul. *Victims and Survivors of Nazi Human Experiments: Science and Suffering in the Holocaust*. London: Bloomsbury Academic, 2015.

---

64. Briggs, *Reproducing Empire*, 22–45.

"CIVILIZING" ADDICTION

FROM LOCAL TO GLOBAL INEQUALITIES IN THE STANDARDIZATION OF OPIUM CONTROLS

In the early twentieth century, governments around the world attempted to address a global crisis: the opium trade and rising addiction levels to the drug and its derivatives. The League of Nations, formed in 1919, convened many commissions in the 1920s and 1930s regarding global restrictions on narcotics. The 1922 Opium Commission's delegates debated the appropriate uses for cannabis, cocaine, and opium, possible restrictions on the volume of trade in these materials, and what other regulations might stem addictions now perceived as a global public health concern.

This was part of the League's efforts to maintain peace in the aftermath of the First World War. The League's functionaries attempted to serve as mediators of all matters facing the "community of nations," ranging from trade disputes to health and sanitation standards. Yet even as this body claimed to institute a new world order, it remained tethered to older, European imperial visions of the world. Examine for a moment the following quote from the *British Medical Journal* on the proceedings of this commission. Thinking back to the last chapter, do any of the words or phrases used to describe India or Indians stand out to you?

> The difficult question was to decide as to the limits of legitimate use. It was said that all opium prescribed by a doctor was legitimate, it must be remembered that, at any rate in some countries, these drugs might be abused by the medical profession. . . . One of the members of the commission asked to what extent Dr. [F. Norman] White thought that the results arrived at for European countries might be safely applied to oriental countries like India, where racial characteristics, habits of life, and incidence of disease were all different. Dr. White replied that in western countries it might be assumed that the use of a drug was legitimate if it was prescribed by a doctor, but in such a country as India, it was necessary to define not merely

legitimate use, but also the doctor.. . . . He agreed that there was a greater tolerance for narcotic drugs amongst the Indian native population than amongst Europeans.[1]

In this report, India is described as "oriental," a dated term used in the nineteenth and twentieth centuries to describe locales across Asia deemed foreign or "exotic" to Europeans. It often had negative connotations, belittling those countries and peoples as "other" or less civilized than Europe. The report confirms the negative connotation by using language to posit "racial characteristics" resulted in different levels of substance abuse. European doctors did not afford Indian "native practitioners" respect as medical professionals and described Indians as likely to use opium in ways deemed "illegitimate" by "western standards."

These attitudes, like the racial assumptions we saw in chapter 2 on "native hygiene," emerged from the history of imperialism. The Indian Raj was the center of the British Empire's century-long export of opium. From this site of production, the British Empire had engaged in a global narcotics trade. From the eighteenth century on, this commerce led to increased addiction levels around the world. By the late nineteenth century, addiction rates in Europe prompted retaliation against British trade and caused governments to reassess narcotics controls at home and abroad.

Drug controls existed in Eurasian societies long before the advent of professional the nineteenth century. Normally a governing elite formed these controls and regulations intending to preserve religious, social, or moral order. After the rise of public health, those medical and governmental officials writing policies purportedly guided by medical and biological concerns were often more heavily influenced by a desire to maintain a specific social hierarchy. In this chapter, we will explore the impact of gender, race, class and other forms of social hierarchy in various states' attempts to regulate opium and opium derivatives such as morphine and heroin. We will examine how regulations pertaining to opium and its abuse evolved from local controls and perceptions to imperial policies and how they finally transformed into a standardized system of global antinarcotics structures.

Our narrative begins by looking at controls implemented in the Kingdom of Burma and the Empire of China from the fifteenth to nineteenth centuries. Officials in both states enacted these regulations in order to preserve gender and social hierarchies in their respective societies, creating and reinforcing their own unique inequalities as attitudes toward opium changed over time. As the British

---

1. A correspondent at Geneva, "The Opium Commission of the League of Nations," *British Medical Journal* 1, no. 3201 (May 6, 1922): 724–25.

Empire grew in the nineteenth and twentieth centuries, Burma was conquered as a British colony and China was forced through military defeat to adhere to Britain's economic interests. Older substance abuse controls in each of these places were destroyed by the arrival of Britain's global trade in narcotics, which increased usage and eroded social norms in each of these countries. Next, we will examine the role of addiction in Britain and how it led to structural changes both domestically and within the empire. British regulators implemented new substance control policies while seeking to preserve ongoing trade. Britain's new health-minded policies in its empire were based on racial pseudo-science and extreme classism. As policymakers in new international organizations such as the League of Nations and later the United Nations and World Health Organization attempted to construct a set of global restrictions on narcotics, their efforts rested upon these imperial foundations. The last part of the chapter will demonstrate how the globalization of those new controls in the twentieth century standardized a set of racist and classist attitudes woven into worldwide narcotics regulations (see Map 4.1).

Buddhism and Bans on Opium: Burma's Drug Controls Prior to British Rule

The Kingdom of Burma, today known as Myanmar, has a long history of opium production and controls. Located in Southeast Asia, Myanmar is part of the "Golden Triangle"—a region of large-scale opium and heroin production spanning the borders of Laos, Thailand, and Myanmar. From the 1950s until the twenty-first century, Myanmar was the world's largest producer of illicit opium. In 2013, according to the United Nations Office on Drugs and Crime, Myanmar was second only to Afghanistan as the largest source of poppy cultivation and heroin production in the transnational drug trade.[2] The former Kingdom of Burma, however, had a different relationship to opium. The rulers of Burma oversaw three stages in Burma's relationship to opium, from religious mores against it across the sixteenth to nineteenth centuries, to becoming a consumer state in the eighteenth and nineteenth centuries, and finally becoming a producer state in the twentieth century. In this section of the chapter we will examine the roles religion, specifically Buddhism, and social rank played in Burmese substance control policy.

Buddhism emerged sometime in the late sixth century BC in what is now Nepal. Buddhism arrived in Burmese territories sometime in the third century BC. One branch, Theravāda Buddhism, was officially adopted by King Anawrahta

---

2. "Myanmar," United Nations Office on Drugs and Crime, accessed June 4, 2018, https://www.unodc.org/unodc/en/alternative-development/myanmar.html.

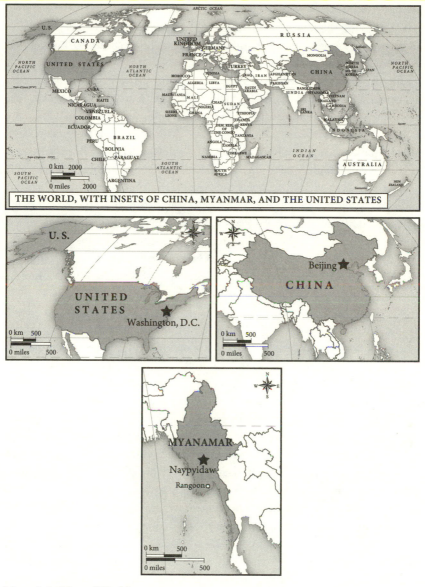

THE WORLD, WITH INSETS OF CHINA, MYANMAR, AND THE UNITED STATES

MAP 4.1 Map of World

(1014–1077, r. 1044–1077) when he united the Burmese under the first Burmese Empire, a.k.a. the Pagan Empire, in 1044.[3] Burmese society, much like other ancient and early-modern cultures, had a system of social rank. We might think of nobles and aristocrats at its top, monks and other religious figures operating in

---

3. Damien Keown, *Buddhism: A Very Short Introduction* (Oxford: Oxford University Press, 1996), 15, 70–74. For more on the religion of Buddhism and its practice, read Keown's very accessible text.

a position of influence, and members of agrarian, merchant, and artisan professions occupying the lowest tier. These social ranks were reinforced by policies derived from interpretations of Buddhist tenants. Opium controls represent one example of this reinforcement.

The first verifiable written reference to opium being traded in Burma by Portuguese and Arab merchants dates to 1519. From then until 1826, when large tracts of the Burmese Empire were annexed by the British East India Company (EIC) and later transformed into a province of British India, Burmese society was antagonistic toward opium. Historians Ashley Wright and Ronald Renard both argue that Buddhism was an essential component of Burmese identity and further suggest that Buddhist mores were the justification for most early bans on opium.[4] Burmese religious leaders, rulers, and members of the higher social ranks adhered to Buddhist injunctions against the consumption of *sura meraya*, which translates to "fermented and distilled liquors." According to Buddhist teachings, those who ingested these substances were blocking their paths to the "attainment of insight" and were creating obstacles to "the unity of the community of monks from whom the Buddha devised his rules."[5]

Although never explicitly mentioned in the Buddha's teachings, many Burmese elites interpreted a section of the fifth precept of Buddhism against the consumption of *sura meraya* to include opium. Kings issued edicts against opium consumption on these grounds throughout the sixteenth and seventeenth centuries, backed by religious spokespersons. King Bodawpaya (r. 1782–1819) categorized intoxicant and stimulant use as capital offenses. Bodawpaya felt the need to take a harsh stance against opium in order legitimize his new dynasty among existing Buddhist elites. He had overthrown his predecessor, King Singu (r. 1776–1782), and wanted to be seen as a truly Buddhist ruler in the first year of his reign.[6] Renard and Wright both argue that evidence suggests taboos against opium were enough to make addiction rare prior to British occupation, but they are also quick to note the religious mores against ingesting opium did not eliminate substance abuse and consumption differed along the lines of social rank. Burmese elites were not immune to opium addiction. Renard contends, however, that opium use in Burma was primarily a habit of the lower social ranks. Elites tended to abstain from use and decry its perceived prevalence among farmers, merchants, and artisans in order to highlight the differences between themselves and the lower social orders.[7]

---

4. Ashley Wright, "Opium in British Burma, 1826–1881," *Contemporary Drug Problems* 35 (Winter 2008): 611–46, 616–17; Ronald D. Renard, *The Burmese Connection: Illegal Drugs and the Making of the Golden Triangle* (Boulder, CO: Lynne Rienner, 1996), 12–16.

5. Renard, *The Burmese Connection*, 14.

6. Renard, *The Burmese Connection*, 14.

7. Renard, *The Burmese Connection*, 15.

By abstaining from opium, by punishing those who distributed, and by making public displays of both, elites highlighted their devotion to Buddhism and solidified their performed role as a more prestigious, moralizing group in Burmese society. Such edicts preserved their own conceptions of respectability and rank. Increased British trade in the region in the nineteenth century led to more widespread—though not epidemic—levels of consumption by members of lower social orders and led to more legislation with stiff penalties against those who used opium for nonmedicinal purposes.[8] Wright points out that Buddhist religious elites imposed restrictions to social mobility related to opium production and use. Families seeking to send their sons to be educated by a Buddhist monk were limited as to which monks could be chosen for their sons based on the family profession. The sons of opium and liquor merchants, as well as butchers and fishers, while still able to attain an education, faced exclusion from the same schools attended by families engaged in more respectable occupations. The loss of educational prospects in turn limited their opportunities to pursue career options other than those into which they had been born.[9]

These bans do not indicate a high level of opium addiction in precolonial Burma. Opium was not the drug of choice and was not yet a major societal problem at the time. Precolonial Burmese were far more likely to smoke tobacco. Tobacco was grown domestically, was far more affordable, and had the added benefit of not being prohibited by Buddhist teachings.[10] Everything changed after the arrival of the EIC in Burma in 1826.

British mercantile interests made opium more readily available in East and South Asia starting in the eighteenth century, with production sites in India and by the nineteenth century in parts of China. The EIC had eyed Burma since the mid-1700s as a new market and a possible site of production for opium. It wanted to compete with its rival, the Dutch East India Company (VOC), which had a monopoly on multiple commodities in Southeast Asia. After the VOC collapsed in 1799, Britain saw an opening to expand. In a series of three wars, the First Anglo-Burmese War (1824–1826), the Second Anglo-Burmese War (1852–1853), and the Third Anglo-Burmese War (1885), the British Empire conquered Burma.[11] The Burmese monarchy, still in place as a figurehead for a time in British dominated Burma, tried to resist militarily and passed more edicts against opium

8. Renard, *The Burmese Connection*, 15.

9. Wright, "Opium in British Burma," 618–19.

10. Ashley Wright, *Opium and Empire in Southeast Asia: Regulating Consumption in British Burma* (New York: Palgrave MacMillan, 2014), 15–17.

11. For more on the Anglo-Burmese Wars: Anthony Webster, *Gentleman Capitalists: British Imperialism in South East Asia 1770–1890* (New York: I. B. Tauris, 1998), 135–66, 209–52.

in the 1850s, but to no avail.[12] After the end of the Third Anglo-Burmese War, Burma was incorporated as a province under the British Raj of India, Britain's main source of opium production. Burma remained part of British India until 1937 and was governed as a separate colony until its independence from Britain in 1948.

From Medicine to Aphrodisiac to Pathology: Opium, Gender, and Class in China

A similar process unfolded in China. The primacy of opium in histories of China is the result of scholars exploring the preludes to and the outcomes of the First and Second Opium Wars. The Opium Wars between Britain and China spanning 1839 to 1860 and China's subsequent subjugation to harsh terms by Britain played a major role in how China interacted with the rest of the world economically, diplomatically, and militarily from the nineteenth century onward.[13] Historian Zheng Yangwen argues, however, that for us to understand China's health and social policies regarding use and control of opium we need to start the narrative much earlier than the nineteenth century. The "social life" and the "political redefinition of opium consumption" resulted in regulations against opium intended to preserve gender and social hierarchies in China; Yangwen contends these originated in the late 1400s during the Ming Dynasty (1360–1644).[14] Unlike in Burma, where religion played a key role in a fairly consistent attitude toward the drug, Chinese attitudes toward opium usage evolved over the course of four centuries as governing officials first viewed it as medicine, then advocated its use as an aphrodisiac, and finally regarded opium as a pathological threat to Chinese society.

Opium was widely available in China for hundreds of years prior to the fifteenth century. Viewed as a medicinal herb, Chinese users ingested opium as *yingsu* soup. The opium from the poppies was boiled and sold in this liquid form as a remedy for ailments such as sunstroke, diarrhea, dysentery, coughs, asthma, and for relief of pain (see figure 4.1).[15] There were no major bans on consumption

---

12. Wright, *Opium and Empire*, 17–60.

13. For more on the Opium Wars see Immanuel C. Y. Hsü, *The Rise of Modern China* (Oxford: Oxford University Press, 2000), 168–220; Julia Lovell, *Opium War* (London: Picador, 2011); and Mao Haijian, *The Qing Empire and the Opium War: The Collapse of the Heavenly Dynasty* (Cambridge: Cambridge University Press, 2018).

14. Zheng Yangwen, *The Social Life of Opium in China* (New York: Cambridge University Press, 2005), 1–11, 87.

15. Yangwen, *Social Life of Opium*, 10–13.

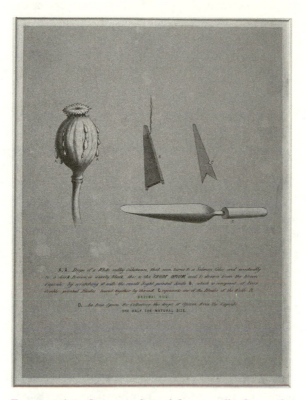

FIGURE 4.1 Opium is derived from a milky, latex substance found in the seedpod of Poppies. Once processed, this liquid, also known as "tears of the poppy," becomes a powerful narcotic that has been used for various purposes, medicinal and illicit, throughout history.
Source: Wellcome Collection. Attribution 4.0 International (CC BY 4.0)

of the substance during this time, though occasionally the Chinese imperial government implemented tariffs and trade restrictions. By 1483, Chinese society regarded opium as a recreational substance. During the Ming Dynasty, Chinese government officials viewed opium as a "spring drug," or aphrodisiac, and considered it part of the "art of alchemists, sex, and court ladies" involved in numerous scandals in the court of the Chenghua Emperor (born Zhu Jianshen, r. 1465–1487).[16]

Fifteenth-century Ming Dynasty court officials paradoxically wanted opium, popularized as a sexual performance enhancer, while simultaneously pushing for reforms to regulate it to prevent courtesans and eunuchs from using the drug

---

16. Yangwen, *Social Life of Opium*, 12–14.

to influence the Emperor and policy.[17] The imperial court of the Chenghua Emperor was fraught with what contemporaries viewed as "sex scandals" threatening to corrupt the imperial court. The emperor was devoted to a senior consort, Lady Wan. Chenghua promoted several of her relatives and friends in his court to please her. Aware of the emperor's obsession with Lady Wan and his fascination with "sex manuals and works of pornography," court officials and Chinese historians and scholars for more than a century later labeled Wan a "sorceress" and spoke of the dangers of opium.[18]

Yin Zhi, Chenghua's Minister of War, wrote how aphrodisiacs became a "ladder of success" for those who took advantage of the emperor's vices. Some officials viewed this path to promotion as eroding the perceived meritocratic system, in which only experts and men of letters could rise to positions of authority. Consorts, eunuchs, and corrupt officials became targets, labeled as the primary peddlers of "spring formulas." (see Figure 4.2) The Chinese government briefly labeled opium as a threat to the social hierarchy and gender norms of the Chinese court. After his father's death, officials wrote to Chenghua's son, Emperor Hongzhi (r. 1487–1505), urging him to fight the "evils of the alchemists" by removing eunuchs and officials who made use of opium spring formula as bribes to improve their careers. Above all, they sought to ban the drug's use as an aphrodisiac to prevent undue influence of women—who were not allowed to hold governmental posts—on the emperor.[19] Emperor Hongzhi used concerns over the drug's detrimental effects on health to rid himself of his father's corrupt ministers and replace them with his own, causing many officials to view him as a great reformer until his death at the age of thirty-five.

Proscriptions against opium as an aphrodisiac during the late Ming Dynasty did not, however, eliminate the drug from Chinese society. Starting in the seventeenth century, smuggling from Portuguese and later British vessels competed with local trade in opium in China and made the drug cheaper and more readily available. In the decade prior to the First Opium War, opium shipments to China from British-controlled Bengal, India increased from 6,000 chests of processed poppies in 1830–1831 to nearly 20,000 chests of the drug by 1837–1838.[20]

As the smuggling increased supply of opium in China, it became cheaper and more popular with lower classes in China who could now afford the recreational narcotic. New users smoked opium instead of ingesting it in liquid or powder

---

17. Yangwen, *Social Life of Opium*, 12–24.

18. Yangwen, *Social Life of Opium*, 13.

19. Yangwen, *Social Life of Opium*, 14–15, 21–22.

20. Michael Greenberg, *British Trade and the Opening of China, 1800–1842* (Cambridge: Cambridge University Press, 1951), Appendix I.

FIGURE 4.2 Moving beyond medicinal syrups and "spring formulas," the implied opium use being depicted here, the recreational smoking of opium, especially by the lower social orders, was viewed by Chinese elites as a sign of societal degradation.
Source: "Opium Smoking Party," *Gaillard's Medical Journal*, Vol. 33, no. 2 (Feb. 1882), p. 102. Courtesy of the Collections of the National Library of Medicine. Public Domain.

form. Governing officials viewed participation by the lower social orders as a "degradation" of opium use. Irritated by the peasants and merchants adopting a recreational pastime of the elite, scholar officials suddenly viewed opium as a visible, disgraceful threat to social order and morality. As historian Zheng Yangwen so eloquently put it, "when [Chinese] men of letters smoked, opium was cultured; when the poor began to inhale, it became a social problem [for China]."[21] With an eye toward justifying opium prohibition in the early nineteenth century, scholar-officials began writing stories of addicts bankrupting their parents, engaging in criminal activities, or being so degenerate they neglected work and could not afford feed themselves—a burden on their communities and the empire.[22]

Set against the backdrop of several regional rebellions in the 1820s and 1830s against Chinese Imperial authority, now the Qing Dynasty (the period from 1644 to 1912), Chinese regulators raised additional concerns about soldiers

21. Yangwen, *Social Life of Opium*, 7.

22. Yangwen, *Social Life of Opium*, 87–90.

using opium. Xi En was appointed governor-general of Guangdong province in order to crush a rebellion there in the 1830s. He wrote of the soldiers: "Although there are more than ten thousand of them, seven out of ten are Guandong natives. They are cowardly and not used to marching in the mountains. Plus, most coastal soldiers are opium smokers."[23] Feng Zhanxun, an imperial investigative censor, reported similar concerns: "Many Cantonese and Fujianese soldiers smoked opium . . . they are cowards and they have spoiled our operation."[24] Take a moment and look at the language used by Xi En and Feng Zhanxun. What stands out to you? We notice they are focused on soldiers from specific regions of the Chinese Empire: Guangdong, Canton, and Fujian. Why would Xi En and Feng Zhanxun single out these regions? If we dig deeper into this period of Chinese history, we notice that all three of those regions had engaged in rebellion against the empire around the time Xi En and Feng Zhanxun were writing.

We can safely conclude these men, as elites and agents of imperial rule, had strong prejudices about individuals from these regions prior to writing their reports. By associating opium usage with these regions, they are associating the drug with the unraveling of social order. These two government officials branded soldiers, likely conscripts, from these regions with "cowardice" and called them "despicable," both of which would have been grave insults to a soldier in China. Xi En and Feng Zhanxun, coming from the social order of scholar-officials in China, were of a higher social standing in society than the soldiers they were critiquing. They themselves had used opium, yet these officials portrayed soldiers using the drug, particularly soldiers from rebellious regions, as a degradation of family and societal norms and a threat to the security of China against enemies both foreign and domestic.

Chinese officials blamed the lower social orders for the rise of this societal ill and simultaneously viewed it as their place to serve as the defenders of high moral principles. Scholar-officials and the imperial court instituted bans against the opium trade and the drug's consumption from 1799 to 1838. In 1810, the Qing Dynasty Jiaqing Emperor (r. 1796–1820) issued an imperial edict against the drug. Note again the specific regional condemnation of Guangdong and Fujian:

Opium is a poison, undermining our good customs and morality. Its use is prohibited by law. Now the commoner, Yang, dares to bring it into the Forbidden City. Indeed, he flouts the law! . . . We should also order the general commandant of the police and police- censors at the five gates to

---

23. Da Manzhoudiguo, Guowyuan, ed., *Da Qing Lichau Shilu: Xuanzong*, vol. CCXVIII (Taipei: Huanlian, 1964), 17 A, as translated in Yangwen, *Social Life of Opium*, 91.

24. Da Manzhoudiguo, 28–29, as translated in Yangwen, *Social Life of Opium*, 91.

prohibit opium and to search for it at all gates. If they capture any violators, they should immediately punish them and should destroy the opium
at once. As to Kwangtung [Guangdong] and Fukien [Fujian], the provinces from which opium comes, we order their viceroys, governors, and
superintendents of the maritime customs to conduct a thorough search
for opium and cut off its supply.[25]

Officials now viewed opium as a severe threat to Chinese society and crafted
punishments including confiscation of property and execution. The goal of these
policies was to eradicate addiction by eliminating the supply. These policies reinforced inequalities of social rank in China, falling more heavily on commoners,
Chinese merchants serving as distributers for foreign merchants of the trade, and
soldiers.

The Qing Dynasty's policies, however, did not last past the 1830s. Prohibitions
on the trade and punishments for use did not decrease demand. Increased smuggling on the black market was now wholly dominated by the British Empire.
Britain's disrespect for the Qing Dynasty's laws throughout the 1830s led to
conflict between the two empires. Commissioner Lin Zexu, appointed by the
Qing Dynasty Daoguang Emperor (r. 1820–1850) to once and for all put an
end to the illegal trade, seized and destroyed one thousand tons of opium held by
British merchants at Humen in June of 1839. The result was Britain instigating
the Opium Wars of 1839 to 1860.[26]

In the 1842 Treaty of Nanjing, which ended the First Opium War, China
ceded Hong Kong and several other Chinese ports to Britain, from which Britain
later processed and distributed opium to Chinese customers in even larger quan-
tities.[27] In the Second Opium War, China tried once again to push back against
Britain's opium dealing and was met with brutal military force between 1856 and
1860. The British, aided by France, Russia, and the United States, defeated China
again and forced it to accept the following terms as part of the Treaty of Tianjin:
cession of more ports, including Tianjin; reparations payments to Britain and
France, allowing Christian missionaries in China; and British ships were now allowed to carry indentured Chinese to work in the Americas, meaning that China
had to legalize the opium trade.[28]

25. Fu, Lo-Shu, ed. *A Documentary Chronicle of Sino-Western Relations, 1644–1820*, Vol. I
(Tucson: University of Arizona Press, 1966), 380.

26. Yangwen, *Social Life of Opium*, 90–115.

27. Hsü, *Rise of Modern China*, 168–95.

28. Hsü, *Rise of Modern China*, 196–220.

"Politics of the Poppy": Substance Control in the United Kingdom

As the British Empire consolidated control over the global opium trade through imperial conquest in Burma and China and increased production in the British Raj in India, attitudes toward opium use and addiction changed in the United Kingdom.[29] In the later half of the nineteenth century, a growing British antiopium movement emerged alongside the already powerful temperance movement advocating abstinence from alcohol. New forms of use, such as hypodermic injection of the opium derivative morphine, led to new concerns in the United Kingdom over the drug's role and purpose in society. The domestic controls in the United Kingdom explored in this section were based on disease theory and the belief some groups were predisposed toward addiction, labeling "vulnerable groups" in a fashion based less on science and more on preexisting gender norms and class tensions.

Recreational and medicinal opium had been common in Britain since the eighteenth century, but as we saw in the previous section on China, changes in use, classism, and gendered assumptions led to the British government imposing more restrictions and controls. Though smoking opium and taking "medicinal syrups" was accepted among aristocrats and the wealthy, those same elite "opium eaters" were mortified by middle- and lower-class individuals increasingly using hypodermic morphine, an injectable opium derivative, for recreational purposes in the early decades of the nineteenth century.

Hypodermic morphine in particular sparked a debate over "proper medical use" of opium across the 1850s and 1860s. This debate emerged less as a result of real concern over addiction and more as a consequence of a rivalry between the professional societies of pharmacists (a.k.a. "chemists") and physicians over which group controlled the lucrative distribution of opium derivatives in British society. Rather than advocating for prohibition, both groups lobbied Parliament to establish controls on distribution and legal parameters for appropriate forms of and grounds for consumption of opium.

The rivalry ultimately led to legislators passing the 1868 Pharmacy Act, which set the limits of proper medicinal purposes for opium and its derivatives and began a process whereby recreational use was increasingly deemed abnormal or a disease of the mind and body.[30] With medical professionals and legislators now defining what constituted appropriate opium use, activists and politicians

---

29. The phrase "politics of the poppy" is borrowed from J. B. Brown, "Politics of the Poppy: The Society for the Suppression of the Opium Trade, 1874–1916," *Journal of Contemporary History* 8, no. 3 (July 1973): 97–111.

30. Virginia Berridge and Griffith Edwards, *Opium and the People: Opiate Use in Nineteenth-Century England* (New Haven, CT: Yale University Press, 1987), 113–50.

preserved the British Empire's economic benefits from the supposedly medicinal global trade in opium and related substances while simultaneously being able to justify domestic restrictions on the drug reinforcing upper-middle-class and aristocratic values which situated the blame for abuse on the lower classes and, in particular, working-class women.

Campaigns against child-doping and opium as a substitute for drink were obvious cases of classism and gender norms influencing antiopium activism and policy in the United Kingdom. Soothing syrups were marketed for use by parents on fussy infants in Great Britain. The most popular, such as Godfrey's Cordial, Daffy's Elixir, and Atkinson's Infants' Preservative, contained opium as a key ingredient. Building upon an older home remedy solution derived from white poppies used for over a century in some rural communities, these new factory-produced syrups brought such curatives to larger urban markets. The advent of mandatory registration of births and deaths brought to light an increase in infant mortalities tied to opium poisoning. Reports made to the Privy Council documented 291 deaths of children under the age of four in Manchester and Wisbech between 1863 and 1867.[31] Public health officials receiving similar reports in the 1860s from other communities raised the alarm and demanded action.

Virginia Berridge argues that "opium was the immediate concern" in classifying child-doping as a social problem, but "the campaign against it criticized basic patterns of working-class child-rearing too." Many working-class mothers, living in conditions like those described in the chapter on cholera, were unable to afford professional child care. Single mothers and married women alike shared this problem. Working-class families could not afford to live on the meager salary of one of the adults in the household, which meant neither parent could stay at home with the children. Infants often came to work with their mothers at the mill or factory. Imagine doing manual labor in harsh factory conditions for twelve hours or more a day. Now imagine doing so with a fussy infant. It makes sense mothers might seek to calm their children, and for decades, the society had encouraged the use of things like Godfrey's Cordial (see Figure 4.3). Even the upper classes and aristocrats, either directly or through their hired nurses and nannies, used such syrups on their children.[32]

Yet often antiopium reformers focused solely on criticizing working-class mothers. Look at how *The Englishwoman's Journal*, a periodical of the Manchester and Salford Sanitary Association, describes child-rearing among "the poor" in 1859:

Few but those who have been much among the poor, know how fearfully mismanaged their little ones are—how the infant shares his mothers'

---

31. Berridge and Edwards, *Opium and the People*, 97–100.

32. Berridge and Edwards, *Opium and the People*, 100–05.

THE POOR CHILD'S NURSE.

FIGURE 4.3 This image, illustrated by *Punch* magazine in 1849, captures the attitudes of the magazine's middle-class and aristocratic readers toward working-class mothers and their perceived overuse of opium as a "failing" in child care. The implication is that the bottle of opium on the table is being used to drug the child into slumber as a substitute for a costly nurse or nanny to watch over the infant.

dram and all her food, from red herring to cucumber—how he takes medicine sufficient homeopathically to treat the whole community—and how, finally, an incautiously large dose of laudanum [an opium derivative] wraps him in the sleep that knows no waking.[33]

The authors of the *Englishwoman's Journal* targeted working-class mothers as killers of their children via opium poisoning, despite statistics collected even in the 1860s showing opium-related infant and toddler deaths across all social classes.

---

33. "The details of woman's work in sanitary reform," *The Englishwoman's Journal* 3 (1859), 223.

Why was one class of women singled out? If we think back to the section on the sanitary movement a few chapters back, we might find our reason. Sanitarians had clear views of the lower class in terms of illness, disease, and life style. They blamed this group's perceived immorality for their poverty and all their health woes. These activists made the same assumption here regarding improper drug use as a moral flaw. The temperance movement against alcohol, the antiopium leagues, and the eventual umbrella group covering all addictions, the Society for the Study of Inebriety, operated on the same prejudices and assumptions about the poor as the sanitarians.

Consider the social makeup of the antiopium and temperance movements in Britain. Much like the temperance movement against alcohol in the United States that yielded Prohibition, the anti-alcohol and antiopium movements in Britain were largely headed by middle-class women. These women, who viewed addiction as a male problem, sought to uplift lower-class women by targeting the perceived bad behavior of working-class husbands, arguing that ending addiction would end domestic abuse. However, these middle-class women had particular views about the family and what constituted proper child-rearing and gender roles. Working-class women did not fit these middle-class values and were severely judged by their middle-class counterparts.[34] We can see this clearly in the hypocritical attitude these social movements took toward opium cordials used on fussy children. Addiction, in the worldview of these organizations, was a bad habit based on poor life choices made by immoral people. The working class, they argued, was quintessentially lacking in morals and therefore a community of addicts more likely to overdose themselves and their children.[35]

The matter eventually came before the House of Commons alongside several highly publicized infant opium deaths and the debate over the 1868 Pharmacy Act, which defined proper medicinal use. The resulting 1872 Infant Life Protection Act instituted nationwide compulsory registration of births and deaths and included a statute against the use of opium derivatives to calm children. However, the act specifically excluded nurses and child-minder professionals from this ban, deeming this to be proper medical use, thus enabling continued sales of syrups like Godfrey's Cordial. The idea was professionals were better able to determine proper use than the self-medicating working class, effectively enacting the restrictions on working-class mothers.[36]

---

34. Virginia Berridge, *Demons: Our Changing Attitudes to Alcohol, Tobacco, and Drugs* (New York: Oxford University Press, 2013), 36–54.

35. Berridge and Edwards, *Opium and the People*, 104–09.

36. Berridge and Edwards, *Opium and the People*, 104–09.

The definitions of proper medical use of opium in the 1868 Pharmacy Act also laid the groundwork for disease theories of addiction in turn leading to elaborate, often racist, classist, and gendered notions of which groups were predisposed to opium abuse. Opium abuse in Britain from the 1880s to World War I was discussed now as a disease. We tend to think of disease as a specific bacterial or viral infection, cancers, or a chronic degradation of function in an organ or body system. In the early days of disease theory in the nineteenth century, however, disease implied a deviation from normal behavior or health. Opium addiction was viewed as an "abnormality," both psychologically and physically. British physician Norman Kerr, who worked for the temperance movement influenced Society for the Study of Inebriety, argued that addiction should be viewed as a disease rather than as a vice. In his opening address before the 1887 Colonial and International Congress on Inebriety he stated: "[Addiction] is a functional neurosis.... We thus have alcohol, opium, chloral, opium, ether, chlorodyne and other forms of the disease."[37]

We might think, in the twenty-first century, that a disease theory of addiction would be beneficial, affording those afflicted with the opportunity for treatment and thereby avoid the label of "moral decline." Sadly, in the nineteenth and early twentieth centuries, the disease theory of addiction retooled morality arguments against the poor into arguments of "biological deficiency." The scientific view of addiction as disease coincided with the rise of eugenics, which we defined and discussed in chapter 3. Medical experts viewed addictions to alcohol and opium and other substances, as "hereditary conditions" of abnormality, much in the same way they viewed criminality, insanity, and poverty. Kerr and other physicians listed factors that "predisposed" individuals to addiction, such as biological sex, age, race, climate, education, and religion, and categorized those who met those conditions as "unfit."

Women, the working class, and those of non-European descent were labeled as the most "at risk" of a "biological predisposition" to the disease of addiction by nineteenth- and twentieth-century British, white, male physicians of a high social standing. Morality arguments about the "unfit" and "debased" actions of these supposedly predisposed groups were not eliminated by disease theory, but instead given spurious scientific and medical respectability. Working-class "addicts" were treated as "predisposed," but also responsible for their addiction, and laws were passed to cut off supply to these communities, even for medical purposes. Upper-class addicts were afforded expensive in-patient treatments and viewed as "victims." Legislation such as the 1879 and 1888 Habitual Drunkards Acts, the 1898 Inebriates Act, and the 1913 Mental Deficiency Act extended the

---

37. Norman Kerr, "Opening Address to the Colonial and International Congress on Inebriety," *Proceedings of the Society for the Study of Inebriety* 13 (1887), 1–3.

definition of intoxicants to include more than alcohol and allowed for the "detention" of addicts for "curative treatment," with such detention being voluntary for upper-class whites but compulsory for all other groups.[38]

"Lady Britannia and Her Children": Substance Control in the British Empire

Notions of predisposition toward addiction developed by doctors in the United Kingdom blended with imperial racial theories in the rest of the empire.[39] In Burma, India, and China, colonial officials directed drug control policies at colonial subjects. They shaped their policies and enforcement of them on racial hierarchies of perceived susceptibility to addiction. British officials convinced themselves their intervention in countries like Burma and China was needed to "civilize" the indigenous populations in these and other colonies. This same arrogance came to bear in drug policy within the colonies as well, but with a hypocritical twist shaped by economic motives.

The British Empire, funded in part by the global narcotics trade, needed opium to be produced in places like India and Burma and consumed at a high rate in China and other markets. British colonial officials and European settlers in these regions profited greatly from the cultivation of opium poppies. Plantation owners, using coerced and/or poorly paid colonial subjects for labor, made large profits selling the syrup from these poppies to companies in Britain, Continental Europe, and the United States, where the raw material was industrially processed into all manner of medicinal and recreational opium derivatives. In India and Burma, British settlers had converted large tracks of agricultural land to poppy cultivation, forcing the indigenous population to abandon necessary production of staple food crops and causing famines in the region. In China and Burma, the British colonial governments dismantled older bans against opium use, even threatening punishment for colonial subjects who spoke out against the British opium trade for creating anti-British sentiment. The hope here was to create large markets for the refined opium and its derivative, increasing profit. They sought to use their colonial subjects both as labor and as captive customers.[40] British colonial settlers and officials, therefore, had little incentive to enforce bans on the drug's use or prohibition of its growth in India, Burma, or China.

---

38. Berridge and Edwards, *Opium and the People*, 159–69.

39. The phrase "Lady Britannia and her Children" is borrowed from the title of the third chapter of Wright, *Opium and Empire*.

40. Wright, *Opium and Empire*, 14–44, 76–107; Renard, *The Burmese Connection*, 16–38; Yangwen, *Social Life of Opium*, 87–145.

Yet the British Empire's role as a global drug dealer, addicting colonial subjects to a narcotic substance increasingly becoming taboo at home, did not easily fit with goals of "elevating" colonized peoples. The Aborigines Protection Society and the Society for the Suppression of the Opium Trade attempted to take the moralization campaigns of the antiopium movement in Britain and apply a condemnation of the opium trade across the entire empire throughout the 1840s, 1850s, and 1860s. A stronger movement, the Anglo-Oriental Society, emerged in 1870. This society argued that opium trade in the colonies hindered the civilizing mission of the British Empire.

These groups were equally arrogant in their assumption the British way was the right way for societies to develop.[41] In the Anglo-Oriental Society's monthly periodical, *The Friend of China*, several British antiopium activists condemned British merchants and large-scale Chinese opium trade networks, which had been growing and competing with British opium imports from India. *The Friend of China* contended temptation of profit through drug production retarded the growth of legitimate trade in items like cotton and textiles and damaged missionary efforts of converting colonial subjects to Christianity in India and China. China, these activists contended, could not fully Westernize and civilize until Britain ended the immoral practice international opium trade. The Anglo-Oriental Society sought total prohibition, a move not popular with British governing officials in the United Kingdom and the colonies who profited from the drug trade.[42] A fight raged between competing visions of what the core mission of the British Empire—profit or European-style developmentalism—across the 1870s, 1880s, and 1890s.

Ashley Wright argues that this dynamic between economic interests, notions of European racial superiority, and the civilizing mission ultimately resulted in a hierarchy of differential controls based on race and—you guessed it—ideas of which groups were more predisposed toward addiction. Wright focuses her argument on Burma and points to a pivotal moment between 1878 and 1880, when Sir Charles Umpherston Aitchison, a former Chief Commissioner of British Burma, worked on a memorandum concerning the opium problem under his immediate superior, Lord Lytton: Viceroy of British India.[43] Aitchison, an ardent missionary, had been working in the North Indian Province of Punjab, but left for the more isolated Burmese province of the Indian Raj after disputes with Lytton over frontier policy.

For Aitchison, like those who wrote for *The Friend of China*, opium was a moral issue and the spike in addiction he observed in Burma needed to be

---

41. Brown, "Politics of the Poppy," 97–99.

42. Brown, "Politics of the Poppy," 100–11.

43. Wright, "Opium in British Burma," 630–38; Wright, *Opium and Empire*, 35–60.

addressed. Aware of the importance of opium exports for the economy of British India, however, Aitchison did not advocate a complete prohibition on opium. He instead constructed a set of policies intended to maintain the economic benefits of moderate, nondestructive, legitimate opium use while preventing abuse. Wright maintains Aitchison achieved this by arguing abuse was determined not by quantity consumed, but by the predisposed risk of the individual based on their ethnicity and race.[44] Look at the following text and see if you confirm Wright's findings:

> The Chinese population in British Burmah, and to some extent also the immigrants from India, especially Chittagonians and Bengalese, habitually consume opium without any apparent ill-effects; those of them who have acquired the habit do not regularly indulge to excess. With the Burmese and other indigenous races the case is different. The Burmese seem quite incapable of using the drug in moderation . . . the *legitimate requirements* of the 200,000 Chinese and natives of Bengal, resident in British Burmah, must be considered and provided for. These, to whom the drug is a *necessary of life*, constitute perhaps the most thriving and industrious section of the population.[45]

Let us unpack Aitchison's memorandum. First, we see he mentioned other populations in British Burma: Chinese and Indian migrants. The diversity of populations within a British colony is the result of the global nature of the British Empire, where peoples and goods frequently moved across the empire in various economic capacities, often as merchants or servants. We note in the text that Aitchison crafted a hierarchy here. The Indian and Chinese migrants, he says, are engaging in legitimate use of opium, whereas he believes the Burmese are "incapable of using the drug in moderation." What did Aitchison mean by legitimate use? Building off of earlier discussions in Britain, we can surmise this means medicinal use, but there is also a cultural component of tolerance for recreational use here. Aitchison believed opium was an inherent part of Chinese and Indian culture. Why might he think that? In part this is because India was Britain's main site of poppy cultivation and where the plant originated, making it easy for British officials to label opium as part of Indian culture and make the excuse regulating its use by Indians would infringe on their culture. China, which

---

44. Wright, "Opium in British Burma," 631–36.

45. Memorandum by C. U. Aitchison, late Chief Commissioner of British Burma, on the consumption of Opium in that province, dated April 30, 1880, submitted with appended papers to parliament, 1881 (Parl. Papers, 1881, LXVIII.643), sect. 4, sec. 13.

was Britain's largest consumer of opium in the nineteenth century, had been subjected to increased imports of opium since the Opium Wars. From the late nineteenth-century British perspective, the Chinese were addicts, but British officials again portrayed opium as part of Chinese culture. Monetary reasons are therefore guiding Aitchison's views of opium use by Chinese and Indian colonial subjects. Critiquing their use would shatter the economic system of the British drug trade at both the site of production and consumption.

The Burmese, on the other hand, Aitchison viewed as engaging in excessive, addictive use. Why? Well, again, economics played a role as well as racism. Burma's productivity as a colony had dropped significantly across the preceding decades due in part to increased opium use, peddled by the British in 1820s to 1870s.[46] Britain had hoped to use Burma for agricultural output, both for more poppy production as well as highly desired spices and palm oil. Chinese and Indian migrants in the colony served as middle men: merchants and/or servants of British officials, whereas the Burmese were largely relegated to forms of manual labor in the British colonial hierarchy. The racial hierarchies of the British Empire created a racialized class system wherein different ethnic groups fulfilled different economic roles in the colony.

This pattern was repeated across every colony in the empire and was even starker in colonies with sizeable white European settler populations, where white Europeans were given primacy in all economic and governing capacities.[47] The decline in labor productivity in Burma hindered the agricultural trade and therefore colonial officials viewed policies restricting use among Burmese laborers as necessary. Aitchison justified these divergent policies through performed cultural sensitivity for colonial subjects and standard imperial racist notions of ranking groups of people in relation to European civilization.

Aitchison submitted his final report in January 1881 to Lytton's successor, Lord Rippon, who used his power as Viceroy to implement policies suggested by Aitchison. Chinese and Indian migrants in British-controlled Burma were allowed to sell and consume opium, but the perception of Burmese subjects as weaker by British officials meant they were the targets of supply-control policies. Ironically, however, in addition to limiting Burmese opium use, well into the twentieth century the British still forbade the Burmese themselves from speaking

---

46. Wright, *Opium and Empire*, 32–60.

47. For more examples of these kinds of hierarchy in the British and other European imperial projects, read these anthologies then explore works they cite: Frederick Cooper and Ann Laura Stoler, eds., *Tensions of Empire: Colonial Cultures in a Bourgeois World* (Berkeley: University of California Press, 1997); Catherine Hall, *Civilizing Subjects: Colony and Metropole in the English Imagination, 1830–1867* (Chicago: University of Chicago Press, 2002); Caroline Elkins and Susan Pedersen, eds., *Settler Colonialism in the Twentieth Century* (New York: Routledge, 2005).

out against the opium trade in all venues of society, from religious events to public demonstrations to the classroom.[48] The British alone guided policy and any critique of any British trade or governing principle by a colonial subject was viewed as an act of rebellion against Britain's purportedly benevolent rule.

The distinctions made by British officials meant they could continue to profit from opium, selling it to races who supposedly could tolerate the substance and use it legitimately, while maintaining the façade they were civilizing other colonial subjects by restricting their access to narcotics. Wright contends the Aitchison memorandum and the policies derived from it in Burma in the 1880s soon spread across the empire. Drug-control policy varied for different ethnicities and different colonies. No uniform system of prohibition existed across the entire empire.[49] Some scholars, such as Liat Kozma and Gabriel Nahas, go further to suggest that in British-dominated Egypt and across the empire, policies on cannabis and opium derivatives and their use made certain races and ethnicities synonymous with lower class, thereby blending racism and classism by conflating the two.[50]

Global Drug Diplomacy: Replicating British Prejudices in Narcotics Control Worldwide

Empire-wide links between ethnicity and addiction, as well as British colonial officials' performances of a fabricated "cultural sensitivity" for their colonial subjects, would later form the basis for international law on narcotic substances in the heavily British-dominated League of Nations following World War I. Look back at the quote on the first page of this chapter: can you now see the origins for the racial assumptions made by Dr. White and his colleagues in 1922? In this last section of the chapter, we will look at how the First World War transformed global debates on drug control and led to pushes for a more comprehensive ban on recreational and addictive narcotics. The British remained a dominant power in international affairs, so the imperial policies and assumptions of British colonial drug policy formed the basis for international drug control regimes in the early twentieth century. This established what historian William B. McAllister calls "drug diplomacy" in global politics whereby economic interests crafted

---

48. Wright, *Opium and Empire*, 46–94; Renard, *The Burmese Connection*, 26–51.

49. Wright, "Opium in British Burma," 635–39; Wright, *Opium and Empire*, 45–95.

50. Gabriel G. Nahas, "Hashish and Drug Abuse in Egypt during the 19th and 20th Centuries," *Bulletin of the New York Academy of Medicine* 61, no. 5 (June 1985): 428–44; Liat Kozma, "Cannabis Prohibition in Egypt, 1880–1939: From Local Ban to League of Nations Diplomacy," *Middle Eastern Studies* 47, no. 3 (2011): 443–60.

diplomatic ties, policies, and narratives about the root cause of the drug problem beneficial to states who were dominant geopolitical and economic powers.[51]

The First World War created a new sense of urgency for states and organizations that wanted to curb the international opium trade. Delegates from a number of countries around the world had attempted to put a cap on opium trade and addiction prior to the war at the 1914 Hague Opium Convention. The outbreak of the war prevented most of the attending countries from ratifying the terms of the treaty, delaying enforcement. During the war, Britain and the United States increased industrial production of opium derivatives, specifically morphine, for pharmaceutical use. Germany, the world's leading pharmaceutical manufacturer at the time, was an enemy of Britain and the United States in World War I and had ceased exports to enemy states, leaving the Allies in need of painkillers and other medications. The large number of injuries meant doctors needed morphine for surgeries on soldiers and for subsequent pain control. After the war, there was a massive spike in morphine addictions across all states involved in the conflict, especially among veterans. Higher levels of addiction created new social problems, particularly in Europe, the Americas, and North Africa, and so the League of Nations quickly adopted many of the proposed limits of the 1914 Hague Opium Convention. It established an Advisory Committee for the Traffic in Opium and Other Dangerous Drugs to debate the issue for the next decade and a half. Every state ratifying the 1919 Treaty of Versailles agreed to adopt these early, vaguely defined attempts to control the trade through tariffs whether they were a member of the League of Nations or, like the United States and Germany, not.[52]

Amplified pharmaceutical productivity during the war made opium cultivation even more lucrative than before. British colonial governments and opium cultivators in India and Burma made a fortune during the war and did not want to see those profits diminish. China, which had seen its government destabilized by the events leading up to the Opium Wars and the continual interference by the British and American governments since the 1850s, was in the midst of a civil war throughout the 1920s between competing "warlords" who sought to rule the entire country. The enticing profits from opium cultivation led various factions in China's civil war using opium cultivation to fund their efforts to come out on top. Remnants of China's previous governmental structure, on the other hand, sought a prohibitionist policy to deprive those seeking power from sources of revenue.[53]

---

51. William B. McAllister, *Drug Diplomacy in the Twentieth Century: An International History* (New York: Routledge, 2000), 1–40.

52. McAllister, *Drug Diplomacy*, 41–102; Nahas, "Hashish and Drug Abuse in Egypt"; Kozma, "Cannabis Prohibition in Egypt"; Berridge, *Demons*, 117–42.

53. McAllister, *Drug Diplomacy*, 43–78; Berridge, *Demons*, 122–30; Wright, *Opium and Empire*, 108–16.

The League held numerous conventions over the issue of opium and other substances, such as cannabis and alcohol, throughout the 1920s. By the time delegates arrived at the 1924 Geneva Conference on narcotics, two ideological camps had emerged. The United States—now a major world power and having enacted prohibition of alcohol as law—and what remained of China's independent government demanded a total prohibition on the production, sale, and consumption of opium and other drugs. Colonial subjects seeking independence from European rule, such as the emerging Burmese nationalist movement and the Kingdom of Siam, favored total prohibition, viewing this as a pathway to independence and noninterference. Major pharmaceutical-producing countries like Germany and France joined Britain in arguing for a limited approach to leave the status quo of colonial and pharmaceutical economies in place.[54]

British officials, who had been instrumental in the construction and administration of the League of Nations and its subsidiary agencies and commissions, used their influence to shift the debate to the supposedly moderate position of tariffs and border control. Individuals like Edwin S. Montagu, the Secretary of State for India under British control, claimed Britain wanted stricter control, but centered the debate on Asian opium-producing states and Germany, all of which supposedly would not agree to international regulations. These officials conveniently ignored the fact Britain itself had transformed India, Burma, and China into opium producing and/or consuming states as part the British imperial economy. Piling a fair amount of blame on China's instability and the production of opium by warlords, these British officials claimed enforceable agreements would be those crafting treaties and diplomatic avenues for each state to police its own borders with stricter customs enforcement.[55]

British medical experts, such as Dr. White who we saw in the quote at the beginning of this chapter, pivoted back to debates over what constituted legitimate medical use and insisted on recognition of racial hierarchies and different definitions of medical use. They argued against prohibition, viewing it as a hindrance to these supposedly appropriate uses of opium and other substances. Racial arguments made by the British in their colonial policies had even successfully infiltrated colonial subjects' resistance movements. Members of the Burmese nationalist movement sought independence from Britain and an end to the opium trade they viewed as the source of Britain's control over Burma. Yet Burmese nationalists, having seen Chinese migrants in Burma operating as middle-men for Britain's opium trade thanks to the racial hierarchies put in place after Aitchison's memorandum, increasingly adopted a racist stance toward those

---

54. Wright, *Opium and Empire*, 108–21.

55. McAllister, *Drug Diplomacy*, 103–212, 247–55.

of Chinese descent in Burma, blaming these migrants for introducing Burmese to the addiction. Britain had successfully turned different groups under its rule against each other, as it had done countless times before in its empire to preserve British dominance in the colonial world. Britain succeeded in creating an international system, grounded in racial assumptions, benefitting its economic interests while still claiming to care about restricting international narcotics. This narrative dominated approaches by the League of Nations and, later, the United Nations and the United States regarding supply-side control in the twentieth and twenty-first centuries.[56]

Conclusion

In this chapter we examined the impact of gender, race, class, and other forms of social hierarchy in various states' attempts to regulate opium and opium derivatives such as morphine and heroin. We explored how regulations pertaining to opium and its abuse evolved from local controls and perceptions in China, Burma, and the United Kingdom into imperial policies and how they finally morphed into a standardized system of global antinarcotics structures. From the 1920s to the 1940s, Britain's racial hierarchies and successful campaign of pinning the blame for global opium addiction on China and other Asian opium-producing states solidified into a standard narrative of drug diplomacy between countries in the League of Nations System. Later United Nations policies from the 1950s onward placed a greater emphasis on border control and limiting supply through customs rather than treatment. Sanctions were declared against states producing opium and other narcotics in the Golden Triangle such as Myanmar, ignoring the historical reason why these countries became so reliant on the drug trade economically. The United States and the "War on Drugs" ignored how US demand for drugs such as cocaine and US policies destabilized Central and South American governments during the Cold War and created the drug problem. Instead, it favored a narrative of drugs as a matter of border patrol and immigration enforcement and still places the blame on countries in the Southern hemisphere.

In the twenty-first century the United Nations began crafting drug control policies to target the extreme poverty and global economic inequality that make the illicit trade profitable and enticing. Such policies attempt to use incentives rather than penalties. "Alternative development strategies" establish international loans and agricultural subsidies encouraging opium growers in impoverished countries to produce badly needed food staples in famine areas instead. These efforts may hopefully succeed, but the damage from decades of imperial-influenced

---

56. Wright, *Opium and Empire*, 108–46.

policy has been done. The twentieth century ushered in a globalization and consolidation of systems of substance abuse control that normalized imperial racial assumptions of drug addiction and reinforced global racial and class inequality. Drug policy is one example of public health officials intentionally or inadvertently reinforcing established power imbalances around the world. In the next chapter, we will explore how well-intentioned HIV/AIDS programs provide a much-needed network of aid, but in doing so the organizations and governments implementing them assign blame to victim groups and reinforce global networks of dependency harkening back to colonial regimes.

FURTHER READING

Berridge, Virginia. *Demons: Our Changing Attitudes to Alcohol, Tobacco, and Drugs.* New York: Oxford University Press, 2013.

Gutzke, David. *Pubs and Progressives: Reinventing the Public House in Britain, 1896–1960.* Dekalb: Northern Illinois University Press, 2006.

Kozma, Liat. "Cannabis Prohibition in Egypt, 1880–1939: From Local Ban to League of Nations Diplomacy." *Middle Eastern Studies* 47, no. 3 (2011): 443–60.

McAllister, William B. *Drug Diplomacy in the Twentieth Century: An International History.* New York: Routledge, 2000.

Nahas, Gabriel G. "Hashish and Drug Abuse in Egypt during the 19th and 20th Centuries." *Bulletin of the New York Academy of Medicine* 61, no. 5 (June 1985): 428–44.

5 THE GLOBAL AIDS CRISIS

STIGMA, PATRONAGE, AND DEPENDENCY NETWORKS

Grouping individuals may be traditional in epidemiology, both as a means of intervention and as an analytic prerequisite. The political or social consequences of such grouping are rarely examined. In this instance, even if this fear of casual transmission could be eradicated, the groups identified would still be seen as bearing a strong negative relationship.

—DR. GERALD OPPENHEIMER, *on the association of Haitians with HIV, 1988*[1]

1982: Community organizations in the United States began promoting safer sex among gay men to prevent the *New York Times* called GRID (Gay-Related Immune Deficiency). That same year, an outbreak of the same symptoms occurred among a small number of Haitian immigrants in Florida. In 1985 in Uganda, doctors described the first cases of a new, fatal wasting disease known locally as "slim." The human-immunodeficiency virus (HIV) was the actual cause of all of these outbreaks. The virus, primarily transmitted through sexual intercourse, attacks the human immune system, creating Acquired Immunodeficiency Syndrome (AIDS): an ultimately fatal illness that leaves the victim open to secondary infections and cancers a healthy immune system could more effectively fight off.

This chapter explores how American and European responses to the HIV pandemic replicated stereotypes and inequalities of race and sexual orientation in the late twentieth and early twenty-first centuries. The European imperial tropes present in these responses became the foundation upon which international agencies based their actions, creating a system of forced dependency that continues to impact national and local responses in African countries like Uganda.

---

1. Gerald M. Oppenheimer, "In the Eye of the Storm: The Epidemiological Construction of AIDS," in *AIDS: The Burdens of History*, ed. Elizabeth Fee and Daniel M. Fox (Berkeley: University of California Press, 1988), 267–300, 283.

This chapter has two parts, each with several subsections. The first part of the chapter will analyze the history of the pandemic itself, the identification of "risk groups," and what anthropologist Paul Farmer calls the "geography of blame" for the illness.[2] It will also explore how some government officials initially responded to HIV. The categorizations of and antagonism they adopted toward the ailment were and are often based on stereotypes about the race and/or sexual orientation of those afflicted and the geographic "point of origin" of the disease. First, we will look at the impact these labels had on discrimination toward gay and bisexual individuals in the United States. Next, we will look at how Haitians became a global target, blamed as vectors for the disease in 1982, and the role racism and anti-immigrant sentiment in the United States played in fostering that image. Then we will examine how older imperial tropes led to a quest for the "origin" of AIDS/HIV in Africa. As we have seen in previous chapters, these sections will outline how media portrayals and fear-mongering "othering" of the sick led to violence against and ostracism of victims of the disease, and sometimes, ironically, increased distribution of HIV as organizations and governments attempted to prevent the spread of a global crisis (see Map 5.1).

The second part of this chapter will look at programs intended to care for AIDS on a global scale run largely by governments and nongovernmental organizations (NGOs), looking at Western-influenced or -dominated programs such as the United States Agency for International Development (USAID) and the Joint United Nations Programme on HIV/AIDS (UNAIDS). The intention and stated goal of these ongoing programs is to help bridge financial disparities and inequalities in access to care across the world. Yet the structure and frameworks of these organizations have reinforced global class inequalities by building and strengthening patron-client relationships on a local, national, and global scale between the Global North and the Global South well into 2017. This half of the chapter will also examine the impact these global responses to and narratives about HIV/AIDS had on national responses to HIV in Uganda from the Ministry of Health and the NGO the AIDS Support Organization in Uganda (TASO).

The Stigma of Disease: Risk Groups and Constructs of Morality

The AIDS pandemic began in the United States. The first confirmed cases of HIV were reported in 1981 in Los Angeles, California, and New York City, quickly followed by a string of individuals testing positive in San Francisco. The victims

---

2. Paul Farmer, *AIDS and Accusation: Haiti and the Geography of Blame* (Berkeley: University of California Press, 1992), 1–17.

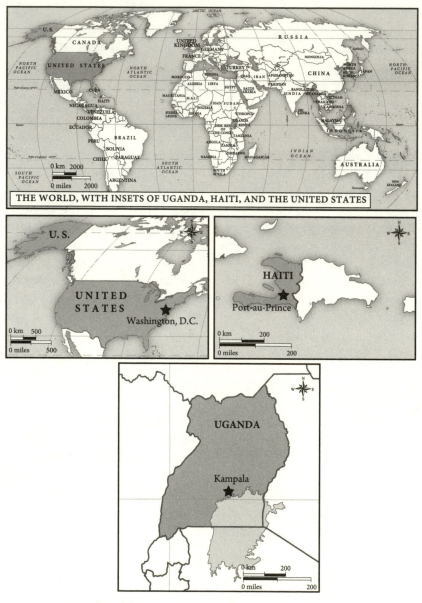

MAP 5.1 Map of World

of the disease in these early cases were white gay or bisexual men. In 1982, an outbreak of cases appeared among black Haitian immigrants in Miami, Florida. In March 1983, as part of an educational effort to halt the spread of HIV/AIDS, the US Centers for Disease Control (CDC) identified and aimed its public campaign at what they coined the "Four H's" or risk groups for the disease: "homosexual men, heroin addicts, hemophiliacs, and Haitians." (see Figure 5.1)

FIGURE 5.1 One of the "Four H's" identified as a risk group by the CDC were heroin users. Look at this image, a public warning and educational poster from the CDC in the 1980s. Think back to chapter 4 when we discussed the stigmatization of drug use and assumptions about addiction and disease. Does this poster perpetuate some of the moral arguments made against drug users from that era? In what ways is it tying them to HIV/AIDs? Consider the tone: Was a person addicted to drugs who saw this image more inclined or less inclined to seek treatment for their addiction and/or HIV/AIDS if they test positive? In your own project you could conduct research on the origins and outcomes of HIV/AIDS prevention targeted at drug users and see what positive and negative changes came from this approach to public health, STD containment, and drug control.

By singling out these groups as the primary populations deemed susceptible to the disease, the CDC inadvertently exacerbated racial tensions, prejudice against gay and bisexual men, and drug-use stigmas. As we have seen in chapters 2, 3, and 4, identification of a health issue with specific segments of the population is not solely derived from a pure idea of the science of health. Such labels are often influenced by societal prejudgments on race, class, gender, or sexual orientation and, even if well-intentioned with the goal of preventing or mitigating a health crisis, have negative outcomes. In this section, we will look at the initial American response to HIV/AIDS, initially called GRID, and the vitriolic stigmas against gay and bisexual men that emerged from Americans associating concepts of sexual morality with disease.

To comprehend why the prejudice against gay and bisexual men who exhibited HIV/AIDS in the 1980s and 1990s was so potent in the American context, we first need to look at the history of homosexuality in the United States. Like many Western European countries, most US states had laws labeling homosexuality—engaging in sexual relations with members of the same biological sex—as a felony. Homosexuality was viewed as a "crime against nature" or "crime against God" or "crime against morality," based on certain American interpretations of the scriptures of the dominant Judeo-Christian religions. "Sodomy laws" made homosexuality an arrestable offense and punishments, if convicted, ranged from fines and jail time to forced chemical castration. It wasn't until 1962 that homosexuality was decriminalized in a US state, Illinois, for the first time.

Building on the foundations of the 1960s civil rights movements and women's rights movements in the United States, gay rights groups emerged, such as the Gay Liberation Front and in New York City, to lobby for the legal rights and freedoms of LGBTQ in the United States. It was not an easy path, as prejudice persisted. The Stonewall Inn Riots of 1969, the assassination of gay San Francisco Board of Supervisors member Harvey Milk in 1978, and police brutality against gay men marked the decades preceding the outbreak of HIV/AIDS in the United States.[3] Still, by the end of the 1970s, many states had decriminalized homosexuality and the gay rights movement had successfully made headway with greater cultural acceptance. Homosexual characters appeared in mainstream television shows like the sitcom *SOAP* and the drama series *Dynasty*. The American Psychological Association, which had previously and consistently labeled homosexuality as a mental illness, removed it as a from its 1973 list of psychological diseases and conditions; homosexuality was now viewed as being within the range of normal human psychological behavior.[4] Progress continued and by 2003, the Supreme Court decriminalized homosexuality in its ruling on the case *Lawrence vs. Texas*. Laws in fourteen US states listing homosexuality as a felony were ruled unconstitutional.[5] Yet prejudice continues to this day and was at its height in the 1980s when HIV/AIDS emerged.

The initial cases in the 1981 and 1982 were identified not by the presence of the HIV virus itself—not yet discovered—but were diagnosed based on symptoms such as secondary infections and cancers, which were results of the disease weakening the victim's immune system. Doctors and the CDC, discovering that the initial patients were men who had engaged in sex with other men—be they gay or bisexual—assumed the connection that explained the illness was the patients' lifestyles. They labeled the syndrome of infections and cancers as "a homosexual disorder," "a rare cancer among homosexuals," GRID, and "gay cancer." They reinforced stereotypes by claiming gays and bisexuals were "prone to multiple sexual partners" and used "poppers"—a slang term for various illegal drugs thought to enhance sexual experiences—and their lifestyles must have suppressed their immune system.

The assumption was HIV/AIDS was limited to the gay community—the result of their supposedly unique "risky" behaviors—confirming the perceptions

---

3. William N. Eskridge Jr. *Gaylaw: Challenging the Apartheid of the Closet* (Cambridge, MA: Harvard University Press, 1999), 1–98, 327–84.

4. Perry N. Halkitis, *The AIDS Generation: Stories of Survival and Resilience* (New York: Oxford University Press, 2014), 4.

5. *Lawrence v. Texas*, 539 U.S. 558 (2003).

and stereotypes about gays held by American politicians, like President Ronald Reagan, and American religious celebrities, like the Reverend Jerry Falwell.[6] These prominent figures and members of the general public labeled gay men diagnosed with HIV/AIDS as "immoral" rather than as victims. Hardly any governmental funding was allocated for medical research to treat and limit the spread of HIV/AIDS. Ninety percent of men diagnosed before 1985 died by 1990.[7] Men discovered to be gay or bisexual, whether infected with the disease or not, were fired from their jobs, blocked from certain employment, prevented from seeking treatment for any ailment at clinics and hospitals, and faced physical assault and abuse: the "gay plague" undid much of the work done toward acceptance in the general public in the preceding decade.

Two major events challenged this initial moralistic conception of the disease. First, in 1982, symptoms of the illness appeared among Haitian migrants in Florida. This led to concerns the disease could spread, but as we will see in the next section, racial and moralistic assumptions by medical and government officials prevented a wider view of the illness as a problem for all. Then, in 1984, a teenager from Indiana named Ryan White was diagnosed with the illness after a blood transfusion.[8] Too young to have engaged in the supposedly risky behaviors and being white, so therefore not labeled Haitian, he did not fit the "normal face of GRID" the CDC had identified. He was nonetheless stigmatized and blocked from going to school or community activities, but it left a question as to how he had caught "gay cancer."

In 1985, French and US doctors identified the virus responsible: HIV-1. They discovered it attacked the T-cells vital to the human immune system's response to disease, causing the symptoms seen in every patient.[9] Testing for the virus and finding it in other populations around the world, including among heterosexuals, led the scientific community to realize anyone could become infected with HIV/AIDS through sexual contact or contact with bodily fluids. In other parts of the world, the disease is primarily a heterosexual one, functioning like a typical STD

---

6. Halkitis, *The AIDS Generation*, 2; J. Goedert, C.Y. Neuland, W.C. Wallen, M.H. Green, D.L. Mann, C. Murray, D.M. Strong, J.F. Fraumeni Jr., W.A. Blattner, "Amyl Nitrate May Alter T Lymphocytes in Homosexual Men," *The Lancet*, vol. 329, no. 8162 (1982): 412–16; M. S. Gottlieb Robert Schroff, Howard M. Schanker, Joel D. Weisman, Peng Thim Fan, Robert A. Wolf, Andrew Saxon, , "Pneumocystis Carinii Pneumonia and Mucosal Candidiasis in Previously Healthy Homosexual Men: Evidence of a New Acquired Cellular Immunodeficiency," *New England Journal of Medicine* 305, no. 24 (1981): 1425, 1425-1431.

7. Halkitis, *The AIDS Generation*, 1–8.

8. For more on Ryan White, see Ryan White and Anne Marie Cunningham, *Ryan White: My Own Story* (New York: Penguin Books, 1992).

9. S. Connor and S. Kingman, *The Search for the Virus: The Scientific Discovery of AIDS and the Quest for a Cure* (New York: Penguin Books, 1988).

in terms of its spread. In the United States, the disease still disproportionately impacts men who have sex with men. One possible explanation for this is that moralizing stigma against HIV/AIDS has again inflamed antagonism against homosexuality, making patients less likely to seek testing and treatment for fear of judgment and reprisals by friends, family, and/or employers. Remember, until 2003 over a dozen states still labeled homosexuality a felony, meaning that giving information on one's sexual activity to one's doctor to receive the appropriate diagnosis and treatment could result in arrest if reported. When it comes to ascribing blame for disease, however, medical and government officials as well as the general public around the world did not stop after the discovery HIV/AIDS was not just a "gay disease." Next, they sought to place moralistic accusations founded in prejudice on other communities in the search for the origins of HIV/AIDS.

The "Geography of Blame": Haiti as the Origin of HIV?

> Hospitals refuse to treat us,
> Immigration is corrupt.
> My friends, let's go back home, let's go back home.
> AIDS, it is a strange thing.
> There is a contagious disease . . .
> Picking humans like ripe mangos.
> Science doesn't yet know its origins,
> But, in the meantime, they say it is Haiti.
> —Ti Manno, *Haitian musician/singer, from his song "Sida," 1982*[10]

As we saw in chapter 3 regarding the origins of syphilis, European and American scientists and doctors quickly began proposing HIV/AIDS originated in the Caribbean, this time Haiti. In this section, I as an historian am not qualified to make a scientific argument about the genetic, evolutionary, or geographic origins of HIV. I can, however, assess the historical prejudices and cultural assumptions influencing American and European scientists in the 1980s and 1990s, their desire to search for an origin point for HIV, and why they so quickly focused their hypotheses and speculation on Haiti.

Our exploration begins with Haiti: a country in the Caribbean that is part of the island of Hispaniola. Today, Haiti is considered one of the poorest countries in the Western Hemisphere. The same was true during the emergence of HIV as a global pandemic in the 1980s. To understand why this was the case, how this

---

10. Translation of lyrics from Ti Manno, "Sida," 1982, Side A, Track 1 on *Ti Manno and his Gemini All-Stars Band*, Cathy's Productions, 1983, LP.

impacted the later rapid spread of HIV/AIDS in Haiti where it likely did not exist at all prior to 1982, and American perceptions of Haitians, you need to know a little about Haiti's history.

In 1492 when Christopher Columbus and his Spanish-funded fleet arrived in the New World, they laid claim to the island and named it the Spanish colony of "Hispaniola"—"New Spain." The island was occupied by Native American groups who the Spanish colonists enslaved and nearly wiped out through massacres and outbreaks of newly introduced smallpox. In search of new labor, the Spanish looked to their outposts in West Africa. They captured Africans and brought them to Hispaniola and elsewhere as slaves, part of the transatlantic slave trade.[11] In 1697, with the Spanish Empire in decline, the island was signed over to the French Empire. The French renamed the colony "Saint-Domingue." Using the colony for sugar and tobacco production, the French increased the forced import of African slaves. Between 1784 and 1791, the fatality rate of African slaves on sugar and tobacco plantations was so high the French annually imported an average of 29,000 new slaves from Africa to replace those who had died under their lashes, the back-breaking labor, and the weight of tropical diseases.[12]

Saint-Domingue gained independence as Haiti in 1791 with the Haitian Revolution. Shortly after the 1789 French Revolution, Mulattos and African slaves, under the leadership of ex-slave Touissant L'Ouverture, successfully revolted against the governing white European settlers and founded a new state. Throughout the nineteenth century, France, Great Britain, Spain, and the United States would try to assert formal control and/or economic influence over the independent Haiti, but Haitians generally repelled these moves, even when the Spanish-speaking half of the island revolted and became its own state—the Dominican Republic—in 1844.

In 1915, however, the United States invaded and occupied the island. This was part of two waves of imperial expansion in the Caribbean. The first wave came after the Spanish-American War (1898), in which the United States took control of Puerto Rico and gained influence over Cuba. Another wave of "gunboat diplomacy" during the First World War secured US military, cultural, and economic hegemony in the Western Hemisphere by invading Haiti and other states in the region. The United States claimed it was occupying Haiti to restore stability after local insurgents had assassinated Haitian President Vilbrun Guillaume Sam. The US occupation and "tutelage" of Haiti and other parts of the Caribbean led to an American colonizing sense of paternalism toward these cultures. American

---

11. For more on the transatlantic slave trade, see David Eltis, *The Rise of African Slavery in the Americas* (New York: Cambridge University Press, 2000).

12. Farmer, *AIDS and Accusation*, 153–64.

tourist guidebooks in the 1930s described Haiti as a "deplorable and almost unbelievable mixture of barbaric customs and African traditions."[13] American troops in Haiti viewed it as developmentally "inferior" and in need of American assistance to improve the island's infrastructure, particularly for the extraction of resources such as sugar, sisal, and cotton.[14]

After US forces left the island in 1934, the United States maintained economic dominance over Haiti. After 1945, Haiti, like Cuba, became a popular American tourist destination. Though this tourism was interrupted by the dictatorship of Haitian President Francois Duvalier between 1957 and 1971, it resumed under the succeeding dictatorship of his son, Jean-Claude Duvalier. Many Americans also assumed, partially erroneously, Haiti was a major site of "sex tourism" and "gay tourism" where prostitution was rampant. This perception arose from guidebooks suggesting Americans looking for sex on their tropical excursions could have their "fantasies come true . . . for a nominal charge" by exploiting the poverty on the island.[15]

While Americans viewed the island as a tropical getaway, Haitians fled the country to escape the terrors of the Duvalier dynasty. The father and son dictators are estimated to have killed 40,000 to 60,000 people they viewed as political dissidents and opponents.[16] Many Haitians tried to migrate to the United States from the 1960s to the 1980s. In the United States, Haitian refugees experienced xenophobia, racism, and were intercepted by the Coast Guard and placed in detention centers awaiting deportation on the order of President Ronald Reagan in 1981's Executive Order No. 12324.[17]

After the outbreak of the disease among Haitian immigrants living in Miami-Dade, Florida in 1982, theories sprang up suggesting the disease must have originated among black Haitians.[18] American doctors and government officials

13. Frank Carpenter, *Lands of the Caribbean* (Garden City, NY: Doubleday, Doran, and Co., 1930), 326.

14. For more on the Haitian Revolution and the subsequent history of the island, see C. L. R. James, *The Black Jacobins: Toussaint L'Ouverture and the San Domingo Revolution* (New York: Vintage Books, 1989); Phillipe Girard, *Haiti: The Tumultuous History* (New York: Palgrave, 2010); Polyne Millery, *From Douglas to Duvalier: U.S. African Americans, Haiti, and Pan-Americanism, 1870–1964* (Gainesville: University Press of Florida, 2010).

15. Farmer, *AIDS and Accusation*, 143–48, 183–89.

16. Michael W. Collier, *Political Corruption in the Caribbean Basin: Constructing a Theory to Combat Corruption* (New York: Routledge, 2005), 85–120.

17. Farmer, *AIDS and Accusation*, 173–90, 212–20; Exec. Order. No. 12324, 46 FR 48109 (Sept. 29, 1981).

18. Rosalind J. Harrison-Chirimuuta and Richard C. Chirimuuta, "AIDS from Africa: A Case of Racism vs. Science?," in *AIDS in Africa and the Caribbean*, ed. George C. Bond, John Kreniske, Ida Susser, Joan Vincent(Boulder, CO: Westview Press, 1997), 165–80.

claimed there was a "thriving gay culture" on the island. Exaggerated caricatures of Haitians emerged in this period. Trying to maintain links between their four risk groups, US and European health experts proposed untested, condescending hypotheses claiming the "primitive" island's "history of voodoo" and "ingestion of pig blood" played a role in the introduction of HIV/AIDS to humans.[19]

After identifying Haitians as a risk group, American media portrayed Haitians as promiscuous and depicted Haitians en masse as a threat to public health. Haitians were upset by stigmatization by medical professionals and the media. Many Haitians and Haitian immigrants in the United States shared the frustrations of the famous Haitian singer Ti Manno, whose song "Sida" ("AIDS" in French/Haitian) appears in translation at the beginning of this section. They were, as you would be, angry at the racist caricatures in US media portraying them as "scantily clad black natives dancing frenetically about ritual fire [or] Haitians with AIDS as illegal aliens interned in detention camps." Haitians, let alone the majority of Haitian AIDS victims, did not and do not fit either stereotype.[20] Some in Haiti were so angry in 1982, they reversed the blame and forwarded conspiracy theories AIDS was an "imperialist plot to destroy the Third World" or a "false disease invented by the American government to take advantage of the poor countries."

Alongside anger came fear of deportation, assault, or loss of income. One Haitian taxi driver in Boston, interviewed on condition of anonymity by Paul Farmer, a medical anthropologist, recounted the fear, shame, and stigma he felt:

My wife and I have lived here [in the United States] for fifteen years, and we speak English well, and I do O.K. driving. But the hardest time I've had in all my life, harder than Haiti, was when people would refuse to get in my cab when they discovered I was from Haiti. It got so we would pretend to be from somewhere else, which is the worst thing you can do, I think.

Their fear was sadly justified. US citizens dehumanized, discriminated against, and assaulted Haitians in the wake of the AIDS outbreak. Employers fired them from their jobs, landlords evicted them from their homes, and federal and state penitentiaries segregated them into separate prisons all out of fear of HIV/AIDS. In 1983 in Brooklyn, vandals spray-painted walls in a predominately Caribbean neighborhood with the hateful and racist message: "Haitians=Niggers with AIDS." Racist groups and individuals sent hate mail to businesses conveying vile

19. Farmer, *AIDS and Accusation*, 2–4, 196–201, 216–38.

20. Jeffrey Vierra, "The Haitian Link," in *Understanding AIDS: A Comprehensive Guide*, ed. Victor Gong (New Brunswick, NJ: Rutgers University Press, 1985), 90–99, 97.

statements like "Hire a Haitian—Help Spread AIDS," or "There were [*sic*] no AIDS in the USA until the illegal criminal Haitian dogs came."[21] In 1984, the City Commission of New York had to establish an AIDS Discrimination Unit to address a devastating number of discriminatory practices and hate crimes against those labeled as risk groups. In New York City, one official explained "Haitian children have been beaten up (and in at least one case, shot) in school; Haitian store owners have gone bankrupt as their businesses failed; and Haitian families have been evicted from their homes."[22]

In 1985, the CDC finally dropped Haitian immigrants in the United States from their list risk groups, "no longer [able to] justify including them on statistical grounds." In 1985, out of 9,405 total cases reported in the United States, only 285 were Haitian patients.[23] Haitians therefore accounted for around 3 percent of all reported cases. Dr. Walter Dowdle—then director of the Center for Infectious Diseases—admitted that Haitian immigrants "were the only risk group identified because of who they were rather than what they did."[24] The CDC had moved too quickly in identifying Haitians as a risk group, clearly indicating racist assumption, not science, had been the determining factor. Even after the CDC altered its risk group definitions, the damage from the stigma and racial associations with HIV/AIDS had already been done.[25] Despite removing Haitians as a risk group, the CDC, along with the US Food and Drug Administration, maintained a ban on Haitians donating blood and renewed it again in 1990. These agencies claimed there was a "lack of effective screening devices" to definitively rule out Haitian blood donors as a potential "risk of transmitting the virus."[26]

There is little evidence to suggest the disease existed in Haiti prior to the earliest identified US cases. However, in Haiti and the Dominican Republic the number of cases skyrocketed in the 1980s. Several factors account for this rapid spread of the disease. American tourists played a role in exposing Haitians to HIV. Immigrants exposed to the disease in the United States and then deported back to or returned to Haiti could also account for several cases. More potent in flaming the epidemic, however, was the lack of access to healthcare due to the

21. Letters signed as from the "United Taxpayers Association" sent to businesses and Social-Service Organizations in South Florida in 1983, as quoted in Farmer, *AIDS and Accusation*, 214.

22. Renee Sabatier, *Blaming Others: Prejudice, Race, and World Wide AIDS* (Philadelphia: New Society Publishers, 1988), 47.

23. "Haitians Removed from AIDS Risk List," *New York Times*, April 10, 1985, p. A00013.

24. "Haitians Removed from AIDS Risk List."

25. Harrison-Chirimuuta and Richard C. Chirimuuta, "AIDS from Africa," 166–67.

26. Farmer, *AIDS and Accusation*, 217–18.

island's poverty: a poverty exacerbated by the Duvalier dictatorships and the various bans on travel to, migration from, and commerce with the nation emerging from the stigma of HIV/AIDS. By 1990, there were 2,331 cases in Haiti reported to the Pan-American Health Organization: almost ten times the number reported among Haitian immigrants in the United States five years prior.[27] By the late 1990s, cases increased to 11,000. Today, the World Health Organization approximates 7,600 cases of HIV in Haiti, making it the nation in the Caribbean hardest hit by the illness.[28]

After Haiti was eliminated as possibility, the quest for the disease's origin began anew. The same 1985 *New York Times* article that announced Haitians and Haitian immigrants had been cleared noted ominously that "the centers have also added one case of a recent immigrant from Africa to [a list of AIDS cases] in which the risk factor is regarded as unknown."[29] Although none of the early HIV patients who were Haitian immigrants in the United States or living in Haiti had ever traveled to or interacted with Africans, despite the identified common link in a 1983 investigation of Haitian contact with North American men or travel to the United States, Africa became the next focus for the search for HIV's origins.[30]

AIDS "Out of Africa": Imperialism's Influence on Scientific Thought

Although cases in Africa were not discovered until after those in the United States, two theories emerged, initially with no evidence, claiming central Africa was the source of the disease. One speculated that a "lost tribe" in Africa had carried the virus for centuries and it was suddenly loosed on the world in the 1980s.[31] Another speculation involving monkeys started gaining traction and acceptance at a faster rate. This hypothesis argued the infection must have come from monkeys some thirty years prior. Starting with a kernel of truth—the presence of similar immunodeficiency syndromes in simians and other primates—some medical professionals started making wild assumptions and leaps. They claimed, with little knowledge of the various cultures of the continent, that "African sexual practices" or diets led to the transmission of the virus to humans and from there, it spread to Haitian migrant workers in central Africa (and no one else, it seems),

27. Farmer, *AIDS and Accusation*, 121.

28. "AIDS info, Haiti Graphs," UN AIDS, last modified 2018, http://aidsinfo.unaids.org/.

29. "Haitians Removed from AIDS Risk List."

30. Farmer, *AIDS and Accusation*, 128.

31. K. M. De Cock, "AIDS: An Old Disease from Africa?," *British Medical Journal* 289, no. 6440 (1984): 306–08.

who in turn brought it back to Haiti and there, or in Africa, infected gay and bisexual American tourists.[32] This late 1980s view was based on certain tropes about Africans, some of which you have read about in previous chapters.

Look at the following quotes from doctors and public health officials regarding the African origin thesis and think about the assumptions and prejudgments impacting their scientific view. The first comes from John Green and David Miller, two early AIDS "experts" from St. Mary's Hospital in London:

> Monkeys are often hunted for food in Africa. It may be that a hunting accident of some sort, or an accident in preparation for cooking, brought people in contact with infected blood. Once caught, monkeys are often kept in huts for some time before they are eaten. Dead monkeys are sometimes used as toys for African children.[33]

Think about the presentation of Africans here. Green and Miller assume all Africans eat primates, which is true of only a few cultures and societies on the continent. There is also a condescending tone expressed by these British doctors when they claim, without evidence, Africans let their children play with dead monkeys—which perpetuates stereotypes of Africans as uneducated, poor parents.

Now read this 1987 letter published in the peer-reviewed British medical journal *The Lancet,* in which a researcher claims a study of African ethnography could explain AIDS's origins:

> Sir: The isolation from monkeys of retro viruses closely related to HIV strongly suggests a simian origin for this virus . . . In his book on the sexual life of people of the Great Lakes area of Africa, Kashamura writes: "to stimulate a man or a woman and induce them into intense sexual activity, monkey blood for a man or she-monkey blood for a woman was directly inoculated in the pubic area and also in the thighs and the back." These magic practices would therefore constitute an efficient experimental transmission model and could be responsible for the emergence of AIDS in man.[34]

32. Vanessa M. Hirsch, Robert A. Olmsted, Michael Murphey-Corb, Robert H. Purcell, and Philip R. Johnson, "An African Primate Lentivirus (SIV$_{sm}$ Closley Related to HIV-2," *Nature* 339 (June 1989): 389–92; R. C. Gallo, "The AIDS Virus," *Scientific American* 256, no. 1 (1987): 39–48; C. F. Farthing, S. E. Brown, and R. C. D. Staughton, *A Colour Atlas of AIDS and HIV Disease,* Slide Set, 2nd ed. (London: Mosby, 1989).

33. John Green and David Miller, *AIDS: The Story of a Disease* (London: Grafton Books, 1986), 66.

34. François Noireau, "HIV Transmission from Monkey to Man," *The Lancet* 1 (27 June 1987): 1498–99.

In both instances, we see European medical professionals imagining a generalized African culture portrayed as primitive, exotic, uneducated, unscientific, and prone to "magic practices." This is a common, ignorant representation of Africa founded on old and persistent stereotypes we see even in news and scholarship today. Take a moment and use the resources at your disposal: libraries, the internet, and professors. Do some research on how the US media depicted Africa and Africans, for instance, during the 2014–2016 Ebola epidemic in Liberia, Sierra Leone, and Guinea. Look up news stories, US government reports, and summaries from the World Health Organization (WHO). Do you see commonalities in the stories on, say, the *Today Show* on NBC or the reports from the WHO and the CDC about Ebola and the representations of Africans in regards to AIDS? Rather than analyzing individual cultures—of which there are thousands— European, American, and Asian scholars, doctors, journalists, and politicians tend to present "Africa" as a monolithic continent. They assume what they see depicted in one location and time is accurate, take it at face value, and consider it representative of the whole without questioning their sources and own personal biases further.

The second quote from the *Lancet* is a perfect example of this tendency. François Noireau, its author, was a French medical scientist with degrees in medicine and public health and was, at the time of the publication of the work in the *Lancet*, working on a PhD in life sciences and health at the University of Sciences and Techniques of Lille. In his letter, he referenced a work by Anicet Kashamura (1928–2004), a Congolese journalist, anticolonial activist, and politician. Kashamura's book on African family and sexual cultures in the Lake Victoria/ Lake Nyanza region of Eastern Africa was written in 1973, a decade before the AIDS outbreak.[35]

Kashamura himself was from the Congo. His "research" into African societies on the opposite side of the continent from his home was drawn from a 1964 work by an Italian Egyptologist. That 1964 work in turn relied on works by ethnographers publishing in the 1920s.[36] Kashamura based his argument on the wrong part of the continent and on an outdated source that itself drew on material from outdated sources. The sources from which Kashamura's source is getting information were written in the 1920s: the height of European imperialism in Africa, when false narratives about racial hierarchy and human evolution were running rampant as eugenics and the "civilizing mission" were common place in European

---

35. Anicet Kashamura, *Famille, sexualité et culture: Essai sur les moeurs sexuelles et les cultures des peuples des Grands Lacs africains* (Paris: Payot, 1973).

36. Boris de Rachewiltz, *Black Eros: Sexual Customs of Africa from Prehistory to the Present Day* (London: Lyle Stuart, 1964).

and American thinking. These are not reliable sources for understanding the various societies, cultures, and peoples of Tanzania, Kenya, and Uganda in the 1980s
during the AIDS crisis.

Derivative, ill-researched scholarship like the *Lancet* piece and the works it
used as sources does not consider the context around its reference materials' creation. The result is that these works create a picture of an Africa culturally and
developmentally static across time and space. They portray the people living there
as one timeless and undifferentiated stereotype—a picture that has stuck in the
general publics of the United States and European states well into the twenty-first
century. This viewpoint sadly even became imprinted in decolonizing societies in
Africa. Many African scholars and elites received their education from European
and American universities and educators during the period of colonial occupation. In the following section, we will see how these oft-perpetuated stereotypes
have influenced international aid groups working across the globe to find solutions for HIV/AIDS.

Good Intentions, Flawed Foundations:
USAID, UNAIDS, and NGOs

As the outbreak of HIV/AIDS turned into a global pandemic in the 1980s
and 1990s, significant ideological differences among governments, the United
Nations (UN), and international NGOs hindered the creation of an effective,
unified global response. The Joint United Nations Programme on HIV/AIDS
(UNAIDS), an effort to create a "synergistic effort," was not created until 1996:
the historical height of the HIV/AIDS pandemic. Africa was, and is, the continent hardest hit by the disease. Made up of newly independent states, liberated
from imperial occupation by Europeans in the preceding decades, these new nations faced several economic and political hardships. These conditions made it
easier for the disease to spread once introduced. African hardships invited intervention from international agencies to contain the disease. International agencies
in turn were and are financially and politically dominated by the US and the same
European countries that had violently conquered and oppressed Africa, Asia, the
Pacific, and the Caribbean for over a century before independence.

From the 1980s to the present, international strategies and policies to contain the disease have transformed. They began by focusing on disease control,
then shifted to community development schemes, and then swung back to a
model emphasizing a medical rather than sociological approach, providing antibiotics for secondary infections and antiretroviral treatments (ART).[37] Though

---

37. Praag, Dehne, and Chandra-Mouli, "The UN Response," 593–99.

often starting from a place of good intentions to assist those in need, variances in governments' and private organizations' willingness to address stigma related to HIV/AIDS made it difficult to strengthen health responses around the globe.[38] These responses, often in the form of financial assistance and direct medical aid, have also had a negative impact on so-called developing countries when they seek other kinds of loans for infrastructure and economic expansion from international finance systems, like the International Monetary Fund (IMF) and the International Bank for Reconstruction and Development (IBRD, a.k.a. the World Bank).[39] In this section, we will look at how these often-well-intentioned forms of international public health assistance can and have perpetuated stigmas related to HIV/AIDS and continue to foster an exploitative global system of dependency between the Global North—a.k.a. the developed or industrialized world—and the Global South—so-called developing countries formerly dominated as colonies by European, American, and other powers of the Global North.

A host of organizations have tried to create a formulaic one-size-fits all international response to the global threat of HIV/AIDS. The chief ones we will address here are UNAIDS, USAID, and the President's Emergency Plan for AIDS Relief (PEPFAR), but we will also identify collective patterns among private NGOs. UNAIDS is the UN program established to unify responses to HIV/AIDS around the globe established in 1996. It works closely with the WHO and several governments. USAID (established in 1961 by President John F. Kennedy) and PEPFAR (established in 2003 by President George W. Bush) are examples of "bilateral aid," where one country assists another through a direct agreement rather than going through a global body like the UN. USAID was originally intended, like the IMF and World Bank we will look at later, to create a "sphere of influence" for the United States as it supplied loans to countries during the Cold War to prevent them from falling under the influence of the Soviet Union.[40] PEPFAR, by contrast, was created to combat health concerns abroad related to HIV/AIDS with the understanding doing so would help "[strengthen] the global capacity to prevent, detect, and respond to new and existing risks—which ultimately enhances global health security and protects America's borders."[41]

---

38. Praag, Dehne, and Chandra-Mouli, "The UN Response," 593.

39. Maureen Lewis and Susan Stout, "Financing HIV: The Roles of International Financial Institutions," in *The HIV Pandemic: Local and Global Implications*, ed. Eduard J. Beck Nicholas Mays, Alan W. Whiteside, José M. Zuniga, . (Oxford: Oxford University Press, 2006), 625–41; Chris Simms, "Donor, Lender, and Research Agencies' Response to the HIV Crisis," in *The HIV Pandemic*, ed. Beck et al., 607–24.

40. Jamey Essex, *Development, Security, and Aid: Geopolitics and Geoeconomics at the U.S. Agency for International Development* (Athens: University of Georgia Press, 2013), 84–128.

41. "About Us," United States President's Emergency Plan for AIDS Relief, https://www.pepfar.gov/about/270968.htm, accessed March 23, 2019.

The chief challenge for UNAIDS has been disagreement between its constituent agencies and the countries contributing to its budget over whether HIV/AIDS response should focus on prevention, treatment, or underlying sociological issues. Officials responding to HIV/AIDS in the 1980s emphasized health education and treatment, but quickly recognized the dominant challenge in many of the countries hardest impacted by HIV/AIDS was their extreme poverty. UN and WHO officials in the 1990s and early 2000s started advising that the roots of this underlying problem needed to be addressed if any real progress was to be made in preventing and containing the disease. Programs and funds coordinated UNAIDS with other UN and WHO programs to improve general education, economic opportunities, women's rights, agriculture, and a host of other sociological factors in countries in Africa and Asia to address these underlying concerns. Some European Union countries and the United States, as well as private lenders from these areas, started to push back on this strategy.

These countries and private lenders argued they had donated the funds for UNAIDS for "healthcare and disease prevention" and wanted an accounting to show their funds were being used for the intended purpose. EU and US officials and institutions viewed poverty as a separate problem rather than a risk factor for HIV/AIDS. The UN Secretariat and UNAIDS governing board, dependent on these cosponsor states for funds, could not exercise any controlling authority over these entities.[42]

The UN and WHO still do their best to address all these issues, but are increasingly hindered by an increase in bilateral agreements bypassing the UN and the Global Fund for AIDS relief. Bilateral assistance networks, like USAID and PEPFAR, and NGOs often come with ideological strings attached hampering responses to the spread of HIV/AIDS in countries receiving their funds and services. USAID, which helps with more than just HIV/AIDS care and prevention, plays a diplomatic role for the United States. This agency prefers more "bang for their buck" approaches, with quick, short-term, high-visibility projects to increase the reputation of the United States abroad, even if high visibility sometimes comes at the expense of effective HIV/AIDS prevention and treatment.

The American PEPFAR and several American Christian faith-based NGOs insist governments and agencies receiving their funds emphasize messages of sexual abstinence as the core of their HIV/AIDS prevention.[43] Faith-based NGOs frequently try to influence laws and other aspects of healthcare in the recipient countries by denying funds to states or clinics where abortion is legalized

---

42. Simms, "Donor, Lender, and Research Agencies' Response," 607–15; Praag, Dehne, and Chandra-Mouli, "The UN Response," 596–603.

43. Simms, "Donor, Lender, and Research Agencies' Response," 616–17.

or practiced.[44] Such morally, ideologically, and politically motivated policies, as well as the oft-used formula "ABC: Abstain, Be Faithful, Use a Condom," are frequently not as effective at reducing harm or spread of the disease as needle-exchange programs, condom donations, or social assistance.[45] Because the donor state, in this case the United States, has to be accountable to its citizens back home, the conditions set for recipients of aid change frequently as the political agendas of donor states and agencies change over time. Though it could be argued a state and its public have a right to attach conditions to the tax dollars they donate to other states as aid, in terms of disease prevention ever-changing donor ideologies can waste valuable time and resources on fundamentally flawed approaches. When these approaches pay scant attention to the unique context of the country receiving assistance or, as is sometimes the case with condoms, object to a proven preventative strategy on ideological grounds, they can do very real harm and lead to further spread of HIV/AIDS.

As private lenders, NGOs, governments, and international agencies donate to HIV/AIDS efforts in low-income countries, they exert more control and can damage these economies. In countries like Tanzania, Uganda, and Mozambique, where donor contributions account for 50 to 70 percent of healthcare expenditures, these lenders exercise considerable leverage.[46] Infusions of cash also cause inflation or sometimes an overvaluation of the country's currency in foreign exchange, damaging its economic growth. For instance, from 1995 to 2000, grants to Uganda grew by 3.5 percent and, despite efforts to manage this new revenue prudently, these funds caused inflation, drove up the exchange rate, and led to an increase in the valuation of the country's agriculture exports. The increase in price led to less demand abroad and created an economic depression in Uganda's agricultural sector.

Large donations can hurt also a country's ability to borrow funds from the International Monetary Fund and World Bank for other projects. The IMF and World Bank were established after the Second World War to create a framework for international capitalist economic cooperation toward a stable and prosperous global economy. The United States was and is one of the dominant countries in both institutions in terms of contribution and voting control over their decisions. The original aim was to facilitate the reconstruction of Europe after the devastation of World War II, but was quickly expanded to rebuilding and developing non-European countries breaking away from European rule and oppression in the 1950s, 1960s, and 1970s. The hope during the Cold War was economic

44. Jon O'Brien, "Can Faith and Freedom Co-Exist? When Faith-Based Health Providers and Women's Needs Clash," *Gender & Development* 25, no. 1 (March 2017): 37–51.

45. Simms, "Donor, Lender, and Research Agencies' Response," 616–17.

46. Simms, "Donor, Lender, and Research Agencies' Response," 607–08.

support from the West would prevent these new states from siding with the international communism of the Soviet Union.

The IMF is chiefly a "lender of last resort" for most countries. It judges nations' creditworthiness if they cannot pursue funds from commercial lenders (private banks). The poorest countries receive three-, four-, or ten-year loans at an interest rate of 0.5 percent on repayment, but not for specific projects. The stopgap loans are generalized and supposed to be a temporary salve, creating opportunities for the receiving government to address underlying economic problems in its country. The World Bank, on the other hand, has a more micro-managing role. World Bank subsidiary agencies give longer-term, targeted loans for specific projects intended to "transform" a country's government and economy into a more "stable" community, as defined by its board. It tends to focus on poverty reduction issues through investment in health, education, and infrastructure and can intervene in the budgetary decisions of a state accepting its funds.[47]

The IMF and World Bank often critique the "absorptive capability of a state": how a country's government manages external influxes of money. If too much money from donors flows in too quickly, the World Bank starts an audit of how the government is managing funds. If a country does not meet certain benchmarks for expenditure or overspends in some sectors, the Bank and the IMF might freeze that country's budget. This was the case with Uganda in 2002/2003, when the World Bank deemed it had received "too much" external aid for HIV/AIDS. Uganda was instructed to "turn down funding from overseas donors that [did] not fall within the government's priorities" as defined by the World Bank, or risk losing funding from IMF and the World Bank.[48] Scenarios like this put low-income countries in a bind, forced to turn down aid for one problem to receive aid for another. Dependency networks put pressure on countries like Ethiopia, Uganda, and Zambia to accept external interference in their cultures and day-to-day governance in exchange for funds desperately needed to encourage their competitive economic status in the world economy or combat a global health crisis. Next, we will examine how these dependencies, and Western narratives and stigmas about HIV/AIDS, have influenced the local and national responses by health officials and politicians of a specific African country: Uganda.

Uganda and TASO: Success, Discrimination, and Dependency

A new disease has been recognized in the Rakai district in South West Uganda . . . the syndrome that is locally known as slim disease . . . It would seem that slim disease is, indeed, recent and that it has spread because of heterosexual

---

47. Lewis and Stout, "Financing HIV," 626–27.

48. Lewis and Stout, "Financing HIV," 630–38.

promiscuity, which is hard to document in a rural community . . . Although the subjects in our study deny overt promiscuous behavior, their sexual behavior is, by Western Standards, heterosexually promiscuous.
            —1985 article on "Slim Disease," a.k.a. HIV, jointly written
                        by twelve Ugandan scientists[49]

It seems odd that Ugandan scientists in the preceding quote would judge the sexual norms of their own society by "Western Standards" when making a case about what caused the spread of "slim disease"—a.k.a. HIV/AIDS. Yet in the contexts of decolonization in the late twentieth century and ongoing global HIV/AIDS responses, this negative portrayal of African culture by Africans themselves is not surprising. The language of American and European responses to HIV/AIDS, coupled with the restrictions on and limitations of international relief programs, had and continues to have an impact on how health agencies of national governments in African countries structure their own HIV/AIDS programs. This is often the result of economic and diplomatic considerations by governments and businesses in African societies hoping to avoid the stigma of HIV/AIDS. These variables have also had an impact on how the disease is portrayed in the media and politicians of these African nations and how their citizens view the disease and its victims.

This is particularly evident in Uganda. In terms of response to the disease, we will examine the presidency of Yoweri Museveni, the Ugandan Ministry of Health, and the AIDS Support Organization in Uganda (TASO), a Ugandan-based nongovernmental organization. TASO is often touted as the archetype for success among African responses to HIV/AIDS, but we will also explore the challenges it has had to confront while we chart the history of how Ugandan government officials and everyday Ugandans have understood and represented HIV/AIDS. Before we do, as with Haiti earlier, you need more information on the longer history of Uganda prior to the outbreak of HIV/AIDS in the 1980s.

The section of Eastern Africa we now refer to as the state of Uganda was a British protectorate—a euphemism for "colony" frequently used by empires—from 1894 to 1962. Prior to the arrival of British colonialism, the region had seen an array of ethnic groups, with different governing structures. The largest and strongest of these kingdoms by the mid-nineteenth century was called Buganda—the kingdom of the Baganda people, one of many Bantu-speaking groups in Eastern Africa. This wealthy state established supremacy over neighboring

---

49. D. Serwadda, N. K. Sewankambo, J.W Carswell, A.C. Bayley, R.S. Tedder, T.A. Weiss, R. D. Mugerwa, A. Lwegaba, G. B. Kirya, R.G. Downing, S.A. Clayden, A.G. Dalgleish et al., "Slim Disease: A New Disease in Uganda and its Associations with HTLV-III Infection," *The Lancet* 326, no. 8460 (19 October 1985), 849–52, as quoted in Maryinez Lyons, "The Point of View: Perspectives on AIDS in Uganda," in *AIDS in Africa and the Caribbean*, ed. Bond et al., 131–48, 135.

communities, enlisting them for labor and military service. The *kabakas* (roughly translated as "kings") of Buganda were elected by representatives from the various societies within the expanded Bugandan state.[50]

Increased contact with Europeans and Arabs in the late nineteenth century resulted in a multiplicity of religions in the kingdom, including multiple denominations of Christianity and Islam. Between 1885 and 1887, factions of Bugandans adhering to Protestantism, Catholicism, and Islam were engaged in a civil war for control of the region, vying to have their leaders selected as Kabaka. British imperialists took advantage of this internal dispute after the Bugandan Protestant faction succeeded. Promising support and negotiating with Apolo Kagwa, a leader of the Protestant faction who became *katikkiro* (prime minister of Buganda), the Imperial British East Africa Company (IBEA) secured administration rights for the territory in 1893. The IBEA transferred those rights to the British government the following year, which grouped Buganda together with other kingdoms, clans, and societies in Eastern Africa—such as the Lango—to establish the Uganda Protectorate as a single colony.[51]

The Uganda Agreement of 1900 established a ranking of "client-chiefs" of the various clans of the colony. The Protestant "Bakungu," Bugandan client-chiefs under the leadership of Kagwa, were favored by the British in this hierarchy due to their Christianity, their history of a working relationship with British imperialists, and their preexisting structures for collecting taxes and tributes from other groups in the colony. These were the same Bugandan "chiefs" cooperating with the British in STD controls you read about in chapter 3. Added to this racial-hierarchy dynamic were white European settlers and Indian merchants, soldiers, servants, and professionals brought to the colony via the various connections of the British Empire. White Europeans dominated the colonial society, and both Europeans and Indians received preferential treatment over indigenous East Africans from British colonial governance.[52]

Starting with British Ghana in 1954, the 1950s and 1960s saw a wave of African states undergoing decolonization from the rule of European powers like France, Portugal, and Belgium.[53] Formal British rule ended in Uganda in 1962.

---

50. Christopher Wrigley, *Kingship and the State: The Buganda Dynasty* (Cambridge: Cambridge University Press, 1996), 57–68, 122–68, 207–29.

51. Richard J. Reid, *A History of Modern Uganda* (Cambridge: Cambridge University Press, 2017), 284–310; Onek C. Adyanga, *Modes of British Imperial Control of Africa: A Case Study of Uganda, 1890–1990* (Newcastle upon Tyne: Cambridge Scholars, 2011), 14–60; Wrigley, *Kingship and the State*, 7–9, 22–34, 99–148.

52. Adyanga, *Modes of British Imperial Control*, 60–135.

53. For more on the history of decolonization and independence movements in Africa, see Frederick Cooper, *Africa since 1940: The Past of the Present*, 2nd ed. (Cambridge: Cambridge University Press, 2019).

The ethnic and religious tensions created and exacerbated by British racial hierar-chy quickly led to conflict in the new state. The result was a series of military dic-tatorships. First came Milton Obote (r. 1966–1971), who suppressed challenges to a unified national identity through force. He was then toppled by Idi Amin (r. 1971–1979), who created a tyrannical government, persecuted his political opponents, and took advantage of ethnic tensions to strengthen his regime.[54]

Amin blamed "Asians" for the exploitation of black Ugandans by the British. "Asians," as defined by Amin, included Indians who had moved to Uganda under British rule or were descended from those who had, as well as Arab Muslim com-munities extant in Uganda long before the arrival of the British. He pointed to Asian complicity in British rule as troops, officials, and merchants. Because of Britain's colonial hierarchies, Indians and Arabs in Uganda had some benefits of education and certain rights black Africans had been denied. It fostered decades of resentment a dictator like Amin could easily exploit to maintain his control. He encouraged violence against Asians, expelled them, and seized their property.

Amin was overthrown by Obote, who returned from exile in 1979 during a war between Tanzania and Uganda. Ruling again for six years, Obote's second administration was marked by a brutal civil war, adding to the destruction of Uganda's economy and infrastructure begun under Amin. The conflict did not end until 1985: that year saw two other attempts at military dictatorships by two other generals before Yoweri Museveni was declared president in 1986, begin-ning a long period of rebuilding for Uganda, alongside ongoing involvement in conflicts in neighboring states, such as the Democratic Republic of the Congo, and rebellions against Museveni's administration.[55]

The period of the Ugandan Civil War is when the Ugandan epidemic of "slim" was first noted. In 1985, four years after the first US HIV/AIDS cases, the outbreak coincided with the moment when American and European doctors dropped Haiti as the origin point for the disease and began focusing on Africa. Economic and government leaders in African states were quick to recognize that accusations of Africa as the source of HIV/AIDS would have deleterious impacts on commerce, tourism, diplomatic exchanges, and aid packages from the United States and powerful European states. Having seen the effect on Haiti and Haitian immigrants, these leaders quickly wanted to control the narrative.

---

54. For more on the dictatorship of Idi Amin, as well as details on how the British and Israeli states provided indirect support for Amin's coup, see Mahmood Mamdani, *Imperialism and Fascism in Uganda* (Trenton, NJ: Africa World Press, 1984).

55. Adyanga, *Modes of British Imperial Control*, 180–205; Phares Mutibwa, *Uganda since Independence: A Story of Unfulfilled Hopes* (Trenton, NJ: Africa World Press, 1992), 58–76; John Kiyaga-Nsubuga, "Managing Political Change: Uganda under Museveni," in *Civil Wars in Africa: Roots and Resolutions*, ed. Taisier M. Ali and Robert O. Matthews (Montreal: McGill-Queen's University Press, 1999), 13–34.

When the Ugandan Ministry of Health funded Ugandan scientists and an-thropologists to investigate HIV/AIDS, it did so with money from the WHO, the US government, and the American-based private donor the Rockefeller Foundation. This money came with ideological strings attached. The anthro-pologists hired to identify risk groups in Uganda did so through the lenses of outdated imperial ethnic groupings and Western sexual mores. They told a narra-tive of entire Ugandan subcultures and ethnic groups, both urban and nonurban, as "promiscuous husbands" and "prostitutes" with "increased numbers of sexual partners . . . a history of sexually-transmitted disease or genital ulcers . . . intact foreskins . . . [and] witchcraft." Seemingly borrowing from the colonial tropes we saw in chapter 3, some even went so far as to equate "bar maids" with prostitutes, implying all working women were, well . . . working women.[56]

It is not surprising Ugandan scientists and doctors, like those in the Serwadda piece quoted here, many of whom were trained and funded directly or indirectly by American and European universities, portrayed Africans as "promiscuous by Western standards" and prostitutes as a source of the problem. Co-opting this Western narrative enabled access to continued funding and support from moral-istic NGOs, international agencies, and governments. It also allowed politicians to transform the "AIDS out of Africa" concept from a global racial discourse to one of gender, morality, and class.[57]

We can see how this adoption and shift of Euro-American rhetoric was used in Uganda's HIV/AIDS response programs in the Museveni administration. Museveni's presidency, which started in 1986, continues into 2020, because he eliminated term and age limits during his reign.[58] His administration has over-seen the country's public health response to the disease in the last three decades. Museveni himself has on multiple occasions adopted the West's moralistic argu-ment about the disease in order to present Uganda as a "modern" state worthy of aid. In doing so, he focused the blame on the poor, the youth, and what he deemed amoral, antimodern "African tradition" in his own country. In 1990, he gave a speech in which he claimed "traditions and customary habits, like polyg-amous marital relations which encouraged the spread of the killer disease. (see Figures 5.2A and 5.2B)"[59]

In Florence, Italy, at the 7th International Conference on AIDS in 1991, Museveni presented this view on the world stage. Distracting from criticisms

---

56. George C. Bond and Joan Vincent, "AIDS in Uganda: The First Decade," in *AIDS in Africa and the Caribbean*, ed. Bond et al., 85–98, 85–90.

57. Lyons, "The Point of View," 132–41.

58. "How Ugandan MPs Voted to Scrap Presidential Age Limit," *The Independent*, December 21, 2017.

59. As quoted in Lyons, "The Point of View," 140.

FIGURE 5.2a   FIGURE 5.2b

Take a moment to look at these two HIV/AIDS educational posters and the info about them in the citations below. Both were produced and/or approved by the Ugandan Ministry of Health in the 1990s. The image on the left even bears the logo of the World Health Organization in the lower right-hand corner. Think about the longer historical context of European/Western influence on African countries, Western stereotypes of all African men as promiscuous and predatory, and Western stereotypes of non-European women as prostitutes in relation to STDs. In either image, do you see any of that historical context represented in these public health educational materials? Discuss with your instructor and classmates after you have considered the images carefully.

Source: (Figure 5.2a) AIDS Control Programme, Ministry of Health, Uganda. Credit: Wellcome Collection. Attribution-NonCommercial 4.0 International (CC BY-NC 4.0)

A groom with his bride and a message to love faithfully and obey the christian way of life and avoid

Source: (Figure 5.2b) AIDS; an advertisement by the Uganda Catholic Medical Bureau. Colour lithograph by A.B.C. Ngónzi, ca. 1990's (?). Credit: Wellcome Collection. Attribution-NonCommercial 4.0 International (CC BY-NC 4.0)

of his own government's ability to respond and trying to portray Uganda as a Westernizing state, he argued the best method to curb HIV/AIDS was morality. He insisted his government would not advocate the distribution and use of condoms. Instead, he argued, "Africans had evolved cultural taboos against premarital sex and strict sanctions had been established against premarital sex or sex out of wedlock," and his regime would pursue a "return to our time-tested cultural practices which emphasized fidelity and condemnation of premarital and extramarital sex. I believe that the best response to the threat posed by AIDS and other sexuality transmitted diseases is to reaffirm publicly and forthrightly the

reverence and respect and responsibility every person owes his or her neighbor."
Lastly, he turned the blame to "foreign cultures" spreading immorality through
"dating culture" rather than "Christian" relations between men and women.[60]

Negative views on condoms were also echoed by Uganda's religious aid organizations, which in turn took their cue from European and American groups.
These groups maintained that condoms would promote immorality and therefore spread the disease. Politicians and advocacy groups in Uganda blamed promiscuity and prostitution as the real threats to the family and future generations
and geared much of their rhetorical and policy solutions in this direction.[61] As
you can see in the pictures of educational posters in Figure 5.2, this has been an
enduring stance of the Ugandan Ministry of Health in its official educational efforts. This agency receives most of its financial support from aid packages from
USAID, and the UK Department for International Development. The Ugandan
government also receives aid from the World Bank and WHO for healthcare
development, often with strings attached, as we saw in the previous section.[62] The
dependency on funding from American and European sources, especially faith-
based or politically motivated bodies with specific ideologies regarding HIV/
AIDS, paired with statements from the Ugandan government, has had an impact
on perceptions by everyday Ugandans. The result is the perpetuation of stigmas
related to the disease hindering the work of containment well into the twenty-
first century.[63]

Outside the Ugandan Ministry of Health, and sometimes despite antagonism from the government, that difficult work has mostly been performed by
NGOs like TASO. This organization was established in 1987, the first full year
after Museveni became president, to combat the everyday stigma created by the
government positions on HIV/AIDS. The organization is still active. It has the
ongoing mission "to contribute to a process of preventing HIV infection, restor-
ing hope and improving the quality of life of persons, families and communities
affected by HIV infection and disease."[64]

The idea for this support network came from Christopher Kaleeba, a radiog-
rapher at Mulago Hospital in Uganda who was diagnosed with HIV. He was

---

60. President Yoweri Museveni, "Opening Speech at the Seventh International AIDS
Conference," June 16, 1991.

61. Lyons, "The Point of View," 138–47.

62. Justin Parkhurst, Freddie Ssengooba, and David Serwadda, "Uganda," in *The HIV
Pandemic*, ed. Beck, et al., 255–69, 260.

63. Bond and Vincent, "AIDS in Uganda"; Parkhurst, Ssengooba, and Serwadda, "Uganda,"
262–64.

64. "About TASO," TASO, http://www.tasouganda.org/index.php/about-taso, accessed
March 20, 2019.

ostracized by his coworkers at the hospital as a result of portrayals of HIV victims as immoral by national and international agencies in the 1980s. Before his death, he hoped a group could be created to fight the stigma and provide the medical and emotional support patients needed, especially those abandoned by families and friends. His wife, Noerine Kaleeba, and a small group of health workers and patients, founded the group and started an HIV/AIDS clinic in space afforded them at the hospital. As of 2005, TASO had opened eleven service centers, four regional offices, and one training center across the major cities and towns of Uganda and has cared for over 300,000 Ugandan HIV/AIDS patients in the thirty-two years it has existed.[65] TASO has been remarkably successful at stepping in where the Ugandan government and other international agencies cannot or will not supply assistance. Many African countries are trying to imitate its model. Scholars in medicine, anthropology, and history have argued, however, that as successful and beneficial as this organization has been, TASO's structure helps replicate a harmful national and global network of dependency.[66] To explore this critique, we must look at how TASO dispenses the aid it offers.

TASO is a membership organization, with certain criteria individuals must meet to subscribe to its network of national and international aid and resources. First, an individual must test positive for HIV. Their photograph is taken and sent to the Ministry of Health by TASO, and then they and their dependents are eligible to become members. TASO's subscribers receive a TASO membership card affording them and their family members access to medical treatment, outreach, home care, education and literacy training, family planning aid (including condoms), food, employment opportunities, counseling, and community activities. These services are in some instances dispensed by TASO or by other partner organizations, particularly when it comes to distribution of things like food and blankets. To achieve this, though, the individual must sacrifice their privacy. Take for instance the case of Martha, a Ugandan woman who explained why she left TASO in a 2005 interview with anthropologist Susan Reynolds Whyte:

> Well, yes, they give free drugs . . . but in TASO, everybody would know because they make you sit there, read files, then call you to pick drugs even after many hours! It is tiresome and unnecessary revealing someone's health status as far as HIV is concerned.

---

65. "About TASO."

66. Susan Reynolds Whyte, Michael A. Whyte, Lotte Meinert, Jenipher Twebaze, "Belonging in Uganda's Projectified Landscape of AIDS Care," in *When People Come First: Critical Studies in Global Health*, ed. João Biehl and Adriana Petryna (Princeton, NJ: Princeton University Press, 2013), 140–65.

Martha went on to explain she was the primary provider for her extended family and did not want her health problems to be "paraded" in front of them. She instead started paying for her treatments through the Joint Clinical Research Center, an agency funded by the American PEPFAR to preserve her privacy. In doing so, she sacrificed the social connections and job opportunities TASO preserves solely for its subscribers, which she and others desperately needed.[67]

Such a system creates the opportunity for what some medical scholars have called "therapeutic clientship"—a term which here means a "a local moral economy [in which] individuals call on networks of obligation and reciprocity to negotiate access to therapeutic resources."[68] In the hierarchical relationship created by this client–patron system, those on the outside are blocked from jobs, nutritional aid, and other resources needed by HIV victims and their relatives. This network of dependency, in which patients feel forced into this clientship as a dependent of TASO to support their own dependents, can be humiliating. Humiliation is exacerbated by the ongoing moral stigma the Ugandan government and public attach to the disease. To avoid this, Ugandan HIV/AIDS victims turn to other organizations that charge for their assistance or, in the worst-case scenarios, turn to an underground network of predatory individuals who acquire the resources from TASO and then dispense them to others in exchange for extortionary favors or fees.[69] The benefits from TASO are immense, its motives are well-intentioned, and the work it does is having a positive influence in reducing the number of HIV/AIDS cases these last three decades. Its structure for accessing care, however, in certain aspects imitates on a smaller scale the global forced dependency of African states to European and American-based patrons we looked at earlier.

Conclusion

In this chapter, we surveyed how initial American and European responses to the HIV pandemic were steeped in prejudices related to race and sexual orientation in the late twentieth and early twenty-first centuries. The stereotypes present in these responses were, sadly, the ideological and fiscal foundations upon which international agencies based their actions. Though many of these governments and NGOs and medical professionals are doing good work, and many are motivated by good intentions in assisting others, the earliest responses to HIV/AIDS have left their impact on the structures of global health response. Among the many negative consequences has been the creation of a system of forced dependency whereby low-income countries like Haiti and Uganda must adopt Western

67. Reynolds Whyte et al., "Belonging in Uganda's Projectified Landscape," 161.

68. Reynolds Whyte et al., "Belonging in Uganda's Projectified Landscape," 149–51.

69. Reynolds Whyte et al., "Belonging in Uganda's Projectified Landscape," 146–65.

systems of disease control and morality in exchange for assistance in fighting a truly global health threat. As of 2017, there were 36.9 million people in the world living with HIV/AIDS. Sixty-nine percent of those victims live on the continent of Africa, 14 percent in Asia and the Pacific, and 6 percent in Europe and North America.

Of those infected as of 2017, 21.7 million (59 percent) were receiving ART. This was an increase of 8 million over the number receiving care in 2010. AIDS-related deaths went down from 1.9 million in 2004 to 940,000 in 2017. Despite this good news, the rate of new infections among adults globally—1.8 million yearly—has not decreased.[70] In the United States, there are approximately 39,000 new cases each year, with over half in the American South in 2017.[71] In 2015 alone, Indiana identified 140 new cases in Scott County.[72] HIV/AIDS has not disappeared, nor has the stigma that prevents one in seven US victims from seeking diagnosis. Officials and volunteers at UNAIDS, TASO and other NGOs, PEPFAR, the WHO, the CDC, and governments around the world are working to combat both, but with a global pandemic a one-size-fits-all approach will not work. In the complex world in which we live, even those with good intentions need to think carefully through the unintended consequences their findings and efforts could have on those impacted by this deadly disease. The history of responses in the past and their consequences might provide them with warnings and lessons about societal responses to disease and their impact on social inequalities.

FURTHER READING

Cooper, Frederick. *Africa Since 1940: The Past of the Present.* 2nd ed. Cambridge: Cambridge University Press, 2019.

Farmer, Paul, Margaret Connors, and Janie Simmons, *eds. Women, Poverty, and AIDS: Sex, Drugs and Structural Violence.* 2nd ed. Monroe, ME: Common Courage Press, 1996.

Halkitis, Perry N. *The AIDS Generation: Stories of Survival and Resilience.* New York: Oxford University Press, 2014.

Langley, Lester D. *The Banana Wars: United States Intervention in the Caribbean, 1898–1934.* Lanham, MD: SR Books, 2002.

Vaughn, Meghan. *Curing Their Ills: Colonial Power and African Illness.* Stanford, CA: Stanford University Press, 1991.

70. "Global HIV/AIDS Overview," HIV.gov, https://www.hiv.gov/federal-response/pepfar-global-aids/global-hiv-aids-overview, last updated November 20, 2018.

71. "U.S. Statistics," HIV.gov, https://www.hiv.gov/hiv-basics/overview/data-and-trends/statistics, last updated March 13, 2019.

72. Shari Rudavsky, "CDC: Indiana Has 'One of the Worst' HIV Outbreaks," *Indianapolis Star*, April 28, 2015.

CONCLUSION

The argument presented in this book is some public health initiatives reinforced societal inequalities based on race, class, and gender around the globe, even in moments when the intent was to challenge those same inequalities. Government officials, doctors, and social movements advocated for and created public health practices that were a product of their cultural, political, religious, demographic, and economic beliefs in each context. At times intentional, at times unintentional, policies based on preset views about race, class, and gender have had a detrimental impact on the equality of care and access to medical to medical treatment by all communities in a given population. This book has emphasized how in an increasingly globalizing society from the premodern era to the present, these inequalities in healthcare persist, in part because the faulty foundations created by scientific and social views steeped in racism, classism, and/or limited perceptions of sexuality and gender roles.

It is not the intent of this book, however, that you the reader take the lessons of this text as encouragement to condemn all of medicine or public health or view these life-saving fields as hopelessly flawed. This book, yes, has repeatedly emphasized the negative consequences for some portions of the population resulting from policies that were directly or indirectly influenced by societal norms that provoked hatred and misconceptions about disenfranchised groups. Public health, particularly in moments of accusation and stigmatization of victims of disease, did play a role in exacerbating prejudice and inequality. Such outcomes from some public health programs and protocols in the past and even in the present does not mean every policy then, now, or in the future will follow that negative pattern.

This book instead maintains that knowledge of the past can make public health in the present and future more effective. As you learn about past examples of flawed policies and ideas about the source of disease in their historical context, you should become more attuned to how prejudices and labels in your own time have the potential to promote similar inequalities in within their communities. Knowledge of past errors can help public health officials and doctors—and even the general public—change their perceptions of risk groups, origins of disease, and modify which policies they implement and how so their actions reduce inequality in the health of all members of their local, national, and global communities. To that end, this book concludes with a brief model for doing your own research on the historical roots of contemporary issues and problems surrounding public health and inequality.

Consider the example I used in the introduction—the deadly 2014 to 2016 Ebola outbreak. If we were to limit ourselves to a Google search using the phrase "2014 Ebola outbreak," major news outlets, government websites, and Wikipedia pages might lead us to believe the roots of this issue only date back to December 2013, with the first cases in the outbreak. Or they might make us believe the events leading to this outbreak only go as far back as 1976, when Ebola was first discovered in the Congo River Basin of Central Africa. Having read this book, though, I'm sure you can think of research questions that would lead to deeper historical investigation of multiple regions and societies. You may even decide to investigate the history of a more recent Ebola crisis. The 2018-2020 Ebola outbreak in the Democratic Republic of the Congo (DRC) and Uganda has claimed 1,400 lives as of June 2019. In either case, your research questions might include the following (see Map 6.1):

- How did Euro-American racial assumptions about Africa as a source of disease, from the STD crises of the nineteenth century to the ongoing HIV/AIDS pandemic, contribute to the stigma faced by African migrants in the United States during the 2014–2016 Ebola outbreak?
- In what ways did the history of humanitarian aid networks and financial relief programs run by American and European agencies help or hinder disease response in the DRC and Uganda during the 2019 Ebola outbreak?
- How did European imperialism and subsequent decolonization impact healthcare infrastructure in Sierra Leone, Guinea, Liberia, Uganda, or the DRC? Limit yourself to looking at no more than two countries to keep your paper focused and brief.
- How were the borders of Sierra Leone, Guinea, and Liberia determined during the era of decolonization and how did this contribute to the rapid spread of Ebola in 2014 to 2016?
- What are the origins of recent conflicts in West Africa and Central Africa that facilitated the spread of Ebola during both outbreaks?

To answer these questions, probably the best place to start would be to read recent histories written by experts on the history of sub-Saharan Africa or specific—even better—countries like Liberia, Guinea, or Sierra Leone, the DRC, or Uganda aimed at students or a general audience. As you search, bear in mind

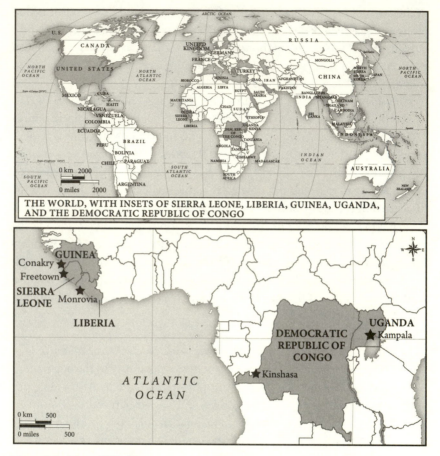

THE WORLD, WITH INSETS OF SIERRA LEONE, LIBERIA, GUINEA, UGANDA, AND THE DEMOCRATIC REPUBLIC OF CONGO

MAP 6.1 Map of World

some of these present-day countries have changed names, borders, locations, and forms of government over the years. The DRC, for example, used to be called Zaire from 1971 to 1997. Before 1964, it was part of the Belgian Congo, the colony the Belgians formed from a collection of precolonial societies and states, including the Kingdom of Kongo, which they brutally conquered during their late nineteenth-century imperial expansion. After answering basic questions and expanding your knowledge of African history you could then read scholarly articles and books that look at specific aspects of these societies' histories, the history of Ebola, and the history of medical care and treatment in these regions of the world.

Finally, I encourage you to pull up a newspaper article or other media story related to a health crisis facing the world today. Try search phrases like "global health issues" or "current world health crises." If you wanted to do another targeted search for a specific health crisis, bear in mind that it is sometimes help-ful to know other terms related to the disease or event. For example, the corona-virus responsible for the pandemic that began in 2019 was called various things in the news and by scientists. COVID-19 was the name given to the severe respi-ratory disease the virus caused. nCoV-2019 and SARS CoV 2 were both names that scientists gave to the virus itself. Remember the concept of the "geography of blame" we discussed in earlier chapters? You might also need to know that some American politicians used racist and derogatory names for the virus, calling it "Wuhan Virus," "China Virus," "Kung Flu," or "China Flu," indicating its point of origin in an accusatory way. Having that baseline of information on the various terms used to describe the event or illness might help you understand why some news pieces bearing such seemingly unrelated headlines are appearing in your search for "coronavirus" or "COVID-19." You may need to try several terms or variations of them as you conduct research online or in your library to strengthen your research results.

To make sure you get a media or news article if you are using Google, hit the "News" tab just below the search bar. Have you found a piece that interests you? Good. Now think about the kinds of questions in the list we posed about the 2014 to 2016 Ebola outbreak. Even if the piece you are looking at relates to a health crisis other than Ebola, can you pose similar questions about what the news is covering? After reading the piece carefully, develop a list of questions the journalist or author of this brief piece did not have the time or space to research and answer.

The exercise you just completed is not about criticizing the author or news source or the brief, click-bait format of some news material online. Journalism plays different (and essential) roles than history in how we present, interpret, and acquire information. The point is to start with what journalism and the inter-net offer and then investigate more into how world history can help you better understand a topic in greater depth. Remember, a Google search or a newspa-per article is only a starting point. Once you start digging deeper, you will start asking different questions at each stage of your research. As you become better informed, you will be in a better position to draw conclusions and make well-reasoned arguments about what historical developments, societal views, and cul-tural factors—both in the past and in the present—are influencing the policies and decisions of today.

INDEX

Note: Page numbers in italics indicate figures.

ABOUT THE COVER

"The Map of Health" by self-styled scientific artist Odra Noel (Ph.D. University of London) was part of an exhibition at the Royal Society of London, a prestigious fellowship of scientists, in 2013. Noel represented each region with bodily cells impacted by diseases common in each location. North America is represented by adipose tissue, Central and South America is depicted as pulmonary tissue, Europe is signified with neural tissue, Southwest Asia and Central Asia are shown as cardiac muscle tissue, Eastern Asia and the Pacific islands are portrayed as pancreatic acinar tissue, and Africa is made up of blood cells, since the majority of Africans die from illnesses, such as HIV and malaria, that are transmitted through bodily fluids during human contact or by the Anopheles mosquito. The author of this book saw the image on display while conducting research in London in 2013 and was immediately struck by how it perfectly captures the "Chronic Disparities" in global health.

Image: "Map of Health. Credit: Odra Noel. Attribution-NonCommercial 4.0 International (CC BY-NC 4.0)"